Bistro Cooking at Home

Bistro Cooking
AT HOME

GORDON HAMERSLEY

with JOANNE MCALLISTER SMART

with WINE ADVICE by FIONA HAMERSLEY

BROADWAY BOOKS
New York

BROADWAY

PRINTED IN CHINA

BROADWAY BOOKS and its logo, a letter B bisected on the diagonal,
are trademarks of Random House, Inc.

Visit our website at www.broadwaybooks.com

Library of Congress Cataloging-in-Publication Data

Hamersely, Gordon.
Bistro cooking at home / Gordon Hamersley with Joanne McAllister Smart.
p. cm.
Includes bibliographical references and index.
1. Cookery, American. I. Smart, Joanne McAllister. II. Title.
TX715.H194 2003
641.5973—dc21   2002043758

Book design by VERTIGO DESIGN, NYC

Photography by Anna Williams

ISBN 0-7679-1276-4

1   3   5   7   9   10   8   6   4   2

FOR *Fiona* AND *Sophie*

AND FOR *Julia*

CONTENTS

PREFACE

SAY THE WORD "bistro" and almost instantly you conjure up an image of a small neighborhood restaurant where regulars drink *vin de table* out of tumblers while enjoying Madame's beef Bourguignon. The word connotes a unique sense of intimacy not found at other types of restaurants. Part of that feeling comes from the traditional bistro arrangement, which finds the owner, *le patron,* cooking at the stove, and his wife, *la patronne,* tending to the dining room. Part of that feeling comes from tables situated close together and a décor that whispers rather than shouts. And part of that feeling comes from the food, which tastes delicious yet comfortingly familiar, as if the chef knew just what you were craving even before you did.

Just before opening Hamersley's Bistro in 1987, Fiona and I lived in Nice for a year. Our neighborhood bistro was a little place called La Ville de Sienne, and it was owned and run by a husband and wife. She ran the front and was French; he ran the kitchen and was Italian. Our apartment looked right at the restaurant's back door, and we would always see a few older men sitting on the back stoop in the late morning drinking coffee and peeling garlic. It was something I found curious. (Who were these guys, and why were *they* peeling the garlic?) The inside of the restaurant was wonderful, everything you imagine a bistro to be, with thick stone walls, a beamed ceiling, wooden tables. We loved to watch the action: the arguments between the chef and his wife. (I would wonder silently if Fiona and I would ever fight in front of our customers. "No," I thought, "no way.") We observed the relationship between the regulars and the owners and how the regulars themselves had a sense of ownership in the place. The menu itself read like a romp through the market, heavy on the meat and game braises but also featuring old-fashioned Provençal fish dishes like a whole daurade with tomatoes, garlic, cloves, and lemon. My favorite was a daube of lamb with gnocchi floating on the top. Chunks of lamb shoulder, carrots, onions, orange, and herbs braised in a clay pot until tender. Then a few light-as-air dumplings placed on top. It was all covered with a dusting of Parmigiano-Reggiano and put back in the wood-burning oven to puff and brown. That dish exploded with flavor and demonstrated a better marriage of French and Italian than the owners themselves displayed.

When I am asked to define bistro cooking, I only need to think back to that daube. Bistro cooking is bold and fully flavored and yet it feels more like the best home cooking than restaurant fare: long, slow-cooked stews; exquisitely roasted chickens; perfectly seared steaks; creamy gratins topped with a crisp crust; vibrant green salads; bright, tangy fruit tarts; and silky smooth custards.

My love affair with bistro food—with good food in general—began relatively late in life. I'm not one of those chefs who as a kid stood on a stool watching Grandma roll out fresh pasta dough by hand. My mother didn't make her own cheese. I envy those chefs who did grow up surrounded by great food lovingly prepared (for one thing, they get to reminisce about their childhoods in the introduction to *their* cookbooks), but I was not one of them. Truth be told, I was never even remotely interested in what went on in the kitchen or what ended up on the table. My dad tells me I was almost always late for dinner, out playing baseball or basketball, and would try to get back to the game as soon as the minimum amount was consumed.

I happened into cooking when my dreams of leading a life in rock and roll slowly fizzled. Because being a roadie (as close as I got to that dream) earned me no money, I took a job washing dishes at a restaurant called Autre Chose, here in Cambridge, Massachusetts. I didn't even know what a bistro was at the time, but this small restaurant was as close as you got to one this side of the Atlantic. Owner Maurice Le Duc, a skilled pastry chef, made a croissant that had people lining up around the block every morning. At night, he cooked home-style dishes, the kind of food his mother made for the family back in France. When Maurice would ask me what I wanted to eat (the extent of my benefits package), I almost always chose the same dish: scallops coated with flour and browned in butter to which Maurice would add chopped garlic, tomato, parsley, and white wine. It amazed me that food so simply prepared could be so full of flavor. Here's how I became a cook there: One night the kitchen got so backed up that Maurice literally threw a bunch of mussels at me to clean. (This was back in the days when mussels came covered with hair, barnacles, and mud; cleaning them was not exactly a quick job.) "What about the dishes?" I asked. "Forget the dishes," Maurice answered, "we're not going to *need* any dishes if we can't feed these people."

After a few more cooking jobs in Boston, which included working for a chef who took perverse pleasure in beating cooks up rather than teaching them, I left in the middle of the blizzard of '78 for sunny California. It was a great move, not the least because it's where I met Fiona. It was also in California that I realized that cooking was not the job I ended up with but the job I love. The realization began at Ma Maison on Melrose Avenue in Los Angeles. The famous little "bistrot," owned by Patrick Terrail, was known for its ability to serve the Hollywood elite with style and just the right balance of attention and arrogance. The star factor was fun, but what really mattered to me was that I was now cooking with a great team of cooks, led by Wolfgang Puck, who at the time was nothing short of revolutionary. Wolfgang and the rest of the cooks in that kitchen opened culinary doors for me that I never even knew existed. Every day I tasted and prepared foods that I had only read about before: black truffles, turbot, Beluga caviar. Even more important, my years cooking under Wolfgang taught me food as a way of life. I began to understand that for many people, food and cooking was a passion that was all consuming.

That newly discovered passion sent us next to France. Susan Feninger, with whom I worked at Ma Maison, suggested I do a *stage,* an apprenticeship essentially, at L'Oasis, a three-star restaurant where she had done one. A connection was made and Fiona and I sold practically everything we owned to pay for an extended trip. (Fiona had lived in the south of France for ten years, so this was sort of a homecoming for her, albeit one with an albatross around her neck, since I spoke very little French.)

When I got to L'Oasis, I learned that due to a mix-up, there was no job waiting for me. Sounds tragic, right? It actually turned out to be one of the best things that ever happened to me. Instead of peeling carrots and watching three-star chefs run around the kitchen, Fiona and I went to farmers' markets, fishmongers, charcuteries, vineyards, and every kind of restaurant. By this point in my life I had mastered the mechanics of cooking, but it was during this trip that I found my inspiration, discovered my culinary "voice," if you will.

Living in Nice changed my life. We lived in the old city about a block from the produce market/flower market, with all the fish and meat places feeding into it like wagon wheel spokes. I shopped every morning and I was able to watch as the produce changed and matured throughout the spring and summer, the first young garlic arriving and then the wild mushrooms. The people I met were passionate about food, but they were also practical. I was excited the first day strawberries showed up and I jumped at the opportunity to buy some. But a woman nearby told me that they were too expensive. "Never buy on the first day," she said. (I couldn't speak much French, but I understood a lot.) "After a couple days the price will come down and *that* is the time to buy." I took her advice, the strawberries were just as delicious, and I think of her now and again when I'm placing orders for the restaurant.

We were living in France with nothing but time on our hands (something I can scarcely imagine now), and so we traveled around and ate at every kind of restaurant possible. Throughout our trip, I was toying with the notion of opening our own restaurant (something Fiona was not aware of, or she likely would have dumped me right there and then). And though dinner at Alain Chapel remains the single best meal of my life so far, I knew the place we would open would be more like the informal, relaxed bistros Fiona and I felt ourselves drawn to again and again.

One particular experience comes to mind as I write this. On a cold night, Fiona and I went to the famous bistro in Paris called L'Ami Louis, which is known for its wood oven, its lively waiters, and its rustic charm. It's also really tiny, with all of the seats elbow to elbow. To save space, coatracks with baggage space like that above the seats on a train frame the dining room. A little woodstove sits in the dining room providing some heat for those sitting in front. A giant wood oven cooks the food and keeps the back of the place cozy all winter. Fiona ordered duck confit to start, and I had escargots so hot and bubbling with garlic butter that it was a full five minutes before I could take a bite without scorching my tongue.

The room was filling up. A crowd of Americans arrived, the men in leather coats and the women in full-length fur. They were greeted with gusto by two waiters who grabbed the women's coats and hurled them skyward over the coatracks. The women screamed to be careful, but nothing could deter the waiters' efficiency and any fears were put to rest when the coats landed perfectly arranged in the upper racks.

As we waited for our entrées, there was more commotion at the door. A huge smile came over Fiona's face as Omar Sharif sat down right next to me. And while having a renowned international actor seated next to you in a bistro in Paris can be quite distracting, it was not enough to keep me from appreciating the wonderful roast chicken served at L'Ami Louis. Alongside the bird was a pile of french fries at least half a foot tall. I could still see the individual crystals of sea salt that had been sprinkled on just seconds before. I was in heaven. When we left, Omar and his friends were still there smoking, playing cards, and looking very, very relaxed. As we left I thought about how remarkable it was that a place like L'Ami Louis could make even Omar Sharif feel so at home. (On a trip back to France in 2001, we went back to L'Ami Louis and could not believe our eyes when in walked Omar Sharif—again! Turns out he, like so many bistro patrons, is a regular.)

When Fiona and I opened our restaurant a few years later, we wanted to create the same kind of comfortable, well-fed, and well-cared-for feeling that we enjoyed at bistros like La Ville de Sienne and L'Ami Louis. Our location, a true neighborhood in Boston's South End; our décor, warm yellow walls, rich wood accents; and friendly attentive service all play a role in nurturing that feeling. And while those are not things you can necessarily re-create at home, a huge factor—the food—is. In *Bistro Cooking at Home,* I share my versions of such bistro classics as frisée aux lardons, onion soup au gratin, pissaladière, and tarte Tatin. Some of the more intimidating traditional recipes, such as duck confit and cassoulet, are tweaked a bit to make them work best for the home cook. But not all of the recipes are so overtly French in origin. As a chef who creates seasonal menus using as much local product as possible, I give many of my recipes a distinctly American accent: hamburgers stuffed with blue cheese, finnan haddie chowder, pear and cranberry crumble. Such recipes, as well as those for curried cauliflower and Moroccan lamb shanks, while not French, are delicious examples of the casual style that bistro cooking celebrates.

Finally, *Bistro Cooking at Home* demonstrates just how liberating bistro-style cooking can be. Many of the methods employed—simmering, braising, roasting—allow for what I call "walk-away" cooking. After some preliminary work, you can simply walk away and tend to the rest of your life while the beef stews or the chicken roasts. Another liberating aspect of bistro-style cooking is that many of the dishes taste better if prepared well ahead of serving. Because bistros are often small, family-run establishments, there isn't a line of chefs preparing the meals *à la minute*. Instead, much of the menu consists of soups, stews, and braises that only get better as they sit, cassoulet being the prime example. These recipes work especially well for entertaining; instead of frantically doing a lot of last-minute cooking you will actually be able to spend time with your guests. This relaxed sharing of great food simply prepared is part and parcel of cooking bistro style. I know I'm happiest when sitting down to a good meal with people I know well, where the food is not being worshiped or fawned over, but rather has just simply taken its natural place in the moment. The message that comes across to the friends gathered at the table is that, yes, delicious food is important, but just as important are the good times involved with the sharing of that food.

ACKNOWLEDGMENTS

Like restaurant kitchens, book projects require a team effort.

Without Joanne Smart this book would not have happened. Thank you, Jo, for your good taste and tenacity.

Doe Coover first asked me to write a book many years ago. Thank you, Doe, for not giving up on me or the book. Your guidance, patience, and caring are boundless.

Thanks to Jennifer Josephy for believing we had a good idea and for all of her good work on the book.

I have learned so much from reading, tasting, and simply watching cooks cook. Thanks to all the great cooks who have influenced my cooking, especially Wolfgang Puck.

Thanks to Jasper White, Lydia Shire, Chris Schlesinger, Todd English, Moncef Meddeb, and Jimmy Burke who began the new wave of cooking in New England many years ago and who continue to cook inspired food. Special thanks to chef Jody Adams for being a rock-solid friend.

Thanks to all the fine people at Hamersley's Bistro, past and present, who work hard every day to make it a great place to have dinner.

Special thanks to chef Michael Ehlenfeldt, whose tireless dedication to high-quality cooking has made ours a well-respected kitchen. Michael's knowledge and hard work inspire me daily and make me a better cook.

Thanks to Sophia Schueler, Heather Stella, Jason Henelt, and Kate Dagle for their loyalty to the restaurant.

Thanks also to Peg Carmen, pastry chef at Hamersley's Bistro for many years, who worked on the dessert recipes for this book.

Thank you, Sandy Block, wine expert extraordinaire.

Thanks to Colleen Duggan and Meg Suzuki for their attention to detail as recipe testers.

Thanks to Charlie Smart, Peter and Joan McAllister, and Jodie and Andy Delohery for eating and opining.

Thanks to my father, Gordon, for not getting too upset when I told him I was washing dishes for a living.

Thanks to Julia Child for her sage advice, undying support, and immense appetite for all things culinary.

Finally, and most important, thanks to Fiona, Sophie, and Chester who saw little of me last summer and still managed to talk to me when I got back. Thanks for all your patience and love.

Bistro Cooking at Home

Introduction

CHANCES ARE

that you already cook in the bistro style
at home but are not aware of it. Chicken
cacciatore, beef stew, and chocolate pudding
could all be candidates for bistro fare. (In
fact, there are versions of each in this book,
but they go by the names coq au vin, beef
Bourguignon, and pot de crème.) Bistro
cooking is delicious, but it's not fussy. You
don't need to be a trained chef to execute it
well, but there are some key things to think
about as you approach these recipes.

SOMETIMES IT'S GREAT ingredients that will make all the difference: dry untreated scallops, good-quality chicken stock, authentic sherry vinegar, ripe pears. Other times technique matters most: keeping duck legs at a slow simmer for confit, whisking eggs and oil properly for aïoli, searing a rib-eye until well browned. Of course, high-quality ingredients combined with informed technique will always give you the best results. In the pages that follow, I talk about the key ingredients used in bistro cooking and describe my approach to various cooking methods.

• *Bistro Techniques* •

SEARING IS BELIEVING. Many bistro recipes begin with this step—essentially browning food in a hot pan coated with a little oil—because it's a great way to build flavor. Searing gives the food, whether it's a rack of lamb, a bunch of mushrooms, or some chicken thighs, a ton of flavor. The browned bits left on the bottom of the pan after searing also add flavor to any sauce that you make in the pan. To sear well, use a pan with a heavy base that's large enough to hold the food without crowding. Heat the pan and then add enough fat—butter, oil, duck fat, or a combination—to just coat the bottom. When the oil is hot—a drop of water will sizzle immediately when added to the pan—add your food to the pan. Don't crowd it in there or it will steam; be sure you can see some of the pan around each piece. Now, here is the important thing: Don't move the food. Let one side get good and brown before you turn the food over. This often takes longer than you think. Then sear the other side (or sides depending on what you are cooking) before moving on to the rest of the recipe.

THE BEST BETS FOR BRAISING. Braising is my favorite cooking method. For one thing, braising transforms tough, cheaper cuts of meat into meltingly tender morsels. For another, braises usually dirty just one pot and taste best when made ahead, all of which add to their efficiency. Most of my braises begin with browning (see Searing Is Believing), which gives the dish a huge head start in flavor. Next comes a sauté of aromatic vegetables. The food is then surrounded by a flavorful liquid, often wine and broth, and left to simmer quietly in the oven, all the while building in flavor. You want to use a heavy-based pan in which the food fits snugly. As is traditional, I cook my braises covered, but I often uncover the pot toward the end of cooking to begin to concentrate the flavors in the liquid and let the contents brown a bit. When the cover is off for an extended period of time, however, you need to baste or turn the meat over, so that the exposed side doesn't dry out.

One mistake often made with braising is thinking the meat is done before it is; the meat should be so tender that you can pull it apart easily with a fork. The time this takes can vary; use the given time as a guide, but use the fork test for best results. Keep this in mind when reheating a braise. Cook it gently and don't call it ready until the meat reaches that same degree of tenderness as when it originally came out of the oven.

Degreasing the braising liquid is crucial, especially when cooking something fatty such as lamb shanks. To degrease the liquid, use a gravy separator to pour off the fat, or allow the liquid to chill and remove the hardened fat with a spoon. Cook the degreased sauce (remove the meat first) until the sauce is reduced somewhat and the flavor is intensified.

"WALK-AWAY" ROASTING MAKES LIFE EASIER. Every chef does things a little differently. For a while, the trend for roasting was to start with the oven on very high heat for a certain amount of time, then lowering it to finish. Another variation has you crank up the heat at the end. I prefer to roast with a moderate oven temperature and the same temperature from start to finish. I can pop the bird or beast into the oven, walk away, and then forget about it for a while. It's not just the ease of preparation that leads me to roast this way; I find that roasting longer at a more moderate temperature gives me juicier results. But because this moderate roasting can result in a less browned exterior, I often sear the meat before roasting it.

There are sensory clues to tell if a roast is done, and I always include them in my recipes. But a sure way is to take its temperature with a meat thermometer. The temperatures given in the recipes are for taking the meat out of the oven. As it rests, it will continue to cook with the residual heat.

"SEAR ROASTING" MAKES ROOM ON THE STOVE AND HELPS FOOD COOK EVENLY. At most restaurants, the stovetop is prime real estate. That's why so many chefs employ a technique called "sear roasting" or "pan roasting." A piece of meat, fish, poultry, or vegetable gets seared on the stove and then finishes cooking, usually for just a few minutes, in the oven. Aside from creating space on the stove, finishing the food in the oven cooks it evenly, and often more gently, for the most tender results. One warning: Be careful of hot handles. You might notice that professional chefs almost always wrap a towel around a sauté pan's handle—whether or not the pan is even near the heat—before picking it up. It's a habit you develop quickly after burning your palm on an innocent-looking yet searingly hot handle. At home, try slipping a pot holder onto the handle as soon as you take the pan out of the oven, so that when you reach for it again you won't yelp with pain.

Sautéing, braising, and roasting may be the main methods employed in bistro cooking, but it's helpful to know some specialized techniques, too.

To blanch means to parcook something in boiling water, usually until just tender. A tip: Have ready a bowl of ice water to immediately stop the cooking.

A chiffonade means leafy greens or herbs cut into thin strips. To cut a chiffonade efficiently, stack the leaves, roll them into a tight cylinder, and slice crosswise with a very sharp knife to create thin ribbons.

To chop an onion efficiently, start with a very sharp knife. Cut the onion in half through the root, leaving the root intact. Put the onion cut side down and make 6 or 7 lengthwise (with-the-"grain") slices up to, but not through, the root to keep the slices together. Turn the knife blade parallel to the cutting board and carefully make 3 or 4 horizontal slices (depending on desired thickness) toward the root end. Finally, slice the onion crosswise. This method also works well on shallots, garlic cloves, and even fennel.

To toast nuts for deeper flavor, spread them on a baking sheet and cook them in a 350°F oven, stirring them once or twice for even cooking, for 5 to 10 minutes, depending on the size of the nut. Or toast them in a dry skillet on the stove over medium heat, shaking the skillet occasionally for even cooking. Either way, check on them often to keep them from burning.

A NOTE ON COOLING FOOD SAFELY: Cool down large amounts of soup or stew before chilling them. Foods spoil most easily at temperatures between 70 and 120 degrees. The faster you cool foods down to below 70 degrees, the less time they will be in the danger zone. Small containers are okay in the fridge, but a large pot will stay warm for a while. Set the food in a container in a larger bath of water and ice; stirring the food will speed cooling. Refrigerate the food only when it reaches room temperature.

· Bistro Tools ·

I am not a gadgety guy when it comes to cooking, and there aren't really any tools specific to bistro cooking, but I do have some opinions on the tools I do use. So here goes:

KNIVES: Buy the best ones you can afford and keep them sharp.

CHEF'S KNIFE: Also called a French knife, it has a wide, heavy blade. Get the biggest size you can handle well; a 10-inch knife works for most people. But obviously hand sizes differ. Before buying a knife, hold it in your hand. It should feel sturdy but not too heavy. It should also feel well balanced. Good-quality knives will have the tail of the blade running the full length of the handle. I find carbon-steel blades easier to keep sharp, and I like that they're a little lighter than stainless steel. When I find one I like, I buy them for the restaurant by the half dozen.

When using a chef's knife, go ahead and choke up on the handle for better control. You can even move your thumb and index finger onto either side of the blade, gripping the handle with the back three fingers. This is a good way to hold the knife for precise cuts. For less precise cutting, such as chopping herbs, move all of your fingers back on the handle. To chop herbs quickly, hold the tip of the knife down on the cutting board with one hand while you lift the handle up and down with the other, sweeping the blade across what you are chopping.

BONING KNIFE: The second most-used knife in my kitchen is a boning knife. It seems this is not a common one in most home knife collections. But its short, sharp, semiflexible blade makes boning a chicken, filleting a fish, or butterflying a leg of lamb so much easier. Once you try one you will be amazed that you ever cooked without one.

PARING KNIFE: Every kitchen has one or more of these knives, which are essential for fine work and peeling. Once again, look for one that feels good in your hand and has a sturdy blade; some versions have very wimpy, thin blades that are almost useless.

A 6-INCH UTILITY KNIFE: For when you don't need the big guns of a chef's knife, and it can stand in for filleting a fish in a pinch.

POTS AND PANS: I love cast iron and cook everything I can in it. It's got a heavy base and conducts heat in a great way. Once it gets hot, it stays hot with no hot spots. I once bought a round, 24-inch cast-iron pan with sides 3 inches high for the restaurant. The cooks looked at me like I was nuts. Two weeks later, they asked me to order two more. We do everything in it, from roasting birds to making polenta. Cast iron is also really cheap. People get nervous about it because you have to season it, but that just means coating the pan with oil and letting it heat in a 375°F oven for a couple of hours. Then you have a virtually nonstick interior that gets better every time you use it. Enameled cast iron, which has a light-colored interior, heats as well as uncoated cast iron and doesn't need to be seasoned. It also won't react with acidic food. It's not cheap, however.

As for the styles of pots and pans you'll need: Heavy-based roasting pans and braising pots (often called Dutch ovens) are especially crucial for the success of the long-cooked roasts and braises. A sauté pan that's large enough to hold your steaks or burgers without crowding—one that's at least 12 inches across if you often cook for four—makes all the difference in getting good browning. In many of these recipes, the sauté pans go into the oven, so be sure yours are ovenproof.

Other "must-haves" include a couple of saucepans. Here is where you might want to opt for a stainless interior instead of cast iron to allow you to see a sauce better, especially important when gauging the color of a caramel, for instance.

A good nonstick pan comes in handy, especially for searing fish and duck. But I don't recommend nonstick interiors for roasting pans; those flavorful juicy bits that stick to a regular pan add flavor to sauces. Speaking of roasting pans, I prefer a flat roasting rack to a V-shaped one.

TONGS: I use tongs so much in the kitchen they are practically an extension of my hands. I use them for the obvious—turning over meat or fish that I'm searing—and the less obvious: fishing for a french fry to taste for doneness, lifting ramekins out of their hot water bath, grabbing baked potatoes out of the oven. Tongs should be long enough to keep your hand away from the heat, but short enough to offer good control, about 12 inches seems right. They must have a spring-action handle. A lock on the handle makes them easy to store, but they'll probably be out all the time anyway.

THERMOMETERS: An instant-read meat thermometer is a handy tool to ensure that you cook a roast safely without overcooking it. As you take the temperature of your foods, also note the physical signs of doneness. Over time, you will need to rely less and less on the thermometer to tell when food is cooked to your liking. A candy/frying thermometer will come in handy for making the pommes frites in this book, and you will likely find other uses for it as well. You might also want to buy an oven thermometer, since oven temperatures can vary widely, affecting cooking times greatly.

• Bistro Pantry •

To cook in the bistro style at home does not require a pantry filled with exotic or unusual ingredients. Most of the items I define and describe here can be found in your supermarket.

As I tested the recipes for this book, I did most of my shopping at the supermarket. (We restaurant chefs can get a bit spoiled; we order the best produce, fish, and meat for the restaurant and just tack a little more on if we want some for home.) What I found as I shopped was that the folks working at the store were more than happy to help. Your supermarket butcher will cut a roast to size, french a rack of lamb, or order a special cut of meat for you. You just have to ask. As with my suppliers for the restaurant, I find that the more genuine interest I show in what they have to offer, the more interest they show in me. So talk to the folks working at the grocery store. If the whole side of salmon they ordered and cleaned for you was fabulous, let them know. If you wish the market carried saffron, chanterelles, or skirt steak, tell the head of the appropriate department. The way most supermarkets are designed, you may have to look hard to actually find the right person to talk to, but you'll be glad you did.

That said, check out what specialty shops are in your area. When you want a really great piece of fish, try a busy fish market. And don't forget ethnic markets. Even if your supermarket carries curry paste, it's likely just one brand and it may not be as authentic as the stuff you can pick up (usually cheaper) at an Asian market. Finally, there is the mail-order option for hard-to-find ingredients. The Internet makes finding and ordering just about anything a snap. If there is an unusual ingredient in a recipe, look to Sources (page 317) for information on how to order it.

What follows is observations about commonly used ingredients in bistro cooking as well as recipes for ingredients that taste much better when homemade, such as bread crumbs, stocks, and roasted peppers.

BUTTER: I always use unsalted butter for cooking and baking. If there is an amount of salt given in a recipe that also contains butter, it's presumed you are using unsalted (sweet) butter. Using salted butter might therefore make the recipe too salty. Also, unsalted butter tends to be fresher than salted because it has a shorter shelf life.

CRÈME FRAÎCHE: When milk is not pasteurized, the cream that floats to the top of the milk is sometimes left to "mature," resulting in crème fraîche, a thick, slightly tangy cream. You can buy approximate versions of it—approximate because most milk in the United States is pasteurized—in specialty markets, or you can make your own version by following the recipe on page 12.

BREAD CRUMBS: You'll find bread crumbs in a lot of bistro dishes. There are a couple of reasons for this. The French are big-time bread lovers, so there is always a loaf that's a day or two old and ready to be made into bread crumbs. Also, a topping of toasty bread crumbs adds a wonderful counterpoint to the many casseroles and gratins featured at bistros, including cassoulet.

Don't use those bread crumbs you get from the supermarket. Always, always make your own. It's so easy: Simply whirl a few chunks of good-quality bread in your food processor. Pulse just a few times for coarse bread crumbs, longer for fine ones. A good habit is to make bread crumbs out of whatever leftover bread you've got and then freeze them so you can always have some on hand. Most of my recipes call for what's called "fresh bread crumbs," meaning they're used as is. If a recipe calls for toasted or dried bread crumbs, simply spread the crumbs on a baking sheet and dry them out a bit in a 350°F oven. I often use seasoned bread crumbs. The recipe is on page 13.

OILS: When a recipe calls for vegetable oil, you can go ahead and use what you have on hand: canola, corn, and grapeseed, for example; all cook well at high heat and are practically without flavor. I don't use olive oil for sautéing, but if you do, don't use extra virgin olive oil because any nuances in this more expensive oil will be lost with the heat. Instead, save extra virgin olive oil for dressings and for drizzling over already cooked dishes. Olive oils can vary tremendously in flavor, some being quite fruity, others being quite peppery, and still others tasting green and grassy. Try some from different countries as well as different brands to see which ones you like.

Nut oils, such as walnut oil and hazelnut oil, are not really for cooking with. They're good in salads and drizzled on cooked foods, especially those dishes that contain nuts, to emphasize the nutty flavor. Once opened, nut oils should be refrigerated for a longer shelf life.

ANCHOVIES: You can buy anchovies packed in oil or salt. Those packed in oil just need a rinse in cold water. Soak salt-packed anchovies in a few changes of water before using them or they will be far too salty. You also need to remove the bones of salt-packed anchovies, an easy task: Gently split them open with your finger and pull the exposed backbone away from the fillet.

VINEGARS: "Vinegar" comes from the French word for sour wine. I like to use a range of vinegars. Red wine, white wine, and Champagne vinegars are the basics. Sherry vinegar has a sweeter, more complex flavor; the best come from southern Spain. Balsamic vinegar has gone from an esoteric, regional ingredient to a staple. The really expensive stuff needs to be rationed: Save it for drizzling on meat or risotto or cheese. Use a more moderately priced vinegar for salad dressings and stews.

LENTILS: I like to use regular brown lentils (which are also called "green lentils") primarily for soup, such as Fiona's Hearty Lentil Soup (page 55). If I'm cooking them as a side dish or making a lentil salad, I prefer the smaller French or European lentils, which hold their shape better, becoming fully tender while staying intact. My favorite French kind are lentils du Puy, which have an even more refined flavor. You can find European lentils at some supermarkets and at gourmet groceries. You can also mail-order them. (See Sources.)

SALT: I generally use kosher salt for all of my cooking, including baking. It has a larger crystal than table salt, and it really brings out flavors. To see for yourself, sear two steaks, one salted with table salt, the other with kosher salt. A similar-sized, good-quality sea salt would also be a fine choice. There are now some really fancy coarse salts available. They're best reserved for using at the table and can be fun to experiment with.

PEPPER: Always use freshly ground pepper. The flavor difference compared to that powdery preground stuff is like night and day. I keep a peppermill at the stove as well as on the table. I generally use black pepper, although white pepper is also delicious, especially with fish.

When a recipe calls for cracked pepper, it means just that. You can crack peppercorns under a heavy pot, or put them in a sealed heavy-duty, zip-top plastic bag and smash the peppercorns with the flat side of a meat mallet or an old rolling pin. As the peppercorns break up, shake the bag to make sure they all get cracked.

WINES AND SPIRITS: Being that I'm a cook inspired by the French, is it any surprise that I use a lot of wine in my cooking? But an ample use of wines and other spirits should not break the bank. Use a wine that you would not mind drinking, but certainly not the best wine on the shelf. French wines labeled *vin de table* usually work well. White wines should be on the dry side, while reds should have some fruit and not be too tannic. It might seem obnoxious to call for a quarter cup of white wine for a braised vegetable dish, but I do find that without it a sauce can seem lackluster. (In such cases, you can turn to a bottle of decent vermouth, a fortified wine that has a longer shelf life than regular white wine.) Other fortified wines I turn to again and again include sherry, brandy, and port. These add a deeper, richer flavor. Again, use good-quality but inexpensive bottles for cooking.

HERBES DE PROVENCE: This is a wonderful, fragrant herb mix from the south of France that includes the herbs that grow rampant there: thyme, tarragon, rosemary, fennel, and lavender.

You can buy cute little crocks of it at gourmet stores, but I find that they're pretty heavy with the lavender. I prefer to make my own mix (see page 14).

QUATRE ÉPICES: French for "four spices." The spices themselves can vary a little; my version (page 13) is pretty standard, although I often see white pepper in the mix instead of the black we use.

ROASTED GARLIC PURÉE: A little roasted garlic purée (see page 15) is one of those secret ingredients that make good food great. It will keep in the freezer, so you can make a lot of it and freeze it in smaller amounts. It's wonderful simply spread on grilled bread. It makes an excellent rub for steaks and chicken, and can go into a vinaigrette or a sauce for a sweeter, more mellow garlic presence.

ROASTED PEPPERS: Roasting bell peppers at home is really easy, and the flavor is brighter than that of jarred roasted peppers. Their sweetly charred flavor adds a real boost to many recipes. You can roast peppers either in the oven or over a flame.

    TO ROAST PEPPERS IN THE OVEN: Stem them, seed them, and cut them in half lengthwise. Line a baking sheet with aluminum foil and flatten the peppers onto the baking sheets. Broil until blackened. Put the hot roasted peppers into a bowl and cover with plastic wrap. The steaming will loosen their skins. Remove the skins from the peppers.

    TO ROAST PEPPERS ON A GAS BURNER: Place the peppers directly on the burner on its highest setting. Use tongs to turn the peppers until they are black all over. Steam as directed above, and then stem, seed, and peel them.

AÏOLI AND ROUILLE: Two garlicky mayonnaises from Provence. I love them with everything from steamed fish and vegetables to french fries. The rouille gets its brilliant color from the flavorful addition of saffron and its heat from cayenne pepper. (See recipes on pages 16–17.)

STOCKS AND BROTHS: According to *The Joy of Cooking,* a stock by definition is made with more bones than meat, and a broth with more meat than bones. Whatever you call them, stocks are a vital ingredient in much of bistro cooking, whether a soup, braise, or sauce. People often say it's a lack of time that keeps them from making stock at home. But I think it's more a fear of doing it wrong. A lot of recipes are insistent upon things like simmering the liquid just so, defatting it as it cooks, and fastidiously straining it. But really, a stock doesn't need such precious treatment.

If you can simmer water, you can make a stock that's better than anything prepackaged. If it's a little cloudy, who cares? For most uses, that doesn't matter. What you're really after is great flavor and, in the case of veal stock, body. So choose a time when you'll be home for a few hours. Stocks do take a while, but it's the kind of time that takes very little baby-sitting.

When you do make stock, make a lot of it (or what's the point?). Freeze the stocks in different amounts, so that when you need a cup for a sauce, you don't have to defrost a lot of it. Freezer bags, quart size and gallon size, work great for this because you can flatten the broth in the bags, stack them for efficient storage, and defrost small amounts in a couple of minutes under hot running water. Before freezing stock, chill it overnight in the fridge and then remove the fat that has solidified on its surface. Stock recipes are on pages 18 to 22.

REDUCE STOCK TO A GLAZE FOR INTENSE FLAVOR: One huge benefit of making your own stock is that you can also make your own glaze, an ingredient used often in restaurants and one of the reasons why pan sauces from a good restaurant often taste so much fuller than those made at home. It's easy enough to do: Simply simmer an amount of degreased chicken, beef, or veal stock until it's reduced to a syrupy glaze. This can take anywhere from 2 to 4 hours depending on how much you started with and the shape of your pan. The glaze will be anywhere from 10 to 20 percent of the original volume and will coat the back of a spoon. Once chilled, it will feel firm to the touch. You can freeze the glaze in even smaller amounts, since a tablespoon or two added to a pan sauce is usually all you need to make the dish taste really fabulous. In the recipes in this book, there's no recipe calling for glaze explicitly, but you can use a tablespoon or so when making pan sauces for a really rich flavor.

A NOTE ON SALT IN STOCKS: I don't generally season meat and poultry stocks with salt as I cook them. If you decide to reduce it at a later point, a salted stock will become overly salty. (But when you taste your stock for flavor, you might want to add a pinch of salt.) If you know you won't be reducing your stock, you can season it with salt at the end of cooking.

IF YOU AREN'T MAKING YOUR OWN STOCK: Any recipe that calls for broth or stock will taste better with a good homemade version. That said, I'm a practical man. As I tested these recipes, I often used supermarket chicken broth to be sure the results would be good—and they were. You must be careful, however, when adding additional salt to a recipe; because most packaged or canned broths are high in sodium, the result, especially for a reduced sauce, can be very salty indeed. Try different brands of broths and stocks to see which you like best. Your local butcher or gourmet store might also make stocks from scratch, which will likely be better than most commercial brands.

HOMEMADE CRÈME FRAÎCHE

A dollop is great on puréed soups. Sweetened and whipped, it's perfect on desserts.

2 cups heavy cream, preferably not ultrapasteurized

¼ cup buttermilk

COMBINE the cream and buttermilk in a glass container (e.g., a jar) or stainless-steel bowl. Cover with cheesecloth or a clean kitchen towel to allow some air to reach the mixture. Let stand at room temperature—about 70 degrees—until thick, 12 to 24 hours. When it has reached the desired consistency, stir until smooth, cover, and refrigerate before using. Crème fraîche will keep in the refrigerator for up to 2 weeks. If any liquid appears on the surface, simply pour it off before using.

SEASONED BREAD CRUMBS

MAKES ABOUT 1½ CUPS

These bread crumbs are especially delicious as a topping for gratins.

1½ cups fresh coarse bread crumbs

1 shallot, thinly sliced

1 garlic clove, finely chopped

½ teaspoon chopped fresh thyme leaves

Kosher salt and freshly ground black pepper to taste

COMBINE all of the ingredients with your fingers.

QUATRE ÉPICES

MAKES A LITTLE MORE THAN 1 TABLESPOON

Freshly grated nutmeg and freshly ground black pepper will give you the most flavorful result.

1 teaspoon ground cloves

1 teaspoon grated or ground nutmeg

1 teaspoon freshly ground black pepper

½ teaspoon cinnamon

COMBINE the ingredients and store in an airtight container.

HAMERSLEY'S HERBES *de* PROVENCE MIX

If you grow lavender, dry the buds yourself for this mix. Otherwise, make sure to get the buds that are dried for culinary purposes, as lavender is often used in making potpourri blends (see Sources).

2 tablespoons dried thyme

2 tablespoons dried oregano

2 tablespoons dried marjoram

1 tablespoon dried tarragon

1 tablespoon dried rosemary

½ teaspoon fennel seeds

Pinch of lavender buds

COMBINE the ingredients and store in an airtight container.

WHOLE ROASTED HEADS *of* GARLIC

My motto at the restaurant is "Life is nothing without garlic." We like to serve the whole heads so people can squeeze the soft, sweet cloves out themselves.

4 to 6 whole heads of garlic

About 2 tablespoons olive oil

1 teaspoon kosher salt

½ teaspoon freshly ground black pepper

HEAT the oven to 325°F. Remove any loose, papery skins and cut off the top ¼ inch of each head of garlic. Line a baking pan with aluminum foil. Put the garlic in the baking pan, cut side up. Drizzle the garlic with olive oil and sprinkle with salt and pepper. Sprinkle each head of garlic with about 2 tablespoons water and cover the pan well with more aluminum foil. Bake the garlic until very tender, 1 to 1½ hours. Remove from the pan with a metal spatula. Let the garlic cool a bit and then squeeze the whole head with your fingers for the garlic purée.

Note: If you want to serve individual cloves of roasted garlic, separate the cloves from the head and bake for less time.

AÏOLI

Bringing the ingredients to room temperature before combining them allows them to emulsify more easily.

1 large egg yolk (see Note)

1 teaspoon Dijon mustard

2 to 3 teaspoons fresh lemon juice

4 to 6 garlic cloves, very finely chopped

Kosher salt and freshly ground black pepper

½ cup olive oil

½ cup canola oil

WHISK together the egg yolk, mustard, lemon juice, garlic, and salt and pepper to taste until smooth. Slowly whisk in the olive and canola oils, a drop at a time at first. When the mixture has begun to thicken, continue whisking in the oils in a slow stream. Taste and add more lemon juice and salt and pepper to taste. Store, covered and refrigerated, for up to 2 days.

Note: Although it's estimated that only 1 in 20,000 eggs from chickens bred in the United States contains salmonella, certain people—the elderly, small children, and anyone with a compromised immune system—should probably avoid eating any raw eggs. In such cases, a pasteurized egg product would be more suitable.

ROUILLE

Sometimes bread crumbs are added to rouille, but I prefer this smooth version. If you like very spicy food, add the entire amount of cayenne.

1 egg yolk (see Note)

1½ teaspoons Dijon mustard

½ to 1 teaspoon cayenne pepper

½ teaspoon paprika

2 garlic cloves, very finely chopped

½ teaspoon kosher salt

3 to 4 teaspoons fresh lemon juice

½ teaspoon saffron threads, crushed in a mortar and pestle or finely chopped

½ cup olive oil

½ cup canola oil

IN a small bowl, combine the egg yolk, mustard, cayenne, paprika, garlic, and salt. Whisk to combine until smooth. In a small saucepan, heat 3 teaspoons of the lemon juice and the saffron until just warm. Let the lemon juice cool and then scrape it into the egg yolk mixture with a rubber spatula. Whisk to combine. Slowly whisk in the olive and canola oils, a drop at a time at first. When the mixture has begun to thicken, continue whisking in the olive and canola oils in a slow stream. Add more lemon juice and salt to taste. Store, covered and refrigerated, for up to 2 days.

Note: Although it's estimated that only 1 in 20,000 eggs from chickens bred in the United States contains salmonella, certain people—the elderly, small children, and anyone with a compromised immune system—should probably avoid eating any raw eggs. In such cases, a pasteurized egg product would be more suitable.

VEAL STOCK

I use knuckle bones plus veal shanks, but you can also cut up a veal breast, both meat and bones, and use about the same amount (around 7 pounds) of that cut.

5 pounds veal knuckle bones, cut into manageable chunks by your butcher

2 to 3 pounds meaty veal shanks (osso buco)

3 cups dry white wine

2 medium onions, chopped

2 medium carrots, peeled and chopped

3 celery ribs, chopped

2 to 3 medium tomatoes, canned or fresh, chopped

1 tablespoon tomato paste

10 peppercorns

2 bay leaves

3 to 4 sprigs fresh thyme or 2 teaspoons dried thyme

1 bunch fresh parsley, washed well

Kosher salt (if not reducing)

HEAT the oven to 425°F. Roast the veal bones and shanks in a roasting pan, stirring occasionally, until well browned, about 1 hour. Transfer the veal bones and meat to a large (about 16 quarts) stockpot. Pour off any fat that has accumulated in the roasting pan and discard. Place the roasting pan on the stove over high heat and add 1 cup of the white wine. Bring to a boil and stir, scraping up any browned bits stuck to the bottom of the roasting pan. Add this to the stockpot. Fill the stockpot with enough cold water to cover the bones by an inch. Bring to a boil and then lower the heat to a slow simmer. Skim the foam that accumulates on the surface during the first 15 minutes of cooking.

MEANWHILE, toss the onions, carrots, celery, and tomatoes with the tomato paste in the roasting pan. Roast the vegetables, stirring every 10 min-

utes, until they begin to brown, about 40 minutes. Remove the vegetables from the roasting pan and put them in the stockpot. Put the roasting pan on the stove over high heat and add 1 cup water. Bring to a boil and stir, scraping up any browned bits stuck to the bottom of the roasting pan. Add this to the stockpot. Add the peppercorns, bay leaves, thyme, parsley, and remaining wine to the stockpot, and let the stock simmer for 4 to 6 hours. As the stock cooks, monitor the heat level so you find the right balance of heat to cooking time. The slower you cook the stock, the clearer it will be; but it all gets strained in the end and for this kind of cooking you don't need to be too meticulous. You want to cook the stock until it tastes quite flavorful, but overcooking it can give it a muddy flavor. One way to tell doneness is to take a bite of some of the meat simmering in the broth; once it's lost its flavor, the stock is done.

STRAIN the stock through a fine-mesh strainer or, for a more clear stock, through a layer of cheese-cloth. Season with salt to taste if not reducing. Cool the stock as fast as possible (see page 4) and refrigerate for up to 3 days. Before freezing or reducing, remove the hardened layer of fat from the stock.

MUSHROOM STOCK

MAKES ABOUT 1½ QUARTS

A rich, full-flavored broth. The leftover mushrooms and onions make a great pasta sauce. Add cream and let it bubble for about 10 minutes, then toss with cooked pasta of your choice.

2 tablespoons olive oil

1 onion, chopped

4 portobello mushrooms, stems and gills removed and cut into quarters

10 white mushrooms, cleaned and chopped

6 garlic cloves, chopped

6 to 8 ounces dried mushrooms, such as porcini, black trumpet, or shiitake

1 cup dry sherry

½ cup soy sauce

Pinch of herbes de Provence (see Bistro Pantry)

Kosher salt

HEAT the olive oil in a large pot over medium heat. Add the onion and cook until tender, about 7 minutes. Add the portobello mushrooms, the white mushrooms, and the garlic and cook, stirring every few minutes, until the mushrooms begin to throw off their juices.

ADD the dried mushrooms, sherry, soy sauce, 2 quarts water, and the herbes de Provence. Bring to a boil and then reduce the heat to a simmer. Cook for 45 minutes. Strain through a fine-mesh strainer and season with salt to taste. Cool and store.

VEGETABLE STOCK

The first version of this stock is very lean; it's made with no oil and only boiled. I like to use it for poaching or blanching vegetables or for poaching fish; it's also nice in a light risotto, such as the Crabmeat Risotto with Peas and Mint on page 138. The roasted variation has much more punch and should be used for heartier dishes; it can be used in just about any recipe that calls for chicken broth. Because I don't reduce vegetable stock, I do add a little salt to bring out the flavor of the stock.

1 medium leek, trimmed, rinsed well, white part and a couple inches of the green, chopped

1 medium onion, chopped

2 carrots, chopped

2 celery ribs, chopped

2 parsnips, chopped

1 medium turnip, chopped

1 tablespoon crushed canned tomato

2 sprigs fresh thyme or 1 teaspoon dried thyme

½ bunch fresh parsley, washed well and roughly chopped

1 bay leaf

6 black peppercorns

1 cup vermouth

1 tablespoon kosher salt

2 to 3 sprigs fresh tarragon

6 to 8 fresh basil leaves

2 sprigs fresh marjoram

PUT the leek, onion, carrots, celery, parsnips, and turnip in a large stockpot. Add the crushed tomato, thyme, parsley, bay leaf, peppercorns, vermouth, and salt. Add water to cover the vegetables by about 2 inches. Bring to a boil and then lower the heat to a simmer. Cook until flavorful, about 1½ hours. Add the tarragon, basil, and marjoram, and let steep for about 15 minutes. Strain and cool.

For Roasted Vegetable Stock: Toss the leek, onion, carrots, celery, parsnips, and turnip with about 1 tablespoon olive oil and season with ½ teaspoon kosher salt. Roast in a 350°F oven, stirring occasionally, until the vegetables take on some color but are not fully cooked, about 1 hour. Put the vegetables in a large stockpot and continue as directed above.

CHICKEN BROTH

When you taste the chicken broth for doneness, add a little salt to your tasting sample to bring out the flavor of the broth and give yourself a true appreciation of its flavor. To make a roasted chicken broth, which has a stronger flavor and makes a good substitute for veal stock, see the Note that follows.

5 pounds chicken parts (backs, necks, wings, legs, or thighs)

1 medium leek, trimmed, rinsed well, white part and a couple inches of the green, chopped

2 medium carrots, chopped

1 celery rib, chopped

2 bay leaves

6 black peppercorns

1 sprig fresh thyme or 1 teaspoon dried thyme

2 cups dry white wine

Kosher salt (if not reducing)

RINSE the chicken parts and put them in a large stockpot. Add cold water to cover the bones by an inch and bring to a boil. Skim the foam off the top of the stock.

ADD the leek, carrots, celery, bay leaves, peppercorns, thyme, and white wine. Bring back to a boil and then lower the heat to a rapid simmer. Cook until the stock tastes of a fairly strong mix of chicken and vegetables, about 2 hours. Strain the stock through a fine-mesh strainer or, for a more clear stock, through a layer of cheesecloth. Season with salt to taste if not reducing. Cool the stock as fast as possible (see page 4) and refrigerate for up to 3 days. Before freezing or reducing, remove the hardened layer of fat from the stock.

> **Note:** For a richer, more deeply flavored stock, chop the vegetables into larger pieces and roast them with the chicken parts in a 400°F oven until well browned. Put the chicken and vegetables into the stockpot, pour off the fat in the roasting pan, and deglaze the pan with a cup or so of water, scraping up the browned bits with a spoon. Pour this into the stockpot, and continue with the recipe as directed.

BEEF STOCK

MAKES ABOUT 3½ QUARTS

5 pounds beef rib bones or knuckle bones, cut into manageable pieces by your butcher

2 pounds beef chuck, cut into 3-inch chunks

3 cups red wine

2 medium onions, chopped

2 medium carrots, chopped

3 celery ribs, chopped

2 to 3 medium tomatoes, canned or fresh, chopped

10 peppercorns

2 bay leaves

3 to 4 sprigs fresh thyme or 2 teaspoons dried thyme

1 bunch fresh parsley

Kosher salt (if not reducing)

HEAT the oven to 425°F. Roast the beef bones and meat in a roasting pan, stirring occasionally, until well browned, about 1 hour. Transfer the beef bones and meat to a large (about 16 quarts) stockpot. Pour off any fat that has accumulated in the roasting pan and discard. Put the roasting pan on the stove over high heat and add 1 cup of the red wine. Bring to a boil and stir, scraping up any browned bits stuck to the bottom of the roasting pan. Add this to the stockpot. Fill the stockpot with enough cold water to cover the bones by an inch. Bring to a boil and then lower the heat to a slow simmer. Skim the foam that accumulates on the surface during the first 15 minutes of cooking.

MEANWHILE, toss the onions, carrots, celery, and tomatoes together in the roasting pan. Roast the vegetables, stirring every 10 minutes, until they begin to brown, about 40 minutes. Remove the vegetables from the roasting pan and put them in the stockpot. Put the roasting pan on the stove over high heat and add 1 cup water. Bring to a boil and stir, scraping up any browned bits stuck to the bottom of the roasting pan. Add this to the stockpot. Add the peppercorns, bay leaves, thyme, parsley, and remaining wine to the stockpot, and let the stock simmer until the broth is quite flavorful and the meat has lost its flavor, 3 to 4 hours. As the stock cooks, monitor the heat level so you find the right balance of heat to cooking time. The slower you cook the stock, the clearer it will be; but it all gets strained in the end, and for this kind of cooking you don't need to be too meticulous.

STRAIN the stock through a fine-mesh strainer or, for a more clear stock, through a layer of cheesecloth. Season with salt to taste if not reducing. Cool the stock as fast as possible (see page 4) and refrigerate for up to 3 days. Before freezing or reducing, remove the hardened layer of fat from the stock.

A Few Words About
Pairing Wine and Food

Sunday dinner at our house might look a little odd to the uninitiated. Fiona (who oversees the wine buying for the restaurant), our daughter, Sophie, and I sit at one end of our old, fifteen-foot-long French dining table. Way down at the other end stands a multitude of wine bottles. In front of the two of us who are of drinking age are five or so glasses, one for each of the various wines that Fiona has chosen for us to taste that night. I often cook things at home that will eventually go on the menu at the restaurant, and I love cooking food with bold flavors for Fiona to fool around with. As she tries each wine, she scribbles down descriptions, often exclaiming either how bad or how good one or the other wine is with what I've cooked. Sometimes she'll throw her pen down in disgust. "How are we supposed to serve wine with food with this much vinegar?" she'll demand. Or she'll practically shout: "Just because asparagus is in season doesn't mean we have to put it in every dish!" At such times, I usually just keep eating knowing that sooner or later she'll find a wine that will work.

Choosing what to drink with most dishes doesn't have to be complicated, though. And even though I am poking a little fun, neither of us gets too crazy about it. If we have any "rules" to suggest, the main one is to drink what you like. And, generally speaking, turn to lighter wines with lighter-tasting foods and heavier wines with more hearty meals.

The wine suggestions included in this book are Fiona's personal suggestions and are meant only as a place from which to start if you are totally perplexed as to what to drink. Fiona has a great palate and knows my food well, having tasted my cooking for many years both at home and in the restaurant, so you are in good hands. If some of these wines, most of which are referred to by their appellation or growing area, seem unfamiliar to you, turn to a well-staffed wine store in your area; they will be only too glad to help with information and tastings. Most important, have fun when pairing wine and food, and don't be afraid to try something a little different from what you might normally.

THE ART
of the SALAD

BISTRO SALADS

have assertive personalities. Most
often served before the main course, they
stimulate the appetite with flavorful greens,
bright vinaigrettes, and additions that are
salty, tangy, crispy—often all three. Frisée
au lardons, a bistro staple, illustrates this
perfectly: frisée, a member of the chicory
family with delicate, curly good looks but
a slightly bitter edge, gets tossed with a
vinaigrette made tangy with ample red wine
vinegar. Then there are the crispy strips
of bacon and crunchy croutons. The salad
is often served topped with a poached
egg, which is how I like it.

WHILE YOU'LL FIND recipes for other kinds of salads elsewhere in the book (such as the lentil salad on page 197), in this chapter I'm focusing on salads made with greens. Because making a green salad seems easy, it's often not given the same care and attention as other food preparation. But when a salad is made just right, people go crazy for it. At a food event for *Food & Wine* magazine, I served lobster and scallop terrine to, oh, a few hundred people. We spent a lot of time on those little terrines, cracking open scores of lobster shells, making the shellfish mousse, wrapping the terrines in leeks, and baking them gently in a water bath so that they were perfectly set. We served slices of the terrine with a spoonful of beet sauce and a small salad on the side. The salad was hardly an afterthought. We worked just as diligently on the salad as we had on the terrine. For each plate, we gently tossed together young arugula, pristine mâche, tender frisée, and whole chervil leaves. We dressed the greens on each plate with a few drops of olive oil, an outstanding Chardonnay vinegar, very finely chopped shallots, and the tiniest bit of sea salt. People loved the terrine, but they raved about that little side salad. Here are some things to think about to help your salads get raves.

BUY THE BEST GREENS AND USE THEM SOON. Because most ingredients that go into a salad are raw, they have to be stellar. You know what to look for: no wilting, no brown spots. Use all of your senses when buying greens and buy only those items that look, feel, smell, and taste best. If you can buy your produce at a farmers' market so much the better. About those premixed bags of lettuces: They can be convenient, but because they're sealed you really don't know what you've got until you get home. A safer bet is to buy a variety of loose greens and mix them yourself. (For a fresh, vibrant note, try adding some whole parsley or chervil leaves to your salad mix. And don't forget watercress; it adds a great, peppery punch.)

WASH GREENS, OFTEN MORE THAN ONCE. Even if your greens don't look dirty, they may be coated with just the slightest bit of sand. When you bite down on even that small amount of grit, the salad is wrecked.

To wash greens, fill a large bowl with cold water. Separate the leaves, discarding any that are tough or wilted, and gently plunge the leaves into the water. (Putting the greens in a colander and running water over them can bruise the leaves.) Swish the greens around a little to loosen the dirt. Next, put both your hands under the greens, and let them rest on your hands as you lift them out of the water. Place the greens somewhere safe—on a clean towel, in the colander of your salad spinner—for a minute. Now look into the bowl of water. See any dirt? If so, pour the water out, making sure the dirt goes with it, and repeat the process until there is no more dirt in the bowl. Often one rinse is enough; other times, especially for greens like spinach, escarole, and herbs (you should wash them well, too) like basil, you'll need to repeat the rinsing a couple of times.

DRY YOUR GREENS REALLY, REALLY WELL. Omitting this step is the reason there are so many bad salads in the world. Wet greens literally weigh your salad down. The greens soak up the extra moisture and become limp, heavy, and flavorless. The excess water infiltrates your dressing and dilutes its flavor. A good salad spinner makes drying greens easy. For the best results, spin the wet greens a few times, dump out the excess water, fluff the leaves, and spin again. Other ways to dry greens include patting them dry (gently) with towels or putting them in a clean pillowcase and spinning the case over your head. (Doing this outside is less messy, of course.) For quicker salad making, wash and dry your greens as soon as you buy them, wrap them loosely in paper towels, and store them in an uncovered plastic container in the salad drawer in your fridge.

DRESS YOUR SALAD WITH A LIGHT HAND JUST BEFORE SERVING. Give the greens plenty of room in a large bowl, and then toss them with some of your dressing. Never dump in all of the salad dressing at once even if you are following a recipe. Why? Because cooking is not an exact science: One type of lettuce contains more water than another, for example, and will absorb less of the dressing. Add some dressing and toss the greens gently (I like to use my hands to do this). Then take a taste. If the salad seems dry, add a little more dressing and toss. The greens of a perfectly dressed salad will glisten but will still feel light, and the flavor of the greens will be detectable under the dressing.

GIVE YOUR SALAD SOME HEIGHT. At the restaurant, I tell my staff to treat the greens of a salad as a garnish even if the lettuce is the main player. This is something you can think about doing at home, too. Place a handful of greens lightly on the plate and they'll naturally mound (as long as they're not overdressed). A hint: If you're serving the salad on a dinner plate, which I like to do, keep the greens heaped in the center of the plate instead of spreading them to the edges. Divide the greens among the plates and then go back for any nuts or crumbled cheese that fell to the bottom of the bowl and divide those bits among the plates. (When I'm adding roasted vegetables or other heavy ingredients to a salad, I usually toss those heavier pieces separately with a little of the vinaigrette.) Either way, don't just plop the heavier things smack-dab in the middle of the greens; this crushes and flattens the leaves. Instead, scatter them about, even under the greens, so that you get a mixture of flavors and textures with every bite.

· How to Make a Great Vinaigrette ·

Modern bistros serve all kinds of salads with all kinds of salad dressings. But the classic red wine vinaigrette, made with a healthy amount of Dijon mustard and chopped shallot, will always be my favorite. As soon as I start chopping the shallot, I'm happy with anticipation of the good meal to come.

A well-made vinaigrette is a balancing act. Too much vinegar and it will grab the glands beneath your jaw and shake them. Too much oil and it will leave your mouth slick. Part of the balancing act includes personal taste. The portions suggested in this book make a vinaigrette that I like. The actual amounts you use will depend on your ingredients—vinegars differ in acidity and flavor, for example—your palate, and the salad that you plan to dress. You might want a sharper vinaigrette to accompany full-flavored greens, for example, and a rounder one for lighter-flavored greens. Taste the vinaigrette as you prepare it, and then taste it again with some or all of the salad components to determine if it's balanced. Add a little more acid if it tastes dull, a little more oil if too astringent. And don't forget the salt and pepper. Salt brings out and melds the flavors of the vinaigrette, so add a good pinch of it. And while you can make a fine vinaigrette without it, I think the shallot is the ingredient that takes a vinaigrette from good to great. Sure, the quality of the oil and the vinegar plays an important role, but the shallot adds an almost indescribable sweetness and depth of flavor.

Finally, the technique for making a vinaigrette is usually to combine all of the ingredients except the oil. The oil then gets whisked into the ingredients in a slow, steady stream to create an emulsion, a temporary commingling of the oil and the vinegar. A successful emulsion will most effectively distribute the vinaigrette's flavor, but it's not as critical here as it is in, say, a mayonnaise or hollandaise sauce, since you don't really see the resulting emulsion and the tossing will help distribute the flavors. A properly combined vinaigrette will become cohesive and slightly thicker as you whisk it. You can also shake the ingredients together in a covered jar to get the same result. As a vinaigrette sits, it will separate; so just whisk or shake it right before dressing your salad.

Once you get the hang of making the basic vinaigrette, you can start playing with the formula. I love the sharp, nutty flavor of sherry vinegar as well as the rich sweetness of a good balsamic (but don't use the really expensive stuff). I sometimes use half extra virgin olive oil and half canola oil in a vinaigrette, especially if the olive oil is extremely fruity or peppery. Adding fresh or dried herbs is another way to tweak the vinaigrette's flavor; some fresh thyme or some dried herbes de Provence feels especially suited to bistro cooking.

CLASSIC BISTRO VINAIGRETTE

This vinaigrette works especially well with heartier greens. To soften the flavor of the shallot a little, let it macerate in the vinegar for a few minutes before adding the oil.

1 tablespoon Dijon mustard

1 shallot, finely chopped (about 1 tablespoon)

¼ cup red wine vinegar

Generous pinch of kosher salt

Freshly ground black pepper

¾ cup extra virgin olive oil

IN a small bowl, combine the mustard, shallot, vinegar, salt, and pepper to taste. Whisk in the olive oil in a steady stream until it's all incorpo-rated and an emulsion forms. It will keep, covered and refrigerated, for up to 3 days.

· A Little Something on the Side ·

Often when I make a simple green salad, I serve with it a slice of toasted baguette spread with a flavorful topping. It's a simple way to add more flavor and texture to a salad. The possibilities for toppings are endless, but here are some of my favorites.

BLACK OLIVE SPREAD

MAKES ABOUT ½ CUP

I like the mellow flavor of this spread, but if you want a more pungent, tapenade-type flavor, add a tablespoon of rinsed capers to the mix.

4 ounces pitted black olives, such as Kalamata

2 teaspoons grated orange zest

2 teaspoons finely chopped garlic

2 to 3 tablespoons extra virgin olive oil

COMBINE the ingredients in a food processor and pulse until you've got a consistent texture. Or mash the ingredients together with a mortar and pestle. Store, covered, in the refrigerator for up to 1 week.

TOMATO SALAD

To lessen the potency of the scallions, blanch them for 45 seconds in boiling water, then cool them under cold running water.

2 medium ripe tomatoes, peeled, seeded, and cut into a small dice

2 scallions, white parts and about 1 inch of the green, thinly sliced

2 tablespoons chopped fresh parsley

1 teaspoon sherry vinegar

1 tablespoon extra virgin olive oil

Kosher salt and freshly ground black pepper to taste

COMBINE the ingredients in a small bowl and allow the flavors to blend.

MUSHROOM DUXELLES

I like to serve this rich, creamy topping with a salad made with hearty bitter greens, such as radicchio and endive.

About ½ tablespoon unsalted butter

3 ounces mixed domestic and wild mushrooms, coarsely chopped

1 shallot, finely chopped

2 tablespoons dry white wine

Kosher salt and freshly ground black pepper

2 tablespoons heavy cream

HEAT the butter in a sauté pan over medium heat until it stops bubbling. Add the mushrooms and shallot and cook, stirring, until the mushrooms and shallot begin to release their juices and the mushrooms lightly brown. Add the wine and season with salt and pepper to taste. Continue to cook until the wine is absorbed and the mushrooms begin to look dry. Place the mushrooms in a food processor and pulse until they become finely chopped but not mushy, or chop finely by hand. Fold in the cream.

CHICKEN LIVER PÂTÉ

A splash of Madeira adds a sweet pungency to rich chicken livers. This pâté is easy to make, will keep for a couple of days in the refrigerator, and is easily doubled.

2 tablespoons unsalted butter, at room temperature

4 chicken livers, drained, trimmed of all fat and sinew, and patted dry

2 shallots, finely chopped

Kosher salt and freshly ground black pepper

½ teaspoon tomato paste

2 tablespoons Madeira

HEAT about 2 teaspoons of the butter in a small sauté pan over medium-high heat. When the butter is hot, add the livers and shallots, season lightly with salt and pepper, and cook until lightly browned on all sides, about 3 minutes. Add the tomato paste and Madeira. Lower the heat and cook for 2 minutes. Take the pan off the heat and allow it to cool for about 5 minutes. Process the livers and the remaining butter in a food processor until smooth. Season with more salt and pepper, if necessary, and transfer to a serving bowl. Chill in the refrigerator until set. Season with additional salt and pepper, if necessary.

MIXED GREENS *with* FRIED WALNUT-COATED GOAT CHEESE *and* SHERRY VINAIGRETTE

This salad is known as salade Cabécou in the southwest of France because it's traditionally made with a local goat cheese called Cabécou. Warm goat cheese rounds are often served with delicate, springtime lettuces. But I think the cheese's crisp crust and creamy, slightly tangy interior are much more interesting when paired with heartier greens, such as escarole and radicchio.

1½ cups fresh bread crumbs (see Bistro Pantry, page 7)

1 cup walnuts, toasted (see page 4) and finely chopped

2 medium shallots, finely chopped

Kosher salt and freshly ground black pepper

10 ounces fresh goat cheese

2 eggs, lightly beaten

2 teaspoons Dijon mustard

3 tablespoons sherry vinegar

¾ cup extra virgin olive oil, plus more oil for frying

About 12 cups mixed greens, including oakleaf lettuce, escarole (tough stems removed), and radicchio, washed and dried well and torn into 2- to 3-inch pieces

IN a shallow bowl or a plate, combine the bread crumbs, walnuts, half of the shallots, and salt and pepper to taste.

USING your hands, form the goat cheese into 6 balls about 1½ ounces each. Dip each ball in the beaten eggs to cover and then roll the ball in the bread-crumb mixture to cover. Press the balls into round disks ¼ to ⅓ inch thick. Refrigerate until cold, about 1 hour.

IN a small bowl, combine the remaining shallots with the mustard and vinegar, and season with salt and pepper. In a thin, steady stream, whisk in ¾ cup olive oil until it's all incorporated and an emulsion forms.

SEASON the goat cheese disks with salt and pepper.

HEAT about 3 tablespoons olive oil or vegetable oil in a large sauté pan over medium-high heat until quite hot (a bit of bread crumb put in the oil should sizzle immediately). Put the goat cheese disks in the pan and lower the heat to medium. (If your pan does not hold all of the disks with room to maneuver, cook them in two batches.) Allow the disks to brown slowly on one side, lowering the heat as necessary. With a spatula, carefully turn the disks over to brown the other side. Reserve in a warm place.

TOSS the greens with just enough of the dressing to coat the leaves lightly. Divide the greens among six plates and top with a warm disk of goat cheese.

HEARTS *of* ROMAINE *and* WATERCRESS *with* CREAMY PARMESAN DRESSING

SERVES 6

Hearty salads are part of every bistro's menu, and it's no exception at Hamersley's. This Caesar-inspired salad comes without the anchovy. Another difference is the addition of watercress to jazz up the flavor of the greens. If you'd like to serve croutons with the salad, try the Shaved Croutons on page 44.

1 large egg yolk or 1½ tablespoons pasteurized egg yolk (see Note)

1 garlic clove, finely chopped

1 shallot, finely chopped

1 teaspoon Dijon mustard

3 tablespoons fresh lemon juice (from about 1 lemon)

1 cup olive oil

¾ cup grated Parmesan cheese, preferably Parmigiano-Reggiano

Kosher salt and freshly ground black pepper

3 small heads of romaine, hearts only

1 bunch watercress, tough stems removed, leaves washed and dried well

COMBINE the egg yolk, garlic, shallot, mustard, and lemon juice in a blender. With the motor running, slowly add the olive oil, ½ cup of the Parmesan cheese, and salt and pepper to taste. Add a little water if the dressing appears thicker than heavy cream. Set aside and allow the flavors to combine for at least 15 minutes; taste again for seasoning. (The dressing, which makes about 1½ cups, can be made a day or two ahead; cover and refrigerate.)

REMOVE any bruised, yellowed, or wilted outer leaves of the romaine. Separate the remaining leaves, rinse them under cold water, and dry them well. Put the leaves in a large bowl. Add a pinch of salt and enough dressing to coat the leaves. Divide the leaves among six plates.

ADD the watercress to the empty bowl and gently toss it with enough of the remaining dressing to lightly coat it. Put some watercress on top of the romaine leaves. Sprinkle with the remaining ¼ cup cheese and season with more salt and pepper as needed.

Note: Although it's estimated that only 1 in 20,000 eggs from chickens bred in the United States contains salmonella, certain people—the elderly, small children, and anyone with a compromised immune system—should probably avoid eating any raw eggs. In such cases, a pasteurized egg product would be more suitable.

AVOCADO *and* ORANGE SALAD *with* HONEY *and* GINGER DRESSING

SERVES 4

I just love how the silky texture of the diced avocado plays off the orange segments in this refreshing salad. Shop for your avocados a couple of days in advance of making this salad; it seems you can never find a ripe avocado at the store on the same day that you need one!

4 oranges, preferably seedless

1 tablespoon finely chopped fresh ginger

3 tablespoons mayonnaise

1 teaspoon Dijon mustard

2 teaspoons honey

Kosher salt and freshly ground black pepper

2 medium shallots, finely chopped

1 to 2 tablespoons extra virgin olive oil

2 avocados

1 tablespoon chopped fresh mint, plus whole leaves for garnish

1 tablespoon chopped fresh cilantro, plus whole leaves for garnish

4 whole leaves of Boston lettuce, washed and dried well

4 whole leaves of red leaf lettuce, washed and dried well

Sliced pickled ginger (optional)

SEGMENT and juice 3 of the oranges in the following way: Cut both ends off one of the oranges and place it, cut side up, on a cutting board. Using a sharp, flexible knife, cut the skin and white membrane from the orange. Use a sawing motion and cut from top to bottom following the contours of the orange. Free the orange segments by cutting along the seams that separate them from each other. Do this over a bowl to collect any juices. Reserve the segments separately and squeeze what's left of the orange over the bowl to collect the juice. Do the same with the remaining 2 oranges. Strain the juice into a measuring cup: You should have about ¾ cup; if not, juice the remaining orange and add as much as needed.

COMBINE the ginger, mayonnaise, mustard, and honey with ½ cup of the orange juice in a small bowl. Season with salt and pepper to taste.

IN a small bowl, combine half of the chopped shallots with 3 tablespoons of the remaining orange juice. Whisk in the olive oil and season with salt and pepper.

CUT the avocados lengthwise up to the large pit in the middle. Gently twist apart the two halves and remove the pit. Wedge a teaspoon between the skin and the flesh and remove the flesh in one piece. Cut the avocados into 1-inch pieces and put them into the bowl with the honey-and-ginger dressing. Add the remaining shallots, the chopped mint, and the chopped cilantro, and mix together lightly so as not to break up the avocados.

WHEN ready to serve, set aside 8 orange segments. Toss the rest with the whole lettuce leaves and just enough of the orange-and-olive-oil vinaigrette to coat. Divide the lettuce and oranges among four plates. Spoon some avocado onto each plate (there will be some dressing left behind in the bowl). Top with the reserved orange segments and drizzle any remaining honey-and-ginger dressing over the salad. Garnish with whole mint and cilantro leaves, and, if you like, some pickled ginger.

ARUGULA SALAD *with* FRESH FIGS, GORGONZOLA, *and* BACON

SERVES 6

Few pairings please me more than blue cheese and figs. That's why I'm glad to see fresh figs turning up at more and more markets outside of California. Look for them from June through October, and plan to use them soon after you buy them. If you can't get your hands on fresh figs, pears also work nicely in this salad (see Note).

3 slices of bacon, cut in half crosswise

¼ cup balsamic vinegar

2 teaspoons Dijon mustard

1 shallot, finely chopped

Kosher salt and freshly ground black pepper

½ cup extra virgin olive oil

12 small fresh figs

6 ounces Gorgonzola or other blue cheese

1 large bunch arugula, tough stems removed, washed and dried well, about 6 cups

1 medium red onion, very thinly sliced

COOK the bacon in a skillet over low heat until crispy, turning it occasionally to brown it on both sides. Drain the bacon on paper towels.

IN a small bowl, combine the vinegar, mustard, and shallot, and season with salt and pepper to taste. Whisk in the olive oil in a steady stream until it's all incorporated and an emulsion forms.

HEAT the broiler.

CUT the figs in half lengthwise. Make a little indentation with your thumb, and press some blue cheese into the indentation. Put the stuffed figs, cheese side up, on a nonstick baking sheet. Broil until the figs are warmed through and the cheese begins to melt, 1 to 2 minutes.

TOSS the arugula and onion together in a bowl. Add just enough dressing to coat lightly, reserving at least a tablespoon of the dressing. Divide the greens among six plates. Use a spatula to remove the figs from the baking sheet and divide the figs among the plates. Drizzle the salads with the remaining vinaigrette. Top each salad with a piece of bacon and serve immediately.

Note: If you use pears in place of the figs, figure on ½ pear per salad. Slice the pears lengthwise and core them. Melt some unsalted butter in an ovenproof skillet and brown the cut side of the pears. Turn the pears cut side up, sprinkle with salt and pepper, and bake in a 350°F oven until they feel tender when pierced with a knife; the time can vary. Place the blue cheese in the holes left from coring the pears and broil the pears until the cheese begins to melt.

TOMATO, BASIL, *and* FENNEL SALAD
with LEMON VINAIGRETTE

For the best flavor, only make this salad when you have perfectly ripe summer tomatoes.

¼ cup fresh lemon juice (from about 1 large lemon)

1 medium shallot, finely chopped

1 teaspoon fennel seeds, lightly crushed

Kosher salt and freshly ground black pepper

½ cup extra virgin olive oil

2 fennel bulbs

4 medium ripe tomatoes

8 fresh basil leaves, washed and dried well and cut into a chiffonade (see page 4)

2 heads of Bibb lettuce, washed and dried well, leaves left whole

IN a small bowl, combine the lemon juice, shallot, and fennel seeds. Season with a pinch of salt and a few grinds of pepper. Whisk in the olive oil in a steady stream until it's incorporated and an emulsion forms.

CUT off the stalks of the fennel bulbs. Slice off about ¼ inch of the tough bottom and remove any tough or discolored outer layers. Slice each bulb in half lengthwise and then slice the fennel as thin as you can. Put the slices in a bowl with room enough to toss them. Stem the tomatoes and cut them into 6 or 8 wedges, depending on their size. Put them in the bowl with the sliced fennel and add the basil. Toss the tomatoes, fennel, and basil with enough of the vinaigrette to coat them well. Season with salt and pepper to taste. Allow the flavors to combine for a few minutes. When ready to serve, toss the Bibb lettuce with enough of the remaining vinaigrette to coat it lightly. Divide the lettuce among six plates, aiming for the leaves to look cuplike. Place the tomato, fennel, and basil mixture on top of the lettuce.

FRISÉE SALAD *with* LARDONS *and* POACHED EGG

This warm, hearty bistro classic appeals to the bacon-and-egg person in all of us. (*Lardons,* by the way, is French for "pieces of fried bacon.") If I'm serving this salad to company, I serve it with the croutons as described below in the recipe because I think it's important to encourage people to enjoy all of the components together. If Fiona and I are having the salad for dinner, however, I'll just toast a couple of thick slices of good bread, which we use to break open the poached eggs and otherwise make a joyful mess of the plate. To make the timing of the salad easier, I'm suggesting that you hold the poached eggs in warm water, which will keep them warm without continuing to cook them, but you can ignore this step. You can also poach the eggs in advance, then put them in cold water and refrigerate them. Reheat them briefly in simmering water just before serving.

About three ½-inch-thick slices of good French or Italian bread, crusts removed and cut into 1-inch squares to make croutons

2 teaspoons olive oil

Kosher salt and freshly ground black pepper

2 slices of thick-cut bacon, cut crosswise into ¼-inch sticks

2 teaspoons Dijon mustard

1 medium shallot, finely chopped

1 garlic clove, finely chopped

1 teaspoon chopped fresh thyme

2 tablespoons red wine vinegar

1 tablespoon white or white wine vinegar

4 eggs

¼ cup extra virgin olive oil

2 heads of frisée (curly endive), outer leaves and tough core removed, remaining leaves separated and washed and dried well

2 tablespoons chopped fresh parsley

HEAT the oven to 350°F. Toss the croutons with the olive oil on a sided baking sheet. Sprinkle with salt and pepper to taste. Toast, turning once, until golden brown on both sides, about 10 minutes.

COOK the bacon in a skillet over low heat, stirring occasionally, until crisp. Lift the bacon out of the pan with a slotted spoon and drain it on paper towels. Reserve the bacon fat and keep it warm.

(continued)

IN a small bowl, combine the mustard, shallot, garlic, thyme, and red wine vinegar.

BRING about 2 quarts water to a boil in a saucepan. Add the white vinegar and lower the heat to a steady simmer. Break each egg into a small cup or ramekin. Fill a medium bowl with warm water and position it near the pot. Gently slide each egg into the saucepan of simmering water by bringing the small cup close to the water's surface and letting the egg slide out. Adjust the heat to just under a boil. Cook the eggs until the whites are cooked and the yolks are just set, about 4 minutes. Lift the eggs out of the cooking water with a slotted spoon and place them in the bowl of warm water. The eggs will stay warm in this water for a few minutes but will not overcook.

WHISK the extra virgin olive oil and about 2 tablespoons of the warm bacon fat into the shallot-vinegar mixture until the fats are incorporated and an emulsion forms. Put the frisée and the croutons in a large bowl and toss with enough vinaigrette to coat lightly. (You should have at least 2 tablespoons left over.) Divide the frisée and the croutons among four plates.

LIFT the eggs out of the warm water with a slotted spoon, let them drain briefly, and trim off any straggly ends. Put an egg on top of the greens on each plate and sprinkle each salad with some bacon pieces and the parsley. Drizzle the remaining dressing over each salad and serve immediately.

HARVEST SALAD *of* ROASTED VEGETABLES *with* ROMESCO SAUCE

SERVES 4

Romesco sauce, which hails from Spain, is a delicious purée of roasted peppers, nuts, and olive oil. Here it's used as a spread for the croutons and a dip for the roasted vegetables. You can change the mix of roasted vegetables to suit your own taste. Try sweet potatoes in place of the parsnips or butternut squash (peeled and cut into pieces) in place of the acorn squash. Though I left them out of the recipe for fear of alienating too many people, I love to add Brussels sprouts to this salad, which, because of their strong flavors, I cook separately by simmering them in water until tender and then sautéing them in a little olive oil until lightly browned. If, like me, you are a fan, go ahead and add them, too.

1 medium red onion, cut into quarters

2 carrots, cut into 1-inch pieces

2 small to medium turnips, peeled and cut into 1-inch wedges

1 acorn squash, peeled, cut into 1-inch rounds, seeds removed

2 parsnips, peeled and cut into 1-inch pieces

Olive oil to coat the vegetables

Kosher salt and freshly ground black pepper

2 leeks, white parts and about 1 inch of the green sliced into ¼-inch rounds, washed and dried well

½ cup plus 2 tablespoons Classic Bistro Vinaigrette (page 29), preferably using sherry vinegar in place of the red wine vinegar

2 tablespoons chopped fresh parsley

½ teaspoon chopped fresh thyme

1 head of loose leaf lettuce, such as oakleaf, red leaf, or green leaf, washed and dried well, and torn into large pieces (about 4 cups)

Shaved Croutons (recipe follows)

½ cup Romesco Sauce (recipe follows)

HEAT the oven to 375°F. Put the onion, carrots, turnips, squash, and parsnips in a single layer on a sided baking pan or in a shallow roasting pan. Toss with enough olive oil to coat well, about

¼ cup. Sprinkle with ½ teaspoon kosher salt and a pinch of pepper. Cook the vegetables, tossing them occasionally, until just about tender, 35 to 45 minutes. Add the leeks and cook until all of

(continued)

the vegetables are tender, about another 15 minutes. Let the vegetables cool briefly in the pan. Drizzle them with about ¼ cup of the vinaigrette and sprinkle them with the parsley and thyme. Allow the flavors to combine for about 5 minutes.

TO serve, dress the lettuce with just enough of the remaining vinaigrette to coat it. Divide the leaves among four plates. Divide the roasted vegetables among the plates and top with a shaved crouton. Divide the sauce among individual ramekins and serve with the salad.

SHAVED CROUTONS

MAKES ABOUT 10 LARGE CROUTONS

You can cut these croutons into any shape that pleases you. We turn them into triangles, rounds, rectangles, or squares. The important thing is that they be thin and evenly cut.

½ round loaf of country-style French or Italian bread

About ¼ cup olive oil

Kosher salt and freshly ground black pepper

HEAT the oven to 350°F. Lay the flat side of the half loaf on a cutting board. Cut the thinnest slices you can by using long strokes with the knife and steady pressure. (Slicing the "short" way, with more crust to guide the knife, makes thin slices possible.) Cut off the crusts, if you like, and cut the slices into the shape you prefer. Toast the slices on a baking sheet until they are golden brown on one side. Turn them over and toast the other side. Remove the slices from the oven, brush them with olive oil, and sprinkle them with salt and pepper to taste.

We always keep some Romesco sauce on hand; it's great with grilled foods, as a spread on sandwiches, tossed with pasta, or drizzled into soups or stews. It'll keep in the refrigerator for 4 days and can be frozen as well.

2 ancho chiles

2 whole canned tomatoes

2 roasted red peppers (see Bistro Pantry), stemmed and seeded

1 cup any combination of some or all of the following: hazelnuts, almonds, and pine nuts, toasted (see page 4)

2 teaspoons chopped garlic

2 tablespoons chopped fresh parsley

3 tablespoons chopped fresh mint

4 tablespoons sherry vinegar

1 tablespoon kosher salt

1 teaspoon freshly ground black pepper

⅓ cup olive oil, more if needed

POUR boiling water over the ancho chiles and let them soak until very pliable and soft, about 20 minutes. Reserve a couple of tablespoons of the soaking liquid. Drain the ancho chiles and chop them coarsely. Seed the tomatoes and drain their juices. Chop the roasted peppers coarsely. Pulse the toasted nuts in a food processor until fairly finely chopped. Add the garlic, ancho chiles, and roasted red peppers. Pulse until combined. Add the parsley, mint, vinegar, salt, pepper, and olive oil, and process until medium smooth. Taste and add more oil, vinegar, salt, or pepper as needed. If very thick, add a little more oil or some of the ancho-chile soaking liquid (or a little of both) and pulse again.

CHOPPED SALAD *of* PEAS, CUCUMBERS, *and* RADISHES *with* TARRAGON VINAIGRETTE

SERVES 6

In this salad, even the greens are chopped. As part of the greens mix, I like to include some fresh parsley; its presence adds a lively freshness.

1 teaspoon Dijon mustard

3 tablespoons Champagne vinegar

1 medium shallot, finely chopped

1 tablespoon chopped fresh tarragon, plus whole leaves for garnish

¼ cup extra virgin olive oil

Kosher salt and freshly ground black pepper

3 cucumbers, peeled, seeded, and cut into a large dice

8 radishes, cleaned and cut into very thin rounds

3 cups fresh peas, boiled for 2 minutes then immediately cooled in ice water

About 4 cups mixed summer greens, such as green leaf lettuce, arugula, mâche, mizuna, and parsley, washed and dried well

IN a small mixing bowl, combine the mustard, vinegar, shallot, and chopped tarragon. Using a whisk, slowly add the olive oil in a thin, steady stream until it is all incorporated. Season with salt and pepper to taste.

TOSS the cucumbers, radishes, and peas together in a serving bowl with enough of the vinaigrette to coat well. Allow the flavors to combine for 5 min-utes. Meanwhile, slice all of the greens into a chiffonade by stacking some of them, rolling them into a cylinder, then slicing the cylinder crosswise at ¼- to ⅛-inch intervals. Repeat until all of the greens are chopped. When ready to serve, add the greens to the bowl and toss to coat, adding more vinaigrette if needed. Divide the salad among six plates and sprinkle with whole leaves of tarragon.

ROASTED BEETS, TOASTED WALNUTS, *and* WATERCRESS SALAD *with* CREAMY HORSERADISH DRESSING

Roasting beets concentrates their flavor, giving them a sweetness that plays really well with the heat of the horseradish.

4 medium beets, trimmed but not peeled

About 3 tablespoons extra virgin olive oil

Kosher salt and freshly ground black pepper

1 large shallot, thinly sliced

1 tablespoon toasted walnut oil

2 tablespoons prepared horseradish, drained

1 tablespoon Dijon mustard

¼ cup heavy cream

About 1 tablespoon fresh lemon juice

1 bunch watercress, tough stems removed, leaves washed and dried well

1 head of loose leaf lettuce, such as oakleaf, red leaf, or green leaf, washed and dried well, and torn into large pieces (about 4 cups)

2 ounces walnuts (about ⅔ cup), toasted (see page 4)

Whole fresh parsley leaves for garnish

HEAT the oven to 350°F. Wash the beets and dry them with a paper towel. Put the beets in a small ovenproof pan, drizzle them with about 1 tablespoon of the olive oil, and season with a little salt and pepper. Cover the pan with aluminum foil. Bake until the beets are tender when pierced with a paring knife, about 1 hour and 15 minutes.

ALLOW the beets to cool. Peel the beets using a small knife and cut them into quarters or sixths depending on their size. (Be careful, as beet juice can stain counters, towels, and even your hands; you may want to wear gloves for this step.) Toss the beets with the sliced shallot and the walnut oil.

IN a small bowl, combine the horseradish, mustard, cream, 1 teaspoon of the lemon juice, and 1 tablespoon of the olive oil. Season with salt and pepper to taste. Mix lightly with a whisk.

COMBINE the remaining 2 teaspoons lemon juice with 1 tablespoon olive oil and season with salt and pepper to taste.

TOSS the watercress and lettuce with enough of the lemon–olive oil dressing to coat the leaves lightly. Divide the greens among four plates, putting them just off to one side of each plate. Arrange the beets near the lettuces where there is the most room. With a spoon, drizzle the horseradish cream onto the lettuce leaves and beets. Sprinkle with the walnuts and the parsley.

Soul-SATISFYING SOUPS

· —————————————————— ·

WALK INTO

any bistro at any hour and chances are
there's a pot of soup on the stove. Almost
de rigueur is soupe à l'oignon au gratin,
otherwise known as French onion soup.
Originally made with plain water
and onions, the soup was regarded as
a restorative—good for curing a cold
and treating a hangover. Over time, chefs
began to deepen the flavor of the soup
by replacing the water with chicken broth
and adding a bit of Madeira, port, or
other fortified wine.

I ADD CHICKEN STOCK and sherry to my onion soup; I find that the sherry adds a fullness of flavor without being too sweet. You might want to try making it with water only, which places even more emphasis on the onions, or "beefing" it up with beef broth and port.

While I present a fairly classic version of this soup, other time-honored soup recipes get tweaked: Potato and leek soup gets a fresh twist from the addition of tarragon and fennel, while herbes de Provence gives familiar lentil soup a subtle floral flavor. You may also notice that most of my soups call for the addition of some wine or other alcohol. I started doing this a while back when I realized that many traditional soup recipes tasted flat to me. The acid in the wine adds a little edge, making the soup taste less round. In some of these soups, such as the cucumber soup, vinegar serves that role. Speaking of bringing out flavor: Don't forget to season your soup with salt as you go.

Whether I use a blender or a food processor for puréeing a soup depends on what I'm looking for in the final texture. A good blender will give you a smoother purée than most food processors. I like the little bits of cucumber that remain when I pulse my cold cucumber soup in a food processor, but I prefer the lighter, silkier texture that the blender gives my creamy garlic soup. You can, of course, try either machine with either soup. And if you are looking for a completely smooth soup, after puréeing the ingredients, press the mixture through a fine-mesh strainer.

I almost always serve soup with a garnish to add another level of flavor and texture, the latter being especially important for puréed soups. At the restaurant, these garnishes can be quite elaborate—a pea-tendril tempura for a spring pea soup, for instance—but something much simpler—fried slices of garlic, toasted bread topped with melted cheese, a chopped tomato salad—accomplishes virtually the same thing and is much easier to do at home.

A WORD ABOUT PORTIONS. Soup can play many roles, from a starter to a light lunch to dinner, and whether you want a lot or a little depends on what's to follow. For each recipe, I include a cup yield as well as a suggested number of servings. If you're having only the potato and leek soup for dinner, you may want more than a cup of it, but if the soup is launching a dinner that includes a salad, a meat course, and dessert, you'll want to serve just a taste.

COLD CUCUMBER SOUP *with* CHOPPED TOMATO SALAD

MAKES ABOUT 4 CUPS; SERVES 4

I make this soup all summer long because it's so fresh, light, and delicious. Blanching the scallions may seem fussy, but it tones them down so that they don't interfere with the crisp yet delicate flavor of the soup. I like the look of the little tomato halves or quarters floating on top of the soup, but you can also chop a larger tomato to use in the salad.

4 medium cucumbers, peeled, seeded, and coarsely chopped

1 garlic clove, coarsely chopped

2 slices of bread, crusts removed and cut into 1-inch cubes to yield about 1 cup

3 tablespoons plus 1 teaspoon red wine vinegar

Kosher salt

5 scallions, white parts and about 2 inches of the green, thinly sliced

½ cup plus 1 tablespoon extra virgin olive oil

2 cups chicken broth (see Bistro Pantry)

Freshly ground black pepper

½ cup cherry or grape tomatoes, halved or quartered, depending on size

About 3 tablespoons crème fraîche (see Bistro Pantry, page 7)

PULSE the cucumbers and garlic in a food processor about 15 times. Transfer them to a sieve and let the excess liquid drain from the cucumbers for about a half hour. Meanwhile, toss the bread cubes with 3 tablespoons of the vinegar and allow the bread to soften for about a half hour.

BRING about 1 cup water to a boil in a small pan. Add a pinch of salt and the scallions. Cook for 45 seconds, drain, and cool under cold running water. Reserve 1 tablespoon of the scallions. Put the rest of the scallions, the cucumbers and garlic, the bread, ½ cup of the olive oil, and the chicken broth in a food processor and process until smooth. (You

may need to do this in batches depending on the size of your bowl.) Season with salt and pepper to taste and refrigerate until ready to serve. (Can be made up to a day ahead.)

WHEN ready to serve, toss the tomatoes with the reserved scallions, the remaining teaspoon of vinegar, and the remaining tablespoon of olive oil. Season with a little salt and pepper and allow the flavors to blend for a few minutes.

SERVE the soup in cold bowls topped with a dollop of crème fraîche and the tomatoes.

PURÉED BEET *and* GINGER SOUP

For a really pretty presentation and an extra boost of flavor, serve the soup topped with a little crème fraîche and a ribbon of pickled ginger (available in some supermarkets and in Asian markets) as well as the fresh tarragon.

¼ cup olive oil

4 medium beets (about 2½ pounds), peeled and cut into quarters

½ red onion, chopped

2 tablespoons sugar

¼ cup chopped fresh ginger

2 tablespoons chopped garlic

1 teaspoon fennel seeds

1 teaspoon dried tarragon

6 cups chicken broth (see Bistro Pantry, page 10)

1 cup fresh orange juice (from about 4 oranges)

¼ cup balsamic vinegar

Kosher salt and freshly ground black pepper

2 tablespoons chopped fresh tarragon

HEAT the olive oil in a large soup pot over medium heat. Add the beets, onion, and sugar, and cook, stirring occasionally, until the onion becomes tender, about 8 minutes. Add the ginger, garlic, fennel seeds, and dried tarragon, and cook, stirring, for another minute or two. Add the chicken broth, 1 quart water, the orange juice, and the vinegar, and season with salt and pepper to taste.

Bring to a boil, lower the heat to a simmer, and cook until the beets are tender, 1 to 1½ hours, depending on the size of the beets.

PURÉE the soup in a blender, in batches if necessary, until smooth. Taste and add more salt, pepper, water, or balsamic vinegar as needed. Serve sprinkled with the fresh tarragon.

CREAMLESS *yet* CREAMY GARLIC SOUP

Blanching the garlic not only makes the cloves easier to peel, but it also protects against the garlic becoming bitter as you sauté it. If you buy garlic that's already peeled, don't skip the blanching step. For a crunchy garnish, cook thin slices of garlic in oil over low heat until crisp. Drain the slices on a paper towel and sprinkle with salt.

4 heads of garlic

1 tablespoon olive oil

1 medium russet potato, peeled and cut into a small dice

1 teaspoon dried thyme

¾ teaspoon kosher salt

½ cup dry white wine

3 cups chicken broth (see Bistro Pantry, page 10)

1 cup thinly sliced spinach leaves, washed and dried well (optional)

BREAK apart the garlic into cloves by pressing firmly down on the side of the head with your hand. Discard any loose skins. Put the garlic in a soup pot; cover with water. Bring to a boil, lower to a simmer, and cook over medium heat for 5 minutes. Drain the water and then rinse the garlic under cold running water for about 30 seconds. When cool enough to handle, remove the skins.

PUT the garlic back in the clean soup pot. Add the olive oil and cook over medium heat until the garlic begins to brown. Add the potato, thyme, salt, white wine, chicken broth, and 2 cups water. Bring to a boil, lower to a simmer, and cook until the potato and garlic are very tender, about 1 hour.

WORKING in batches, purée the soup in a blender until smooth. Return the soup to a clean pot, add the spinach, if using, and bring to a boil. Serve the soup topped with sautéed garlic slices, if you like.

POTATO *and* LEEK SOUP *with* TARRAGON *and* FENNEL SEEDS

MAKES ABOUT 4 CUPS; SERVES 4

This is one of those soups where a little bit of wine really makes a difference in the flavor.

3 to 4 medium leeks, green tops and roots cut off

1 tablespoon unsalted butter

2 tablespoons olive oil

1 medium russet potato, peeled and cut into a small dice

1 cup vermouth

4 cups chicken broth (see Bistro Pantry, page 10)

1 bay leaf

1 teaspoon dried tarragon

½ teaspoon fennel seeds, crushed

Pinch of cayenne pepper

1½ teaspoons kosher salt

¼ teaspoon freshly ground black pepper

1 cup light cream

CUT the leeks in half lengthwise and then crosswise into ½-inch pieces. You want about 4 cups chopped leeks; a little more or a little less won't hurt anybody. Wash the leeks well in a bowl of warm water and lift them out of the water, leaving the dirt behind in the bottom of the bowl.

HEAT the butter and olive oil in a soup pot over medium heat. Add the leeks and potato, and cook until the leeks become vivid green and begin to wilt, about 5 minutes. Add the vermouth, chicken broth, bay leaf, tarragon, fennel seeds, cayenne, salt, and pepper. Bring the soup to a boil, lower to a simmer, and cook until the potatoes are tender, about a half hour. Remove the bay leaf.

PULSE the soup in a food processor until smooth. (You may need to do this in batches depending on the size of your food processor bowl.) Pour the soup back into a clean pot, add the cream, and bring to a simmer. Season with more salt and pepper as needed.

Note: For an elegant contrast to the puréed leeks and potatoes, try serving this soup topped with shrimp or lobster sautéed with some fresh tarragon. Or top with a little caviar; it would counter the peasant origins of the soup, but would be fabulous nonetheless.

FIONA'S HEARTY LENTIL SOUP *with* BACON *and* ASIAGO CHEESE

Fiona cooks this soup on Sunday afternoons in the winter, and it makes the house smell great. This recipe tweaks traditional lentil soup by adding ample herbes de Provence. The result is a soup that tastes both new and comfortingly familiar.

1 teaspoon vegetable oil

6 slices of bacon, cut into a small dice

1 medium onion, cut into a small dice

2 carrots, cut into a small dice

3 garlic cloves, finely chopped

2 cups kale, washed, tough stems removed, and cut or torn into 1-inch pieces

2 cups lentils, rinsed and picked over for stones

2 teaspoons herbes de Provence (see Bistro Pantry, page 9)

4 cups chicken broth (see Bistro Pantry, page 10)

1 tablespoon kosher salt

Pinch of red pepper flakes

6 to 8 slices of Italian or French bread

4 to 6 ounces Asiago cheese, grated

HEAT the vegetable oil in a soup pot over medium heat. Add the bacon and cook, stirring, until most of its fat has rendered, 5 to 7 minutes. Add the onion, carrots, garlic, and kale, and cook, stirring occasionally, until the onion is just tender, about 5 minutes. Add the lentils, herbes de Provence, 6 cups water, and the chicken broth. Raise the heat and bring to a boil. Reduce the heat to a simmer and cook until the lentils are tender, 35 to 50 minutes. Add the salt and the red pepper flakes.

WHEN ready to serve, toast the bread under the broiler on both sides. Divide the Asiago cheese among the slices of toasted bread and broil briefly until the cheese is just melted. Top each bowl of soup with the bread and cheese.

Note: This soup is also delicious with shredded Duck Confit (page 193) in place of the bacon. Start with sautéing the vegetables, then add the duck along with the lentils and the remaining ingredients.

ONION SOUP AU GRATIN

SERVES 4

Browning the onions slowly over low heat is the key to the sweet, rich flavor of this classic French soup. If you want to hurry things along, sprinkle the onions with about ½ teaspoon of sugar as they cook. I like using sherry and chicken broth together for a lighter soup, and port and beef broth for a richer, darker soup.

2 tablespoons unsalted butter

3 medium onions, thinly sliced

Kosher salt and freshly ground black pepper

½ cup dry sherry or port

5 cups chicken broth or beef stock
(see Bistro Pantry, page 10)

1 baguette

2 small garlic cloves, very finely chopped

1 teaspoon olive oil

6 ounces Gruyère cheese, shredded

MELT the butter in a wide soup pot over medium heat. Add the onions, season them with a little salt and pepper, and cook over medium-low heat, stirring occasionally, until the onions slowly brown. This will take 30 to 45 minutes; the longer the onions cook and the lower the heat, the darker and sweeter they will become.

WHEN the onions are browned to your liking, add the sherry or port, the chicken broth or beef stock, and 3 cups water to the pot. Stir, scraping up any browned bits stuck to the bottom of the pan. Bring the soup to a boil, lower to a simmer, and cook for

about a half hour to meld the flavors. Taste and season with more salt and pepper if needed.

WHEN ready to serve, heat the broiler. Cut the baguette into slices about ⅜ inch thick. You want enough slices to cover the soup bowls, usually about 2 slices per bowl depending on the size of the bread and the bowls. Put the slices on a baking sheet and toast them lightly under the broiler. Mix the garlic with the olive oil and spread a thin layer over each toasted bread slice.

SET four ovenproof soup bowls (see Note) on the baking sheet. Ladle the soup into the crocks. Put a slice or two of the baguette on top of the soup. You want to cover the surface almost entirely without any overlap—cut the slices to fit, if need be. Sprinkle the toast with a handful (about 1 ounce) of Gruyère cheese each. Carefully slide the baking sheet (it will be heavy) into the oven and melt the cheese under the broiler until it just starts to brown in spots, about 2 minutes. Serve immediately, remembering that the bowls are extremely hot.

Note: I use crocks made specifically for onion soup. They hold about 1½ cups and have a nice, wide mouth (see Sources). Any relatively wide-mouthed, low-sided soup bowl will work fine as long as it's ovenproof. And be sure to put the hot bowls on a plate so as not to ruin your table.

HAMERSLEY'S RED ONION SOUP

Yes, another onion soup, but with a much different texture and flavor. This one is a little more refined and definitely less messy to eat.

4 medium red onions, cut into a large dice

2 carrots, cut into a medium dice

3 garlic cloves, cut in half

½ russet potato, peeled and cut into a medium dice

2 to 3 tablespoons vegetable oil

2 tablespoons tomato paste

1 teaspoon herbes de Provence (see Bistro Pantry, page 9)

½ teaspoon kosher salt

⅛ teaspoon freshly ground black pepper

1 cup red wine

2 cups beef stock (see Bistro Pantry, page 10)

3 cups chicken broth (see Bistro Pantry, page 10)

Slices of French baguette

4 ounces Asiago cheese, grated

HEAT the oven to 350°F. Toss together the onions, carrots, garlic, potato, vegetable oil, tomato paste, herbes de Provence, salt, and pepper in a roasting pan. Cover the pan with a lid or aluminum foil and cook in the oven until the onions are tender, about 1 hour.

REMOVE the pan from the oven and transfer the contents of the pan to a soup pot. Add the red wine, the beef stock, the chicken broth, and 3 cups water, and bring to a boil on top of the stove. Lower the heat to a simmer and cook for another 45 minutes. Strain over a clean pot and reserve the vegetables and the broth separately.

PURÉE the cooked vegetables in a food processor until smooth; they will reduce to about 2 cups purée. Add this back to the broth and whisk to combine. Bring to a boil, lower to a simmer, and cook the soup for about 5 minutes. Season with more salt and pepper to taste.

TOAST the French bread slices under the broiler on a baking sheet. Ladle the soup into warm bowls. Place a piece or two of toasted baguette on top of each bowl, sprinkle with some Asiago cheese, and serve immediately.

MUSSEL *and* FINNAN HADDIE CHOWDER

Finnan haddie is haddock that's been partially boned, lightly salted, and smoked. Though it hails from Scotland, where it was originally smoked over peat fires, finnan haddie has become a New England favorite. If you see it, buy it and make this delicious chowder. If you can't find it, ask the fish person at your market to order some for you.

2 pounds mussels (about 50), washed well, beards pulled or snipped off

3 cups (almost 1 bottle) dry white wine

Pinch of red pepper flakes

1 teaspoon dried thyme

2 tablespoons unsalted butter

2 tablespoons vegetable oil

1 medium onion, cut into a small dice

3 celery ribs, cut into a small dice

1 bay leaf

3 garlic cloves, cut into slivers

2 medium russet potatoes, peeled and cut into a small dice

$\frac{1}{4}$ tablespoon all-purpose flour

1 pound finnan haddie, bones and skin removed and cut into a large dice

4 cups light cream

Kosher salt and freshly ground black pepper

3 scallions, white parts and about 2 inches of the green, thinly sliced

PUT the mussels in a large soup pot. Add the white wine, 1 cup water, the red pepper flakes, and the thyme, and bring to a boil. When the mussels open, remove them with a slotted spoon, leaving the liquid in the pot. Strain the liquid through a fine-mesh strainer into a bowl, leaving any sediment behind in the pot. You should have 3½ to 4 cups liquid. When the mussels are cool enough to handle, take them out of the shells and reserve them.

IN the same pot, cleaned and dried, heat the butter and vegetable oil over medium heat. Add the onion, celery, bay leaf, garlic, and potatoes. Cook, stirring, until the onion begins to soften, 8 to 10 minutes. Add the flour and cook, stirring well with a wooden spoon to distribute the flour and remove any lumps that might form, about 5 minutes.

ADD the reserved mussel liquid to the vegetables and bring to a boil. Lower the heat and simmer until the potatoes are tender, about 10 minutes. Add the finnan haddie and continue to cook until the fish is heated and its smoky flavor has permeated the soup. Add the cream and heat to just below the boiling point. Lower the heat to a simmer, add the reserved mussels, and let them reheat briefly. Season with salt and pepper to taste. Remove the bay leaf, divide the soup among bowls, and sprinkle each with some scallions.

LOBSTER, FENNEL, *and* ORANGE SOUP

Serve this soup with some toasted baguette slices. Better yet, slather those baguette toasts with some garlicky aïoli (see Bistro Pantry, page 10).

2 lobsters, about 1½ pounds each

Kosher salt

3 tablespoons olive oil

2 fennel bulbs, top stalks and any tough outer layers removed, cut into a small dice

1 onion, chopped

2 garlic cloves, chopped

3 medium tomatoes, quartered, or 2 cups chopped canned tomatoes

1 tablespoon tomato paste

1 cup vermouth

½ cup Pernod

1 cup fresh orange juice (from about 2 oranges)

2 teaspoons dried tarragon

Pinch of red pepper flakes

Freshly ground black pepper

½ tablespoon unsalted butter

1 orange, skin and pith removed and cut into sections (see page 36)

2 teaspoons chopped fresh tarragon

FOR THE BROTH

In a pot large enough to hold the lobsters, bring about 6 quarts water to a boil. Add the lobsters and about a teaspoon of salt. Bring the water back to a boil and cook the lobsters for 5 minutes. (You are not trying to cook the lobsters completely here; the meat will finish cooking when added to the hot soup.) Remove the lobsters from the pot and let them cool on a sided dish or sheet pan. Reserve 3 quarts of the lobster cooking water.

WHEN you can handle the lobsters, twist off the tails and claws from each and reserve them on the sided dish. Rinse the bodies under cold running water and reserve them separately. Remove the lobster meat from the tails and the claws (see Note). Do this work over a bowl or sided baking sheet to collect the juices. Reserve the lobster meat, well covered, in the fridge for up to 1 day.

HEAT the olive oil in a large soup pot over high heat. Put the lobster bodies in the pot and cook, stirring occasionally, for about 5 minutes. Reduce the heat to medium-high and add half of the fennel, the onion, garlic, tomatoes, and tomato paste. Continue to cook, stirring, for another 10 minutes. The lobster shells will darken and the mixture will become drier.

ADD the vermouth and Pernod to the pan. Bring to a boil over high heat, being alert to the chance that the Pernod can ignite. (This is actually a good thing as the slight char on the lobster bodies adds flavor; if the pan does flame, simply allow the flames to die down.) Let the Pernod boil away for a minute or two, stirring occasionally, and scraping up any bits stuck to the pan. Add the reserved lobster cooking water, orange juice, dried tarragon, and red pepper flakes. Also add any liquid that was collected while cutting up the lobster and gathering the meat. (Strain the liquid into the pot if there is sediment or bits of shell in it.) Bring to a boil over high heat, lower to a simmer, and cook the soup for 45 minutes.

REMOVE the lobster bodies from the pot—lifting them head up so that any liquid in the body cavity will drain back into the broth—and discard. Strain the broth into a clean pot, pressing down on the solids to squeeze out any liquid and flavor. Add more salt, and black pepper to taste. (This broth, which makes about 2 quarts, can be made a day ahead.)

TO SERVE

Heat the butter in a small sauté pan over medium-high heat until hot. Add the remaining fennel and cook until the fennel is tender, about 10 minutes. Add the orange sections and fresh tarragon and remove from the heat. Cut the lobster meat into small pieces and add it to the fennel mixture. Add the fennel, lobster, and orange mixture to the hot broth and allow the flavors to combine over medium heat for a few minutes before serving.

> **Note:** Most of the meat of the lobster resides in the tail. An easy way to get at it is to roll the tail on a hard surface while pressing down on it with your hand to crack the shell. Then, using both hands, pull the sides of the lobster away from each other to expose the meat. (If you see a dark-looking vein, remove and discard it.) You can also use kitchen scissors to cut the shell away. To remove the meat from the large claws, wiggle the smaller pincer from side to side and then pull it off. Crack the claw below the pincer by giving it a good hit with an old chef's knife or cracking it with a nutcracker. Twist open the shell to pull the meat out. Use a nutcracker or scissors to crack open the large knuckles. There won't be too much meat in the legs of smaller lobsters, but you can push out what's in there by rolling over the legs with a rolling pin; the meat should pop right out.

SPICY TRIPE SOUP *with* MINT *and* COUSCOUS

Tripe, which is the stomach lining of a cow, has a big flavor that stands up well to a spicy broth. I use honeycomb tripe, which is readily available and thicker than the other types—pocket tripe and smooth tripe. Because tripe needs a soak before cooking, begin this soup at least a day before you plan to serve it. And for the best results, be sure the tripe is very tender before serving the soup.

12 ounces tripe, preferably honeycomb

Kosher salt

3 tablespoons vegetable oil

1 onion, cut into a large dice

6 garlic cloves

1 tablespoon Gordon's "Famous" Spice Mix (recipe follows)

1 Scotch bonnet or other hot, fresh chile, stem, ribs, and seeds removed and finely chopped

2 teaspoons dried mint

2 tablespoons tomato paste

2 cups dry white wine

6 cups chicken broth (see Bistro Pantry, page 10)

2 cups Israeli couscous

2 carrots, cut into a small dice

8 fresh mint leaves, washed, dried, and torn into pieces

PUT the tripe in a bowl and add enough water to cover. Allow it to soak, refrigerated, for 24 hours. Drain the tripe and cut it crosswise into 2-inch strips. Put the sliced tripe in a pot, cover with water, and add a tablespoon of salt. Bring to a boil and then lower the heat to medium. Cook for 5 minutes. Drain the tripe and rinse it under cold running water.

IN a clean soup pot, heat the vegetable oil over medium-high heat. Add the onion, garlic, spice mix, Scotch bonnet chile, dried mint, and tomato paste. Cook over medium heat until the onion becomes tender, about 7 minutes. Add the tripe, white wine, chicken broth, and 4 cups water. Bring to a boil, lower the heat to a simmer, and cook until the tripe is tender—the best test is tasting it—2½ to 3 hours. Add the couscous and carrots and continue cooking until both are tender, about 15 minutes. Add the mint leaves and serve in warmed bowls.

This spice mix, an adaptation of a Cajun mix, is great to keep on hand. Try it on baked chicken, grilled pork tenderloin, or even tuna.

4 teaspoons paprika

1 teaspoon cayenne pepper

½ teaspoon fennel seeds

1 teaspoon ground cumin

½ teaspoon coriander seeds

¼ teaspoon kosher salt

¼ teaspoon freshly ground black pepper

1 teaspoon sugar

¼ teaspoon red pepper flakes

COMBINE the ingredients and store in an airtight container.

CHAPTER

3

Small
PLATES

I'D BE LYING

if I said that Fiona and I entertain a lot at
home. But when we do, or when we're
lucky enough to have someone cook for
us in his or her home, there's rarely a formal,
"sit-down" appetizer. Instead, what we do,
and what most of our friends tend to do, is
offer nibbles away from the dining table. At
our house, I'll usually put some pâté with
toasts, mustard, and cornichons on the coffee
table in the living room. Fiona will pour
some wine, and our guests will relax and
chat and help themselves to some of the
pâté while I finish off the work on the
main course in the kitchen.

IN A KITCHEN with a more open layout than ours, guests might hang out around a counter near the cook, sharing in a big steaming bowl of mussels or clams. This very casual approach, with the emphasis on enjoying each other's company while enjoying some great food, feels perfectly bistro to me.

What most of the dishes that fall into the small plate category have in common is that they are designed to stimulate the appetite with flavors that are bright, crisp, and fresh (think oysters and celery root remoulade) or quite salty (as in pissaladière or brandade). They can also be flexible in how you might want to serve them. You could, for example, serve the Open-Faced Roasted Red Pepper and Goat Cheese Sandwich with Black Olive Spread (page 98) cut into small pieces as one of several hors d'oeuvres for a large party, or slice it into bigger pieces as the only starter for a smaller crowd. You could also serve a few of these dishes at once or in successive courses, tapas-like, and have that be your meal. (Go out to dinner with a bunch of chefs and watch how they order. Many times we'll forgo the formal "main course" and instead taste as many different dishes as the chef has as appetizers.) Finally, some of these small plates, such as the Open-Faced Omelet with Morels, Dandelion, and Scallions (page 74) or the Soft-Shell Crab Sandwich on page 99, can become "large plates" for lunch or a light dinner if served to fewer people than the yield suggests. I mean, how can you beat a slab of pâté, a nice green salad, and a beer? Just remember how great that sounds as you're putting out the pâté for your guests. You might be wise to put a couple of slices aside in case there are no leftovers!

MUSSELS STEAMED *in* WHITE WINE *with* SAFFRON

Mussels are inexpensive and easy to cook. What a *terrific* combination. The saffron, which adds a wonderful lift to the sweet mussels, is used often in the bistros of France. Don't forget chunks of crusty bread to go with this one.

1½ to 2 pounds mussels

2 to 4 tablespoons unsalted butter

1 medium onion, thinly sliced

2 garlic cloves, sliced

1 medium carrot, cut into julienne

1 celery rib, cut into julienne

¼ to ½ teaspoon chopped saffron

Pinch of fennel seeds

Pinch of red pepper flakes

1½ cups dry white wine

2 tablespoons chopped fresh parsley

WASH the mussels in cold water and remove the beards by pulling them from the top to the hinge of the mussel.

IN a large, heavy-based pot, heat 2 tablespoons of the butter over medium heat until hot. Add the onion, garlic, carrot, celery, saffron, fennel seeds, and red pepper flakes. Cook, stirring, for 2 to 3 minutes. Add the mussels and white wine. Cover the pot and raise the heat to high and cook until the mussels open. Add the remaining 2 tablespoons butter, if you like, and continue to cook, tossing the mussels with the broth and the vegetables until the butter is incorporated. Serve the mussels and broth in large warmed bowls sprinkled with chopped parsley.

SIZZLING CLAMS *with* GARLIC-HERB BUTTER

SERVES 4

This is one of my favorite ways to prepare clams. You can vary the flavorings as you wish, but this classic version is well worth the first try. You can shuck the clams and spread the butter on a couple of hours before you plan to serve them. Put the clams right on the baking sheet and refrigerate them until you are ready to cook them.

3 garlic cloves

Pinch of kosher salt

4 tablespoons unsalted butter, softened at room temperature

Pinch of cayenne pepper

1 teaspoon fresh lemon juice

1 teaspoon chopped fresh rosemary

1 teaspoon chopped fresh thyme

¼ cup plus 2½ tablespoons chopped fresh parsley

20 littleneck clams, washed well in cold water

Lemon wedges

Slices of crusty bread

CHOP the garlic finely. Sprinkle the salt over the garlic and continue to chop it, occasionally smashing and smearing the garlic with the flat side of your blade, until the garlic becomes pastelike. (Alternatively, smash the garlic and salt together in a mortar and pestle.) Place the garlic paste in a small bowl and add the butter, cayenne, lemon juice, rosemary, thyme, and the 2½ tablespoons parsley. Mash together with a fork. Refrigerate and reserve.

SHUCK the clams (see Note) and place each clam on the deeper half shell. Press about 1 teaspoon of the flavored butter onto the clam. Refrigerate until ready to cook.

HEAT the broiler. Place the clams on a sided baking sheet and broil until the butter is melted and sizzling and the clam is cooked through, 3 to 5 minutes. (The cooking time will vary depending on the kind of broiler you use.) Sprinkle with the remaining chopped parsley and serve immediately with lemon wedges and crusty bread to soak up the extra butter.

Note: To shuck a clam, insert a clam knife at its "top," opposite the hinge. Turn the knife to pry open the clam. Scrape the knife along the top and bottom shells to remove the clam, being careful not to cut the meat itself.

OYSTERS *on the* HALF SHELL

Well-chilled oysters on the half shell, with their crisp, refreshing flavor, are a wonderful, almost invigorating way to begin a meal. But which kind of oyster to buy? There are five different species grown commercially in the United States: the Pacific, the Eastern, the European Flat (or Belon), the Olympia, and the Kumamoto. More often than not, these species are identified by the area from which they come. Hence, you have your Hog Island oysters from northern California, your Quilcenes from Washington State, and your Cotuits from Massachusetts. What's fun to do is to grab a variety of species from a range of places and compare them. You'll be amazed at how different one oyster can taste from another, even one of the same species grown in different waters. After you've relished the flavor nuances of your unadorned oysters, go the next round with one or more of the following sauces. Because of their strong flavors, you'll need just a bit for each oyster; each sauce makes enough for about 1½ dozen oysters. For information on shucking oysters, see page 71.

TRADITIONAL MIGNONETTE

5 to 6 tablespoons red wine vinegar

1 teaspoon cracked black pepper
(see Bistro Pantry, page 9)

2 teaspoons finely chopped shallot

COMBINE the ingredients and serve.

GREEN PEPPERCORN SAUCE

5 to 6 tablespoons white wine vinegar

1 teaspoon green peppercorns, crushed

1 teaspoon finely chopped shallot

COMBINE the ingredients and serve.

HOT PEPPER SAUCE

5 to 6 tablespoons white wine vinegar

1 teaspoon finely chopped shallot

¼ teaspoon minced jalapeño chile, Thai chile, or red pepper flakes, or more to taste

⅛ teaspoon sugar

COMBINE the ingredients in a small sauté pan. Bring to a boil and immediately turn off the heat. Let the mixture cool before serving.

PICKLED CARROT MIGNONETTE

5 to 6 tablespoons rice vinegar

1 teaspoon finely chopped shallot

1 tablespoon very finely diced carrot

Pinch of red pepper flakes

COMBINE the ingredients in a small sauté pan. Bring to a boil and immediately turn off the heat. Let the mixture cool before serving.

CIDER AND CRISP APPLE MIGNONETTE

5 to 6 tablespoons apple cider vinegar

Pinch of cracked black pepper (see Bistro Pantry, page 9)

1 teaspoon very finely chopped shallot

1 tablespoon very finely chopped peeled Granny Smith apple

COMBINE the ingredients and serve.

Note: How to Shuck an Oyster: To shuck an oyster, you'll need an oyster knife, which has a strong pointed blade. Put the oyster, wrapped in a towel to protect the hand holding it, on a table or counter. (Placing the oyster on a hard surface instead of holding it gives you more control.) Slip the tip of the oyster knife into the hinge between the two shells. Turn the knife so that it acts as a wedge, forcing the upper shell to open enough so that you can cut through the hinge muscle. Run the knife point flat against the top shell to detach the oyster from the shell, and remove the top shell. Detach the oyster from the bottom shell in the same way, leaving the oyster, and all of the liquor that you didn't spill, in the shell.

SEARED SCALLOPS *with* CHANTERELLES *and* HEARTY AUTUMN GREENS

The natural sweetness of the scallops is paired here with the woodsy earthiness of the chanterelles and the natural bitterness of the greens. Serve this in the late summer or fall when the mushrooms are at their best. When buying scallops, look for ones that have not been chemically treated. Often called "dry" scallops, they brown better and have more flavor.

16 large sea scallops (1 to 1¼ pounds), side muscle removed

Kosher salt

Coarsely ground white pepper

2 tablespoons vegetable oil

6 tablespoons unsalted butter

4 medium chanterelles, brushed clean and cut into slices

1 shallot, thinly sliced

½ teaspoon chopped fresh marjoram

1 leaf of radicchio, washed and cut into julienne

½ head of Belgian endive, washed and cut into julienne

1 leaf of escarole from the inner part of the head, cut into julienne

½ cup dry white wine

PAT the scallops dry and season them well with the salt and white pepper. Heat the vegetable oil in a large sauté pan over medium-high heat until very hot. Add the scallops to the pan, leaving space between them. Cook without moving them until well browned on one side, 2 to 3 minutes. Remove them from the pan and reserve.

ADD 2 tablespoons of the butter to the sauté pan. When it stops bubbling, add the chanterelles and the shallot. Sprinkle with additional salt and pepper and cook over medium-high heat, tossing and stirring, for about 4 minutes. Add the marjoram,

radicchio, endive, and escarole, and toss to combine. Cook until the leaves are wilted, about another 2 minutes. Add the white wine and bring it to a boil. Cook, stirring occasionally, until most of the liquid has evaporated. Add the remaining 4 tablespoons butter and the scallops to the pan. Stir until the butter has been incorporated into the liquid and the scallops have heated through. Taste and season with additional salt and pepper if needed. Divide the scallops, mushrooms, and greens among four plates and serve immediately.

SOUFFLÉED ROQUEFORT *and* HAZELNUT CUSTARD

SERVES 6 TO 8

This wonderful creamy custard is great dinner-party fare. I like to serve it spooned right on top of a green salad lightly dressed with Classic Bistro Vinaigrette (page 29). You could also serve it as a sumptuous side to grilled steak.

4 ounces Roquefort cheese, softened at room temperature

1 tablespoon unsalted butter, softened at room temperature

3 large eggs, separated

¼ cup plus 2 tablespoons all-purpose flour

1 cup heavy cream

½ cup milk

1 tablespoon finely chopped shallot

½ teaspoon chopped fresh thyme

Pinch of kosher salt

About ¼ teaspoon freshly ground black pepper

2 ounces hazelnuts, toasted (see page 4) and finely chopped to equal about ½ cup

USING the paddle attachment of a stand mixer, cream together half of the Roquefort cheese and the butter until well combined, about 3 minutes.

ADD the egg yolks, one at a time, mixing briefly after each addition. Add the flour until just incorporated. Add the cream and milk and mix on low until they are just barely incorporated.

CRUMBLE the remaining Roquefort and stir it into the mixture. Add the shallot, thyme, salt, and pepper, and stir to combine.

HEAT the oven to 350°F. Beat the egg whites by hand with a whisk or with the whisk attachment on an electric mixer, until they can just hold a peak. (Do not overbeat them.) Using a large, flexible spatula, gently fold about one-third of the egg whites into the cheese mixture. Then gently fold in the remaining egg whites until just combined.

Some of the whites may still be floating on the top, which is just fine; overmixing will prevent the whites from puffing up nicely.

POUR the custard into a 9-inch round cake pan that's at least 2 inches high. (Or use a different pan that has about the same volume; just be sure the sides are at least 2 inches high.) Put the cake pan into a larger pan, such as a roasting pan, and fill the roasting pan with enough water to come halfway up the sides of the cake pan. Bake for 20 minutes. Sprinkle the hazelnuts over the top of the custard and continue baking until the mixture is just set, an additional 10 minutes. Remove the baking dish from the roasting pan. Let stand for about 5 minutes before serving. To serve, use a large spoon or spatula to scoop out the souffléed custard, making sure each serving gets some of the puffed-up top and some of the creamy custard.

OPEN-FACED OMELET *with* MORELS, DANDELION, *and* SCALLIONS

SERVES 8 TO 10

Cutting this omelet into small wedges makes it just right for an appetizer, but it's also a satisfying lunch or light supper for four when served with a green salad.

12 large eggs

Kosher salt and freshly ground black pepper

1 tablespoon unsalted butter

1 tablespoon vegetable oil

6 ounces fresh morels

2 garlic cloves, finely chopped

3 scallions, both white and green parts, trimmed and cut into thin rounds

3 to 4 dandelion leaves, washed and dried well and finely chopped

1 teaspoon chopped fresh thyme

3 ounces Gruyère cheese, grated

1 tablespoon grated Parmesan cheese, preferably Parmigiano-Reggiano

1 tablespoon chopped fresh parsley

IN a medium bowl, whisk together the eggs, a teaspoon of salt, and some pepper.

HEAT the butter and 1 tablespoon of the vegetable oil in a large ovenproof nonstick sauté pan or a well-seasoned cast-iron pan over medium heat. Add the morels and season with salt and pepper to taste. Cook, stirring, for about 3 minutes. Add the garlic and continue to cook for 2 minutes. Add the scallions, dandelion leaves, and thyme and continue to cook until the scallions are tender, about 3 more minutes.

HEAT the oven to 325°F. Add the Gruyère cheese to the eggs, give the eggs a final whisking in the bowl, and add them to the pan. Allow the eggs to form a crust on the bottom. Put the pan in the oven and cook until the eggs are gently set, about 12 minutes.

REMOVE the pan from the oven. Release the eggs from the side of the pan by running the tip of a heatproof, flexible spatula around the edge of the pan. Invert the omelet onto a serving platter. Sprinkle with the Parmesan cheese and parsley. Cut into wedges and serve.

GOUGÈRES

These classic cheese puffs are great with cocktails before dinner. They taste best fresh out of the oven, but you can freeze them, well wrapped, and reheat them with good results.

6 tablespoons unsalted butter, softened at room temperature

½ cup milk

½ teaspoon kosher salt

1 cup all-purpose flour

4 large eggs

¾ cup grated Gruyère cheese

¼ cup grated Asiago cheese

IN a saucepan, combine the butter, ½ cup water, the milk, and the salt. Bring to a boil over medium-high heat. As soon as the mixture boils, add the flour all at once. Remove the pan from the heat and beat the mixture vigorously with a wooden spoon or a firm, heatproof spatula. The dough will become smooth and will pull away from the sides of the pan. Put the pan back on medium heat and cook the dough, beating it vigorously once again, until the mixture looks a little drier and more matte, about 30 seconds.

TRANSFER the mixture to a bowl to halt its cooking. Add the eggs, one at a time, stirring vigorously with each addition. As you add each egg, the mixture will look loose, with pieces floating in it. As you continue to beat the mixture, it will come together again and look smooth. Add the Gruyère cheese and beat it in well.

LIGHTLY grease two baking sheets. Heat the oven to 400°F. Drop heaping teaspoons of the dough onto the sheets, leaving some room for the cheese puffs to grow. Sprinkle with the Asiago cheese. Bake for 15 minutes; the gougères will puff up and color during this time. Lower the heat to 350°F and continue to bake for another 15 to 20 minutes to dry the interior. Serve warm. (If you would like to make these ahead, store them in an airtight container for 1 day or freeze them, well wrapped in plastic wrap, and thaw when ready to serve. Recrisp the gougères in a 350°F oven for about 5 minutes before serving.)

COUNTRY PÂTÉ

Of all the pâtés we make at the restaurant, this classic—yet less refined one—remains my favorite. The texture is slightly chunky and the flavor is full. Serve it with toasted bread, cornichons, and mustard. You need to make the pâté at least a day ahead of when you plan to serve it. It will keep for up to 5 days if well wrapped in plastic and refrigerated.

2 tablespoons vegetable oil

1 small onion, finely chopped (about ½ cup)

1 shallot, very finely chopped

2 garlic cloves, very finely chopped

1 tablespoon tomato paste

½ cup chicken broth (see Bistro Pantry, page 10)

½ pound slab bacon, rind removed

1 pound ground pork

½ pound chicken livers, drained, trimmed of their fat, and cut into a small dice

4 teaspoons kosher salt

½ teaspoon coarsely ground black pepper

Pinch of ground allspice

¼ cup Madeira or brandy

3 large eggs, lightly beaten

1 cup fresh bread crumbs (see Bistro Pantry, page 7)

8 slices of thin-cut bacon (about ½ pound)

1 bay leaf

1 sprig fresh thyme

BEFORE YOU BEGIN

Cut a piece of cardboard to fit inside a 1½-quart pâté mold (or similar-sized loaf pan). Wrap the cardboard well with aluminum foil.

HEAT the vegetable oil in a large sauté pan over medium heat. Add the onion, shallot, and garlic, and cook until softened, about 5 minutes. Add the tomato paste and chicken broth. Bring the liquid to a boil and cook until most of the liquid has evaporated but the mixture is still moist. Allow to cool to room temperature.

WHILE the onion mixture cools, cut the slab bacon into cubes measuring about ½ inch. Pulse the bacon in a food processor until it is finely chopped, almost ground but not pastelike. In a large bowl, combine the bacon and the ground pork. Add the chicken livers, salt, pepper, allspice, Madeira or brandy, and the cooled onion mixture. Add the eggs and bread crumbs and mix everything together gently but thoroughly with a rubber spatula or your hands. Do not overmix the ingredients.

TO test the flavor of the pâté, heat 1 teaspoon oil in a small sauté pan. Take a tablespoon of the meat mixture and form it into a patty. Cook it on both sides as you would a hamburger until it is medium well done, about 5 minutes. Allow it to cool and then taste it for salt and pepper. Add more of either or both if needed.

HEAT the oven to 325°F. Line the pâté mold crosswise with 6 of the bacon slices so that they overlap slightly. (You may need to stretch the bacon a little. Do this by pressing with your fingers from the center of each strip out toward the ends.) Let the slices hang over the outside of the mold. Fill the mold with the meat mixture. Tap the mold on the counter a few times to "settle" the mixture. Fold the overlapping bacon slices onto the top of the mixture. Place the bay leaf and fresh thyme on top. Cover the top of the pâté with the remaining 2 strips of bacon and then cover the pâté with aluminum foil.

PLACE the pâté mold into a larger pan. Fill the pan with warm water so that it comes halfway up the sides of the pâté mold. Bake the pâté until its juices run clear when pierced with the tip of a small par-

ing knife and its internal temperature is between 140° and 150°F, 1½ to 1¾ hours. Remove the mold from the pan of water and remove the foil. Remove the top 2 slices of bacon, the bay leaf, and the thyme sprig. Cool for 30 minutes at room temperature.

PLACE the foil-covered cardboard on top of the pâté and then weight the pâté with a can or a brick wrapped in foil. Refrigerate the weighted pâté overnight. This will press the meat so that the pâté will hold together well when cool.

REMOVE the weight and the cardboard and run a knife between the pâté and the sides of the mold. Invert the pâté onto a serving platter. If it does not come out easily, immerse the outside of the mold in hot water for a few seconds and try inverting it again; the pâté should slip right out. Wipe the pâté of excess cooled fat using a spatula, a small knife, or your hands.

SLICE the pâté into ¼-inch slices. Place the pâté slices on plates and serve with cornichons, mustard, and toasts.

CHICKEN LIVER MOUSSE

I like to shape this mousse in a small, narrow terrine and serve it unmolded so that people can slice it themselves. But you can also put it in a pretty bowl.

4 tablespoons vegetable oil

1 pound chicken livers, drained, trimmed of their fat, and patted dry

½ teaspoon kosher salt

Pinch of freshly ground black pepper

½ medium red onion, cut into a small dice

2 tablespoons tomato paste

½ teaspoon herbes de Provence (see Bistro Pantry, page 9)

¼ cup brandy

3 tablespoons unsalted butter, softened at room temperature

Shaved Croutons (page 44)

Cornichons

HEAT 2 tablespoons of the vegetable oil in a large sauté pan over high heat until very hot. Add the livers, spreading them out so they lie flat in the pan in one layer. Season with the salt and pepper. Sear over high heat on both sides for about 3 minutes. The livers should be browned but still quite rare. Remove the livers from the pan and reserve.

WIPE the pan clean and add the remaining 2 tablespoons oil. Add the onion and cook, stirring, for 5 minutes. Stir in the tomato paste and the herbes de Provence. Return the chicken livers to the pan, remove the pan from the heat, and add the brandy. Return the pan to the flame and cook over medium-high heat until the brandy has almost completely evaporated and the livers are medium, about 5 minutes. Using a rubber spatula, scrape the liver mixture into the bowl of a food processor. Add the butter and process until smooth.

USING a rubber spatula, scrape the liver mixture into a 2-cup terrine mold (or a bowl that holds the same volume). Tap the mold lightly on a hard surface to settle the contents. Cover loosely with plastic wrap and let cool for 10 minutes. Cover the terrine tightly with the plastic wrap and place the mold in the refrigerator for 2 to 3 hours or overnight to set.

RUN a warm knife around the edge of the liver mousse. Turn the mousse out onto a serving platter. Sometimes the mousse comes out easily; if not, immerse the outside of the mold in warm water for a few seconds and try again. Serve with Shaved Croutons and cornichons.

ALMOST EVERY BISTRO IN FRANCE serves foie gras every night in some form or another. Whether served as slices of a melt-in-your-mouth terrine or seared until its exterior is deliciously browned, foie gras is a special treat. Even though I serve it at my own restaurant, I can rarely abstain from ordering it myself when I dine out.

In France, foie gras means duck or goose (usually goose) liver from a bird fed in such a way as to cause its liver to grow to an amazingly large size. However, because just about no one in the United States eats goose (meaning there's little market for other parts of the bird) the fresh foie gras we can get here is from duck.

Foie gras is very, very expensive. There's just no way around that fact. But it offers a lot of bang for the buck because there's nothing else like it. With its much milder flavor, it doesn't taste at all like other kinds of liver. As for its texture, words don't do it justice; it must simply be experienced to understand what all of the fuss is about. So if you can splurge, have some good (very good) friends over, sear up some slices of foie gras, and watch them

A Few Words About FOIE GRAS

swoon. (Uncork a bottle of Sauternes to go with it; the wine's deep, elegant sweetness makes it the undisputed match for foie gras.)

Fresh foie gras weighs between 1 and 1½ pounds and comes in a few grades. Grade A is the best and therefore the most expensive, but go ahead and buy grade B, if it's available, for less money. Grade B foie gras is just slightly less perfect; it's often a little smaller than Grade A and has traces of blood in it.

If you live near a store that carries foie gras, lucky you. Otherwise, you can easily mail-order some (see Sources). When mail-ordering, you often have to buy the whole liver, which is made up of a larger and smaller lobe. If you do not use all of the liver, freeze what's left over. The quality suffers a little bit, but it will still be delicious. And don't toss out those bits and pieces left from slicing it or preparing it for a terrine. Freeze those as well, and use them to make the most amazing pasta sauce: Simply sear the pieces with a little chopped onion (they will practically melt away), deglaze the pan with a little booze, add some chicken stock, and toss the sauce with hot pasta.

SALT-CURED FOIE GRAS *with a* SLICED PEACH, ARUGULA, *and* WALNUT SALAD

SERVES 6

I first tasted salt-cured foie gras at the market in Aix-en-Provence. When I asked the guy at one of the stalls what it was, he simply shaved off a piece for me. It's quite salty, rich, and luxurious, and easy as sin to make. You need to start a few days in advance to cure the foie gras, but it will last for days after. This recipe will make more foie gras than you need for this salad. If you want to make less, cure just one lobe of the liver, following the same directions, and use the other lobe for another recipe, such as the seared foie gras on page 86.

FOR CURING THE FOIE GRAS
1 fresh foie gras, about 1½ pounds (see Sources)

About 2 cups milk

Kosher salt

Pinch of quatre épices (see Bistro Pantry, page 10)

FOR THE PEACH SALAD
1 tablespoon rice vinegar

3 tablespoons toasted walnut oil

Kosher salt

¼ teaspoon chopped fresh thyme

About 3 cups arugula, washed and dried well

1 shallot, very thinly sliced

2 ripe peaches, washed, pitted, and very thinly sliced

3 ounces toasted walnuts (see page 4), broken into small pieces

Freshly ground black pepper

LAY the foie gras on a kitchen towel and pat it dry. Separate the liver where the large and small lobes make a natural break. Make a slice in each lobe vertically, from one end to the other, to expose the veins. Using needle-nosed pliers or the tip of a small knife, remove the veins from the foie gras as best you can. The foie gras will become a bit messy and broken up as you work, but don't worry, as it will be pressed back together later on. Put the foie gras into a bowl, cover it with the milk, and refrigerate for about 3 hours, turning once, to remove any excess blood.

HAVE ready a large double-layer length of cheese-cloth that will hold the foie gras with room to spare at each end. Also have handy some butcher's twine. Lift the foie gras out of the milk, pat it dry, and sprinkle it with 1 teaspoon salt and a pinch of quatre épices. Lay it on the cheesecloth and piece the foie gras more or less back together. Roll the foie gras up in the cloth and then twist each end until it becomes taut. (Two people make this job easier.) The foie gras will look like a thick cylinder. Tie the ends with a length of butcher's twine. Cut off all but 3 inches of the cheesecloth on each end.

MAKE a 2-inch bed of kosher salt in a high-sided bowl or baking dish large enough to hold the foie gras easily. (I use a big stainless-steel bowl for this.) Press the foie gras into the salt and then cover the foie gras completely in more salt. Place a weight on the foie gras. (Being a professional cook, I use a brick from my back alley wrapped in plastic wrap, but any noncorrosive weight will do.) Refrigerate the weighted foie gras for 3 days.

TO SERVE

Whisk together the rice vinegar, walnut oil, salt, and thyme. In a large bowl, combine the arugula, shallot, peaches, and walnuts. Toss with just enough of the vinaigrette to coat lightly. Divide the salad among six plates.

UNWRAP the foie gras from the cheesecloth. Gently wipe the outside of the foie gras with a damp towel to remove the excess salt. Using a vegetable peeler or a paring knife, shave very thin slices of foie gras onto each salad (a little goes a long way). Sprinkle with freshly ground pepper and additional salt to taste. The foie gras will keep, well wrapped in plastic wrap and refrigerated, for 5 days.

TERRINE *of* FOIE GRAS *with a* SHAVED APPLE *and* ENDIVE SALAD

Huge slabs of foie gras terrine are a favorite indulgence of mine. Begin making this at least a day before you plan to serve it.

1 fresh foie gras, about 1½ pounds
(see Sources)

About 2 cups milk

Kosher salt

¼ cup Sauternes or Muscat Beaumes-de-Venise

Freshly ground black pepper

Pinch of quatre épices (see Bistro Pantry, page 10)

1 tablespoon coarse-grain mustard

¼ cup white wine vinegar

¾ cup olive oil

2 crisp apples, such as Granny Smith, peeled, quartered, cored, and very thinly sliced

2 heads of Belgian endive, root ends removed, cut into julienne

1 bunch watercress, 2 inches of stems removed, washed and dried well

Sea salt

Slices of toasted French bread or brioche

LAY the foie gras on a kitchen towel and pat dry. Separate the liver where the large and small lobes make a natural break. Make a slice in each lobe vertically, from one end to the other, to expose the veins. Using needle-nosed pliers or the tip a small knife, remove the veins from the foie gras as best you can. The more small veins you remove, the smoother the terrine will be. Don't worry if it looks a little beat up, as it will come back together later on. Put the foie gras into a bowl, cover it with the milk and 1 tablespoon salt, and refrigerate for about 3 hours, turning once, to remove any excess blood.

LIFT the foie gras out of the milk and pat it dry. Put the foie gras in a bowl or sided pan and drizzle the Sauternes or Muscat Beaumes-de-Venise

over it. Sprinkle with about 1 teaspoon salt, 1 teaspoon pepper, and the quatre épices. Let the foie gras marinate for 3 to 4 hours in the refrigerator, turning it every 30 minutes or so.

HEAT the oven to 225°F. Remove the foie gras from the bowl and press it lightly into a 1½-quart pâté mold or similar-sized loaf pan. (You want the mold to hold the foie gras easily and have about 1 inch to spare on top.) Cut a piece of parchment paper to fit the top of the mold. Lay it on top of the foie gras and gently press it down. Put the mold into a larger roasting pan or baking dish and fill the roasting pan with hot tap water so it comes three-quarters of the way up the sides of the mold.

COOK the terrine until it registers 120°F with a kitchen thermometer, 40 to 60 minutes, depending on the mold you've used. Remove the terrine from the water and remove the parchment. Pour off the accumulated fat and juices into a bowl; the juices and solids will sink and the fat will rise. Reserve. Chill the terrine for at least 1 hour. When cool, spoon some of the reserved fat over the terrine and cover by about ⅛ inch. Cover the terrine with plastic wrap and refrigerate overnight or up to 3 days.

TO SERVE

Unmold the terrine by submerging the bottom of the mold in a bowl of warm water for about a minute. Run the tip of a small knife around the edge of the mold and invert the terrine onto a serving plate. Cut it into ¼-inch slices.

COMBINE the mustard and vinegar in a small bowl. Add a pinch of salt and pepper. Whisk in the olive oil in a slow, steady stream until an emulsion forms. Toss together the apples, endive, and watercress with just enough vinaigrette to coat them lightly. Season with salt and pepper to taste. Divide the salad among six or eight plates and arrange a slice of the foie gras terrine next to it. Serve with sea salt and toasted French bread or brioche.

SEARED FOIE GRAS *with* MAPLE-PARSNIP PURÉE *and* PORT SAUCE

SERVES 6

This is a great early spring dish. To slice foie gras cleanly, dip a sharp knife in hot water. Wipe it clean after each slice before dipping it again in the hot water. Refrigerate the slices for at least 10 minutes and up to 8 hours before searing so that they don't melt immediately upon meeting the heat of the pan.

2 tablespoons unsalted butter

3 medium parsnips, peeled and cut into 1-inch rounds

Kosher salt and freshly ground black pepper

2 tablespoons real maple syrup

3 to 4 tablespoons heavy cream

About 2 teaspoons vegetable oil

1 shallot, finely chopped

½ cup port

½ cup chicken broth (see Bistro Pantry, page 10)

6 slices of foie gras, each slice about 1 inch thick (see Sources)

Sprigs fresh parsley

HEAT the butter in a large sauté pan over medium heat. Add the parsnips, season with salt and pepper, and cook until the parsnips are a golden brown, about 10 minutes. Add ¾ cup water and the maple syrup and cover the pan. Reduce the heat to low and cook until the parsnips are very tender, about another 10 minutes. Transfer the contents of the pan to a food processor, add 3 tablespoons cream, and process until smooth, adding more cream, if necessary. Taste, season with additional salt and pepper if needed, and keep the purée warm.

IN a small saucepan, heat about 1 teaspoon of the vegetable oil over medium heat. Add the shallot and cook for about 1 minute. Add the port, bring it to a boil, lower to a simmer, and cook until it's reduced by three-quarters. Add the chicken broth and continue to cook over high heat until the sauce is again reduced by about three-quarters. Season with salt and pepper to taste, and remove from the heat.

HEAT about 1 teaspoon of the oil in a large non-stick sauté pan over medium heat. Season the foie gras slices on both sides with salt and pepper. When the oil is hot, add the foie gras, leaving room between the slices. Cook until well browned on one side, about 1 minute. Turn the slices over and cook until well browned on the other side and medium rare inside, 1 to 2 minutes.

REMOVE the foie gras slices from the pan and keep them warm. Pour off all but about 1 teaspoon of the fat from the pan. Add the sauce to the foie gras pan to reheat and to incorporate some of the foie gras flavor.

HEAP 2 to 3 tablespoons of the parsnip purée onto each plate. Lean a slice of foie gras against the parsnip purée and spoon some sauce over and around the foie gras. Decorate with parsley sprigs.

SEARED FOIE GRAS *with* SAUTÉED PLUMS *and* CANDIED PISTACHIOS

SERVES 6

This is a sweet little foie gras dish that is worth making when plums are perfect and ripe. The rich pistachios act as a counterpoint to the fruit. To slice foie gras cleanly, dip a sharp knife in hot water. Wipe it clean after each slice and before dipping it again in the hot water. Refrigerate the slices for at least 10 minutes and up to 8 hours before searing so that they don't melt immediately upon meeting the heat of the pan.

About 2 tablespoons vegetable oil

About 1 teaspoon unsalted butter

3 ripe plums, cut in half, pits removed

Kosher salt and freshly ground black pepper

1 shallot, finely chopped

¼ cup Sauternes or Muscat Beaumes-de-Venise

¼ cup veal stock or chicken broth (see Bistro Pantry, page 10)

6 slices of foie gras, each slice about 1 inch thick (see Sources)

2 ounces Candied Pistachios, crushed (page 293)

6 sprigs watercress, washed and dried well

HEAT 1 tablespoon of the vegetable oil and the butter in a sauté pan over medium-high heat. Sprinkle the cut side of the plums with salt and pepper. Add the plums, cut side down, to the pan and cook until they are somewhat browned. Turn the plums over, lower the heat to medium, and cook until tender, 3 to 5 minutes. Keep the plums warm.

IN a small saucepan, heat about 1 teaspoon of the oil over medium heat. Add the shallot and cook for about 1 minute. Add the Sauternes, bring it to a boil, lower to a simmer, and cook until it's reduced by half. Add the veal stock and continue to cook over high heat until the sauce is again reduced by about half. Season with salt and pepper to taste, and remove from the heat.

HEAT about 1 teaspoon of the oil in a large non-stick sauté pan over medium heat. Season the foie gras slices on both sides with salt and pepper. When the oil is hot, add the foie gras, leaving room between the slices. Cook until well browned on one side, about 1 minute. Turn the slices over and cook until well browned on the other side and medium rare inside, 1 to 2 minutes.

REMOVE the foie gras slices from the pan and keep them warm. Pour off all but about 1 teaspoon of the fat from the pan. Add the sauce to the foie gras pan to reheat and to incorporate some of the foie gras flavor.

DIVIDE the plums among six plates. Lean a slice of foie gras against each plum. Pour the sauce onto and around the foie gras. Sprinkle with the Candied Pistachios and garnish with a sprig of watercress.

BRANDADE *with* ROASTED RED PEPPERS *and* TOASTS

This may be the ultimate bistro appetizer. Some folks like it really, really garlicky, but I like it less so; I prefer to taste more of the fruity olive oil and the fish, especially if I'm using the more subtly flavored homemade salt cod, described on page 165. Brandade is quick to make, but the salt cod needs a preliminary soak, so begin a couple of days before you plan to serve it.

8 ounces salt cod (see page 165), soaked in cold water in the refrigerator for 2 days

½ large russet potato, peeled and cut into 1-inch pieces, about 4 ounces

½ cup heavy cream

1 to 2 garlic cloves, chopped

¼ cup extra virgin olive oil, plus some for serving

Kosher salt

1 roasted red bell pepper (see Bistro Pantry, page 10), cut into thin strips

Toasted slices of French bread or Shaved Croutons (page 44)

Coarsely ground black pepper

PUT the salt cod in a sauté pan and cover with fresh water. Bring to a boil and then lower the heat to a simmer. Cook the cod until it flakes easily, 5 to 7 minutes. Lift the cod out of the pan and put it in a mixing bowl. Check for any stray bones.

WHILE the fish is cooking, put the potato in a small saucepan and cover with water. Bring to a boil, lower to a simmer, and cook until very tender. Drain the potato and put it into the bowl with the cod.

IN a separate small pan, bring the cream and garlic to a boil. Turn off the heat and reserve.

PUT the cod, potato, olive oil, and the cream and garlic into the bowl of a food processor. Pulse the

mixture until smooth, 8 to 10 times only. (Be aware that too much pulsing will cause the brandade to go from silky to gluey.) Season with salt, perhaps generously, depending on the fish and how much salt flavor was lost during soaking. Serve the warm brandade immediately or cover it and refrigerate it until ready to serve. (Reheat the brandade before serving, adding a little cream if necessary.)

TO serve, place a generous spoonful of brandade in the middle of each plate. Decorate the top with the pepper strips and arrange the toasts or croutons around the salt cod. Drizzle the brandade with additional olive oil and sprinkle with some coarsely ground black pepper to taste.

RILLETTES *of* DUCK

Rillettes hail from the Loire region of France, and are a staple on our menu in Boston. Whether you make a straight pork version or mix it up with rabbit, duck, or goose is up to you. You can vary the amount of fat you add to make the dish richer or leaner, but I like it on the rich side. Serve rillettes as you would a pâté—with crusty bread and a small salad—or as one of a few different pâtés at a party. Although rillettes are traditionally pulled apart with a fork, I like to use the food processor when making them, but don't overdo it or the result will be a paste with no texture. Rillettes are a wonderful treat and will keep for about 5 days in the refrigerator.

8 ounces pork butt, trimmed of most fat and cut into 2-inch pieces

½ teaspoon quatre épices (see Bistro Pantry, page 10)

Kosher salt

8 ounces Duck Confit (page 193), skin and bone removed and cut into 2-inch pieces

1 tablespoon cracked black pepper (see Bistro Pantry, page 9)

3 to 6 tablespoons cold rendered duck fat (see page 193)

PUT the pork into a saucepan and cover with water. Add the quatre épices and salt, and bring to a boil. Lower the heat to a simmer and cook the pork until it is very tender, about 2 hours. Strain the liquid, put the pork in a bowl, and allow it to cool.

ADD the Duck Confit to the bowl and shred the meats together into a rough, chunky texture. By tradition, the meat is shredded using two forks, but if you prefer, you can pulse it 4 to 5 times in a food processor; just be careful not to overprocess it.

ADD the pepper and duck fat to the meats and fold together until well incorporated. Season with salt to taste. Put the rillettes in a small bowl and cover with plastic wrap. Refrigerate for at least 2 hours or overnight. Using a large soup spoon or ice cream scoop, place some of the rillettes onto small plates. Serve with toasts and a small green salad.

CELERY ROOT REMOULADE

I got the notion of adding pear or apple to this traditional bistro dish from my friend Jasper White; the fruit adds a slightly sweet note. It can be served on its own as a starter, but it also makes a great accompaniment to pâté.

1 large egg yolk or 1½ tablespoons pasteurized egg yolk (see Note)

2 tablespoons Dijon mustard

1 tablespoon red wine vinegar

¼ teaspoon kosher salt

Pinch of cayenne pepper

½ cup extra virgin olive oil

1 medium celery root (about 8 ounces), peeled and cut into fine julienne

½ Bosc pear or ½ Granny Smith apple, peeled and cut into fine julienne

2 tablespoons chopped fresh parsley

IN a medium bowl, combine the egg yolk, mustard, vinegar, salt, and cayenne. Whisk in the olive oil, a few drops at a time, until the mixture thickens and begins to stiffen. Add the oil more steadily as you continue whisking.

ADD the celery root, pear or apple, and parsley to the sauce. Mix together well, cover with plastic wrap, and refrigerate for about 2 hours before serving.

Note: Although it's estimated that only 1 in 20,000 eggs from chickens bred in the United States contains salmonella, certain people—the elderly, small children, and anyone with a compromised immune system—should probably avoid eating any raw eggs. In such cases, a pasteurized egg product would be more suitable.

PISSALADIÈRE

This is the ubiquitous olive-and-anchovy tart from the Côte d'Azur. Nothing beats its full-flavored saltiness as an hors d'oeuvre served with a glass of crisp white wine or a dry rosé. If you use salt-packed anchovies, soak them in a few changes of water to rid them of their excess salt.

FOR THE DOUGH

3 cups all-purpose flour

1 package dry active yeast

1 teaspoon sugar

2 tablespoons plus ½ teaspoon extra virgin olive oil

FOR THE TOPPING

About 3 tablespoons extra virgin olive oil

2 large onions, thinly sliced

⅛ teaspoon freshly ground black pepper

3 garlic cloves, finely chopped

1 tablespoon anchovy paste

3 to 4 ounces oil-cured olives, pitted and roughly chopped

3 to 6 anchovy fillets, well rinsed (or soaked if salt-packed), patted dry, and cut in half

TO MAKE THE DOUGH

Put the flour in a large bowl. In a small bowl, combine 1 cup warm water with the yeast and sugar. Let the yeast proof for about 8 minutes then add the 2 tablespoons olive oil and stir to combine. Pour the yeast mixture over the flour, stirring well to combine. When the dough pulls away from the sides of the bowl, turn it out onto a floured surface and knead the dough until it is smooth and elastic, 5 to 7 minutes.

PUT the dough back into a clean large bowl and drizzle with the ½ teaspoon olive oil. Cover the bowl with plastic wrap and let the dough rise in a warm spot until just about doubled in size, about 1 hour. Another way to tell if it's properly risen: When you poke it with the tip of your finger the dough will not spring back.

TO MAKE THE TOPPING

While the dough rises, heat a couple of teaspoons of olive oil in a large sauté pan over medium heat. Add the onions and pepper and cook, stirring every few minutes, until tender, 7 to 9 minutes. Lower the heat to medium-low and let the onions cook until they become golden brown and very soft, another 30 to 40 minutes. Add the garlic, stir to combine, and cook an additional 2 minutes. Let the onions cool.

TO ASSEMBLE AND BAKE

Heat the oven to 425°F. Oil a 10 × 15-inch sided baking sheet with about 2 teaspoons olive oil. Punch the dough down and turn it out onto a lightly floured surface. Roll the dough out into a

(continued)

rough rectangle measuring about 12 × 18 inches. Fit the dough into the baking sheet, letting the ends of the dough ride up onto the sides of the baking sheet. Drizzle the top of the dough with 2 to 3 teaspoons olive oil. Spread the olive oil over all the dough including the edges. Cover the dough again with plastic wrap and let it relax for about 5 minutes.

SPREAD the top of the dough with a thin layer of anchovy paste. Spread the onions over the anchovy paste in one layer. Scatter the olives over the top and lay the anchovy pieces—as many as you want—on top of the tart intermittently.

BAKE until the crust is browned and crisp, 15 to 20 minutes.

WILD MUSHROOM *and* ROASTED GARLIC SANDWICH

SERVES 6

Mushrooms are one of those foods for which proper technique makes all the difference. Cooked correctly—browned well, juices evaporated, and amply salted—they're full of flavor. Cooked badly—underseasoned and steamed instead of seared—they're slimy and insipid. The trick is to resist moving the mushrooms around in the pan. Cook them until they have colored on one side, then cook them on the other side, until their juices are almost completely gone, which concentrates their flavor. Seasoned well with coarse salt, they're irresistible.

About ¼ cup extra virgin olive oil

2 tablespoons unsalted butter

1 pound mixed wild and domestic mushrooms, such as shiitakes (stems removed), creminis, portobellos, oyster mushrooms, and chanterelles, cleaned and cut into 1-inch pieces

Kosher salt and freshly ground black pepper

2 garlic cloves, finely chopped

1 shallot, finely chopped

1 teaspoon chopped fresh thyme

¼ cup dry white wine

2 tablespoons chopped fresh parsley

12 slices of country-style bread, about 3 inches long and ⅓ inch thick

4 whole heads of roasted garlic (see Bistro Pantry, page 10), cloves squeezed to remove the softened garlic

FOR THE MUSHROOMS

In a large sauté pan, heat 3 to 4 tablespoons of the olive oil and 2 tablespoons of the butter over medium-high heat until the butter is very hot. Add the meatiest of your mushrooms, such as the creminis and portobellos, and cook them on both sides until they brown lightly and begin to lose their juices, about 5 minutes. Add the rest of the mushrooms and season with salt and pepper to taste. Continue to cook over medium heat, stirring the mushrooms every few minutes, for about another 5 minutes.

ADD the chopped fresh garlic, the shallot, and the thyme, and cook until fragrant, about 2 minutes. Add the white wine and continue cooking the mushrooms until they are tender and most of the wine and mushroom juices have evaporated, about another 10 minutes. Season with more salt and pepper. Add the parsley and keep the mushrooms warm until ready to serve.

TO ASSEMBLE THE SANDWICHES

Toast the bread on both sides either under the broiler or on a grill until golden brown. Spread each piece generously with some roasted garlic. Top 6 of the slices of bread with the mushrooms. Cover with the remaining slices of bread, garlic side down.

OPEN-FACED ROASTED RED PEPPER *and* GOAT CHEESE SANDWICH *with* BLACK OLIVE SPREAD

The perfect Provençal sandwich.

4 to 5 ounces fresh goat cheese

1 teaspoon finely chopped shallot

Kosher salt and freshly ground black pepper

1 loaf of French, country-style, or Italian bread

About ½ cup Black Olive Spread (page 30) or your favorite tapenade

1 bunch arugula or watercress, washed and dried well, stems removed

3 roasted red bell peppers, sliced about 1 inch thick (see Bistro Pantry, page 10)

1 to 2 teaspoons extra virgin olive oil

PUT the goat cheese, shallot, and salt and pepper to taste in a small bowl, and stir lightly to combine. Let the flavors infuse for at least 30 minutes.

HEAT the broiler. Split the loaf of bread in half and toast it, cut sides up, under the broiler. Take the bread out and reduce the oven heat to 450°F.

SPREAD the olive spread on both halves of bread and then put the bread on a baking sheet. Top with the arugula, red peppers, and dot with the goat cheese. Drizzle with the olive oil. Bake until the goat cheese becomes very soft, about 5 minutes. Cut into pieces and serve.

SOFT-SHELL CRAB SANDWICH
with SPICY ROUILLE

SERVES 4

I love how the rouille gives this American classic a French accent. The best soft-shell crab comes from Maryland, and its season runs from May through September.

2 tablespoons cornmeal

2 tablespoons all-purpose flour

½ teaspoon kosher salt

½ teaspoon freshly ground black pepper

Pinch of cayenne pepper

4 soft-shell crabs, prepared for the pan by your fishmonger (to do this yourself, see Note)

4 to 6 tablespoons vegetable oil

About ¼ cup rouille (see Bistro Pantry, page 10)

8 slices of sandwich bread, cut in triangles and toasted

A few leaves of delicate lettuce, such as Boston or Bibb, washed and dried well, and torn into large pieces

Lemon for squeezing

ON a plate, combine the cornmeal, flour, salt, pepper, and cayenne. Coat the crabs with this cornmeal mixture and shake off any excess.

HEAT a few tablespoons of the vegetable oil in a large sauté pan over high heat until it is hot but not smoking. Add the crabs, shell side down, lower the heat to medium-high, and cook until they turn red and become crispy, 3 to 4 minutes. Turn the crabs over and lower the heat to medium. Add any additional oil, if necessary, and continue to cook until the crabs are crisp on the other side, another 3 to 4 minutes. (Be aware that the moisture in the crabs can make them sputter and spurt while you cook them.)

SPREAD some rouille on the toasted bread. Top with some lettuce and then the crispy soft-shell crab. Add a squeeze of lemon to each crab, top with the remaining toasts, and serve immediately.

> **Note:** Cleaning a live soft-shell crab is not difficult, but it's also not for the squeamish. Using a pair of kitchen scissors, snip off the eyes and mouth in one piece. Pull apart each side of the top shell and pull out and discard the inedible gills. Turn the crab over and pull off the little flap called the apron.

SAVORY GRATINS,
GALETTES, AND
Tarts

$\bullet$ —————————————————— $\bullet$

TARTS AND GRATINS
feel similar in the role they play in the
meal and how they are created. Both
can work well in many guises: on their
own as an appetizer, as lunch accompanied
by a salad, or as a side dish to an entrée.
Texturally they are also similar: Often
a creamy, or at least tender, filling contrasts
with a crumb topping, in the case of
gratins, or a flaky crust, in the case of
tarts. Both dishes allow for a lot of
flexibility and creativity.

I GENERALLY make two kinds of tarts. One is filled with a savory custard. (When I would describe this kind as "quiche" on my menu, they never sold. I switched to using the word "tart" and they sold like crazy.) In the quiche-style tart, the dough is fitted into a tart pan so that the sides of the tart can hold the custard. The other kind of tart is free-form and goes by the name "galette." In this type of rustic-looking tart, a round of dough gets placed on a baking sheet, the "filling" is piled on, and the sides are folded up to make a rim. Gratins are like tarts without the crust. Instead, ingredients are layered into a shallow baking dish and baked until the flavors meld together and the tops are brown and crispy.

A FEW TIPS ABOUT MAKING TARTS AND GRATINS:

- Season the various components—the vegetables, the custard, the bread crumbs— as you go so as to make the tart or gratin flavorful throughout.

- Cook vegetables that throw off a lot of moisture before adding them to a tart.

- Shallow, round, or oval baking dishes will give you the best results for gratins, as square pans tend to overcook the corners of the gratin.

- I like to use tart pans with a removable bottom; I find it's much easier to slice the tart out of the pan.

- Fill the tarts with the custard mixture or the cream right to the top; the tarts settle as they cook. But don't let the custard overflow or it will make the crust soggy.

- When slicing potatoes—a gratin staple—by hand, make a small slice on the bottom of the potato so it will lie flat and not roll around as you slice. (If you have a mandoline, go ahead and use it for these tarts.) However you slice the potatoes, be sure to do it thinly or they won't cook. If you are unsure of just how thin ⅛ inch is, take out your ruler and measure.

The possibilities of filling combinations for tarts and gratins are endless, and once you get the hang of making them you can experiment with your favorite vegetables, seasonings, herbs, meats, and seafood.

GRATIN *of* POTATOES *and* CARAMELIZED ONIONS

This is not a creamy potato gratin. (That one is on page 106.) It gets a lot of its flavor from onions that have been cooked until they're a deep brown and are deeply flavored. Try serving this with a standing rib roast; the jus mixing with the potatoes and onions is fabulous and just what you need on a cold winter night.

2 tablespoons unsalted butter

2 medium onions, thinly sliced

3 garlic cloves, finely chopped

Kosher salt and freshly ground black pepper

½ teaspoon chopped fresh thyme

½ cup dry white wine

½ cup chicken broth (see Bistro Pantry, page 10)

3 russet potatoes, peeled and thinly sliced to about ⅛ inch thick

¼ cup seasoned bread crumbs (see Bistro Pantry, page 7)

About 1 teaspoon olive oil

MELT the butter in a large sauté pan over medium heat. Add the onions and garlic, season lightly with salt and pepper, and cook over medium-low heat, stirring occasionally, until the onions slowly brown. This will take at least 45 minutes; the longer and slower the onions cook, the darker and sweeter they will become. Add the thyme and stir to combine. Add the white wine and the chicken broth, bring to a boil, lower to a simmer, and cook another 3 to 4 minutes.

HEAT the oven to 350°F. Add the sliced potatoes to the caramelized onions. Season with more salt and pepper to taste and toss them together gently but thoroughly. Put the onions and potatoes in a 1½-quart gratin dish, cover the pan with aluminum foil, and bake until the potatoes are tender, about 35 minutes.

SPRINKLE the gratin with the bread crumbs, drizzle with a little olive oil, and bake, uncovered, until the bread crumbs become golden brown, about another 8 minutes. Let sit for at least 5 minutes before serving.

GRATIN *of* MUSSELS, COUNTRY HAM, *and* POTATOES

SERVES 6 AS A MAIN DISH

The work for this recipe can be spread out through the day if you like. Like many of the recipes in the book, this gratin is great with a crisp salad, crusty bread, and a glass of wine.

40 to 50 mussels, about 2 pounds

1½ cups dry white wine

Pinch of chopped fresh thyme

Pinch of red pepper flakes

Pinch of fennel seeds

1 medium onion, thinly sliced

1½ cups heavy cream

1 tablespoon unsalted butter

1 tablespoon all-purpose flour

Kosher salt and freshly ground black pepper

5 ounces spinach, large stems removed, well washed, and excess water shaken off

8 ounces country ham (see Note) or other smoked ham, chopped into a ½-inch dice

2 medium russet potatoes, peeled and sliced into ⅛-inch rounds

1 cup coarse fresh bread crumbs (see Bistro Pantry, page 7)

1 tablespoon extra virgin olive oil

WASH the mussels in cold water and remove the beards by pulling them from the top to the hinge of the mussel. In a large pot or Dutch oven, combine the mussels, white wine, thyme, red pepper flakes, fennel seeds, and onion. Cover and bring to a boil. Cook the mussels until they open, about 5 minutes. Lift the mussels and onion out of the liquid with a slotted spoon and allow to cool. Strain the liquid through a fine-mesh strainer into a saucepan and reserve. Remove the mussels from their shells and reserve in a medium bowl. Pour any liquid left over from removing the mussel shells into the saucepan; you should have about 1½ cups liquid.

COOK the mussel liquid over medium-high until reduced to about 1 cup. Add the cream, lower the heat to medium, and reduce over low heat to 2 cups, about 10 minutes. Reserve.

IN another medium saucepan, melt the butter over low heat. Add the flour and cook, stirring constantly, for about 4 minutes. Slowly whisk in the mussel cream until well combined. Cook over medium-low heat, stirring constantly, until the liquid has thickened, about 10 minutes. Season with salt and pepper to taste, but remember that the ham, especially country ham, will be quite salty.

HEAT the oven to 350°F. In a nonstick sauté pan, cook the spinach over medium-high heat until wilted. Strain and press the excess water out of the spinach. Coarsely chop the spinach if the leaves are large. Toss together the spinach, mussels, and ham. Line the bottom of a 10-inch round casserole or similar-sized dish with a single layer of potatoes. Place half of the mussel mixture on top of the potatoes in an even layer. Place another layer of potato slices on top of the mussels (you may not need all of the potatoes). Place the remaining mussel mixture on top of the potatoes.

POUR the cream sauce over the mussels. With the back of a large spoon, press down lightly on the gratin to distribute the sauce evenly. Bake until the potatoes are tender, about 45 minutes.

RAISE the oven temperature to 425°F. Sprinkle the bread crumbs over the gratin. Drizzle with the olive oil and bake until the crumbs are browned, about another 10 minutes. Allow the gratin to rest and cool for 5 to 10 minutes before serving.

Note: Country ham, such as Smithfield ham, has been brined and smoked. It's easy to find in the South where it's produced, and less so in other areas of the United States. You can mail-order it (see Sources), which I highly recommend; the ham is great with biscuits and added to soups and egg dishes.

CREAMY BISTRO POTATO *and* LEEK GRATIN

SERVES 6

This is the creamy gratin. We serve it with all kinds of roasts at the restaurant. As with most creamy dishes, it needs a lot of seasoning, so be generous with the salt and pepper. If you'd like to make the gratin ahead by a couple of hours, just let it sit at room temperature and reheat it at 350°F, adding a little cream if necessary.

2 tablespoons unsalted butter

2 large or 3 medium leeks, roots and dark green leaves cut off, white and light green parts thinly sliced, washed well, and patted dry

3 garlic cloves, finely chopped

½ teaspoon chopped fresh thyme

Kosher salt and freshly ground black pepper

2 cups heavy cream

3 russet potatoes, peeled and thinly sliced

1 cup grated Gruyère cheese

HEAT the oven to 350°F. Melt the butter in a large sauté pan over medium-low heat. Add the leeks, garlic, and thyme, and season lightly with salt and pepper. Cook, stirring occasionally, until the leeks are tender, 7 to 10 minutes. Add the cream and bring it to a boil. Reduce the heat to a simmer and let the cream and leeks bubble for about 3 more minutes. Season the cream with more salt and pepper. Turn off the heat and add the potato slices to the leeks, tossing them gently but thoroughly to combine.

LAYER half of the potato-leek mixture into a 1½-quart gratin dish and sprinkle half of the Gruyère cheese over the mixture. Add the rest of the potatoes and leeks to the dish and top with the remaining cheese. Bake until the potatoes are very tender and the cheese has melted and turned golden brown, 45 minutes to 1 hour. Let the gratin sit for at least 10 minutes before serving. Or let it sit for a couple of hours and then reheat it to serve.

GRATIN *of* ARTICHOKE *and* SWISS CHARD

This is an earthy dish that I make over and over again all through the fall.

Juice of 1 lemon

Kosher salt

4 large artichokes

4 tablespoons unsalted butter

1 medium onion, thinly sliced

Freshly ground black pepper

6 whole Swiss chard leaves, well washed, excess water shaken off but leaves not dried

1 cup heavy cream

½ cup grated Parmesan cheese, preferably Parmigiano-Reggiano

½ cup seasoned bread crumbs (see Bistro Pantry, page 7)

BRING a large pot of water to a boil. Add the lemon juice and 2 tablespoons salt.

SNAP off the stems of the artichokes and reserve. Trim the artichokes of all but their innermost leaves. Cut about 2 inches off the top of each artichoke and discard. Add the artichokes to the boiling water. Peel the tough outer skin off the stems and add the stems to the water. Place a small bread plate or other weight on top of the artichokes to keep them submerged. Lower the heat to a slow boil and cook until the artichokes' bottoms are just tender when pierced with the tip of a small knife through the bottom, about 15 minutes. Drain and let cool.

TRIM the rest of the leaves off the artichokes and scrape out the chokes—the fuzzy centers—with a spoon. Cut the bottoms into quarters and the stems into ¼-inch rounds.

HEAT the oven to 375°F. Heat 2 tablespoons of the butter in a sauté pan over medium-high heat. Add the onion and lower the heat to medium. Cook, stirring, until the onion is tender, about 7 minutes. Add the artichokes, season with salt and pepper, and continue to cook for an additional 3 to 4 minutes.

STRIP the leaves away from the stems of the Swiss chard. Cut the stems into ½-inch pieces and the leaves into 1-inch pieces, but keep the stems and leaves separate. Heat the remaining butter in another sauté pan over medium-high heat. Add the chard stems and cook for about 5 minutes. Add the leaves and continue to cook until the stems and leaves are tender. Season with salt and pepper. Drain the chard and add it to the artichokes and onion and toss to combine.

PUT the artichokes, onion, and chard into a 1½-quart gratin dish. Drizzle the cream and sprinkle the Parmesan cheese over the vegetables. Season with salt and pepper. Bake until the cheese is melted and the cream is bubbling, about 15 minutes. Raise the heat to 425°F, sprinkle on the bread crumbs, and cook until the bread crumbs are browned and the inside of the gratin is hot, another 7 to 10 minutes. Serve immediately.

TIAN *of* SUMMER VEGETABLES PROVENÇAL

While the word "gratin" refers to any dish topped with cheese or bread crumbs and then baked, a tian is actually a simple vegetable gratin. Because the colors of the vegetables are so striking in this dish, you might want to arrange them in rows of the same type and color. Start at one end of the gratin dish and lean the slices at a bit of an angle. Add the next vegetable type, overlapping by about two-thirds, and continue this way until the dish is full.

Olive oil for sautéing and frying

2 medium leeks, roots and dark green leaves cut off, white and light green parts thinly sliced, washed well, and patted dry

3 garlic cloves, finely chopped

Kosher salt and freshly ground black pepper

About 5 tablespoons all-purpose flour

1 medium eggplant, peeled and cut into ⅛- to ¼-inch-thick slices, salted, if necessary (see Note)

2 to 3 medium tomatoes, stemmed, cored, and thinly sliced

1 medium yellow squash, thinly sliced on the diagonal

1 medium zucchini, thinly sliced on the diagonal

1 teaspoon chopped fresh thyme

½ teaspoon chopped fresh marjoram

¼ cup dry white wine

2 tablespoons grated pecorino cheese, preferably Pecorino-Romano

HEAT about 2 tablespoons olive oil in a large sauté pan over medium-high heat. Add the leeks and garlic and cook, stirring, until the leeks are tender, about 7 minutes. Season with salt and pepper and spread them on the bottom of a 1½-quart gratin dish.

HEAT the oven to 375°F. Put the flour on a plate. Heat 2 more tablespoons olive oil in the same pan over medium-high heat. Lightly coat a slice of eggplant with flour on both sides, shaking off the excess, and add it to the pan. Do the same with just enough slices of eggplant so as not to crowd the pan. Brown the eggplant slices—in batches and adding more olive oil as needed—on both sides and drain on paper towels.

LAYER the tomatoes, squash, zucchini, and eggplant into the gratin dish on top of the leek mixture.

(continued)

Sprinkle the thyme, marjoram, and white wine over the vegetables. Season with salt and pepper and bake until the vegetables are tender and much of their released juices have evaporated and become more concentrated, about 40 minutes. Sprinkle with the pecornio cheese and let rest at least 5 minutes before serving.

> **Note:** If you think your eggplant might be old—its flesh will look dark—and possibly bitter, you may want to salt it. Put the uncooked eggplant slices in a strainer and toss with ample salt. Let the eggplant drain for about 20 minutes. Rinse the eggplant under running water and pat dry with a kitchen towel.

CREAMY GRATIN *of* CELERY ROOT, ONIONS, *and* BLACK TRUFFLES

You don't need to track down a fresh truffle for this dish to be delicious. When testing this recipe at home, I used truffles jarred in olive oil and they worked really well. If you'd like to make the gratin ahead by a couple of hours, just let it sit at room temperature and reheat it at 350°F, adding a little cream if necessary.

2 tablespoons unsalted butter

1 medium onion, thinly sliced

Kosher salt and freshly ground black pepper

3 medium celery roots

Juice of 1 lemon

2 to 3 tablespoons black truffle slices (jarred truffles are fine)

¾ cup plus 2 tablespoons heavy cream

¼ cup grated Parmesan cheese, preferably Parmigiano-Reggiano

½ cup fresh bread crumbs (see Bistro Pantry, page 7)

MELT the butter in a sauté pan over low heat. Add the onions and season them with a little salt and pepper. Cook, stirring occasionally, until the onions are soft and browned, 25 to 30 minutes. Meanwhile, peel the celery root and cut it into thin rounds. Sprinkle the celery root with the lemon juice and reserve.

HEAT the oven to 350°F. Add the black truffles to the onions and stir to combine. Put half of the onions and truffles on the bottom of a 1½-quart gratin dish. Top with half of the celery root. Add the remaining onions and top with the remaining celery root.

HEAT the cream over medium heat until it comes to a simmer. Season the cream with salt and pepper and pour it over the top of the vegetables, letting it seep into the layers of celery root and onions.

BAKE until the celery root is easily pierced with the tip of a small knife, 35 to 45 minutes. Toss the Parmesan cheese and bread crumbs together and sprinkle this mixture on the top of the gratin. Bake until golden brown, another 8 to 10 minutes. Let the gratin rest for 5 to 10 minutes before serving. Or let it sit for a couple of hours and then reheat it to serve.

AUTUMN VEGETABLE STEW *with* CHEDDAR-GARLIC CRUMBLE CRUST

SERVES 6

Not quite a gratin, this cobblerlike dish nonetheless feels at home in this chapter. There's a bit of peeling and chopping to do here, so you'll definitely want to feature this as the star of the meal. A good Côtes-du-Rhône would pair nicely with this vegetarian (if you don't use chicken broth) main dish.

FOR THE CHEDDAR TOPPING

2 cups all-purpose flour

1 teaspoon kosher salt

1 tablespoon plus 1 teaspoon baking powder

6 tablespoons unsalted butter, cut into small cubes and well chilled

1 to 1⅓ cups heavy cream

1½ teaspoons finely chopped garlic

Pinch of coarsely ground black pepper

½ cup grated sharp Cheddar cheese

FOR THE VEGETABLE STEW

About 3 tablespoons extra virgin olive oil

About 3 tablespoons unsalted butter

1 red onion, cut into 1-inch pieces

2 medium carrots, cut into 1-inch rounds

1 medium celery root, peeled and cut into 1-inch pieces

1 acorn squash, peeled and cut into 1-inch pieces

1 parsnip, peeled and cut into 1-inch pieces

2 garlic cloves, finely chopped

1 cup dry white wine

3 tablespoons tomato paste

3 cups chicken broth, vegetable stock (see Bistro Pantry, page 10), or water

1 tablespoon chopped fresh marjoram

Kosher salt and freshly ground black pepper

TO MAKE THE TOPPING

Sift the flour, salt, and baking powder together into a bowl. Cut in the butter, using a pastry cutter or two knives, until the mixture resembles coarse meal. Add the cream, garlic, and pepper. Add the Cheddar cheese and mix lightly with a wooden spoon until it just holds together. Let rest.

TO MAKE THE STEW

Heat the oven to 400°F. In a large sauté pan, heat about half of the olive oil and half of the butter over medium-high heat. Add the onion, carrots, and celery root, and cook, stirring occasionally, until the vegetables are browned, about 7 minutes. Transfer the cooked vegetables to a large (13 × 9

(continued)

inches) casserole dish or a small roasting pan. Add the rest of the oil and butter to the skillet. Add the acorn squash and the parsnip and sauté until they are lightly browned, about 7 minutes. Add the garlic and cook for another couple of minutes, and then add all to the casserole dish.

INCREASE the heat to high and add the white wine, tomato paste, and broth or water to the sauté pan. Bring to a boil, scraping up the browned bits stuck to the bottom of the pan, lower the heat, and simmer for about 3 minutes. Add this liquid to the casserole, sprinkle with the marjoram, and season with salt and pepper to taste. Cover the casserole with aluminum foil and bake until the vegetables are just tender, about 30 minutes.

REMOVE the foil. Using a large spoon, dot the surface of the vegetables with Ping-Pong ball–sized dollops of the Cheddar topping. The top of the casserole should look like the surface of the moon; bumps and craters are ideal. Return the casserole to the oven, uncovered, until the topping is cooked and browned, about 25 minutes.

HAMERSLEY'S BISTRO TART DOUGH

This flaky and light pastry dough works for savory as well as sweet tarts.

1½ cups all-purpose flour

½ teaspoon kosher salt

10 tablespoons unsalted butter, cut into small cubes and well chilled

4 to 5 tablespoons ice water

IN a mixing bowl, combine the flour and the salt. Quickly cut the butter into the flour, using a pastry blender or your fingers, until the butter pieces are the size of large peas. (Alternatively, cut the butter into the flour by pulsing it 8 to 10 times in a food processor, being careful not to overheat and overmix the butter.)

DUMP the mixture out onto a clean surface and make a well in the center of the flour. Pour the ice water into the well. Using just your fingertips and working quickly, combine the flour mixture and the water. Work just until the water is absorbed. The dough will be ragged but should hold together when you squeeze it. If it seems dry, sprinkle on a few more drops of water.

FORM the dough into a log shape about 8 inches long and parallel to the edge of your work surface. With the heel of your hand, push down and away from you all along the line of dough. With a pastry scraper, gather up the dough, shape it back into a log, and repeat the smearing action. This technique, known as *fraisage,* will form sheets of butter in the dough, creating a light crust almost like puff pastry.

WITH the pastry scraper, gather the dough up into a ball; it's fine if the dough does not come together completely at this time. Wrap the dough well in plastic wrap, flatten it a bit, and let it rest in the refrigerator for at least a half hour before rolling. The dough will keep in the refrigerator for up to 2 days. You can also freeze the dough, well wrapped; allow it to defrost for a day in the refrigerator before using it.

ROLL and shape the dough according to your recipe's direction.

NEW POTATO GALETTE *with* CRÈME FRAÎCHE *and* OLIVES

SERVES 6

Provence is the name of the game here. I serve larger slices of this tart with a green salad for an appetizer, but smaller bites are also great with cocktails.

1 recipe Hamersley's Bistro Tart Dough (page 115), divided into 6 equal pieces

Flour for rolling out the dough

2 tablespoons unsalted butter

1 large onion, thinly sliced

Kosher salt

3 garlic cloves, finely chopped

1 tablespoon chopped fresh oregano or marjoram

⅓ cup dry white wine

About 3 medium new (red) potatoes (about 1 pound)

Freshly ground black pepper

3 ounces pitted black olives, roughly chopped (about ½ cup)

1 egg yolk

3 tablespoons crème fraîche (see Bistro Pantry)

3 tablespoons heavy cream

3 ounces feta cheese, crumbled

LINE a baking sheet with parchment paper. On a lightly floured surface, roll each piece of dough out into a round about 7 inches across. Place each round on the baking sheet—they don't need much room between them—and refrigerate until needed.

HEAT the butter in a large sauté pan over medium heat. Add the onion, season with salt, and cook over medium heat, stirring every few minutes, until the onion starts to brown. Lower the heat and continue to cook until the onion is soft and well browned, about 25 minutes. Add the garlic and the oregano and continue to cook for another couple of minutes. Add the white wine and cook, scraping the bottom of the pan with a wooden spoon to release the flavorful browned bits, until most of the liquid has evaporated.

MEANWHILE, put the potatoes in a medium saucepan and cover with water. Add 2 teaspoons salt and bring to a boil. Lower the heat to a simmer and cook until the potatoes are tender when pierced with the tip of a small knife. Drain and let cool. Cut the potatoes into ¼-inch slices.

TO ASSEMBLE AND BAKE THE TARTS
Heat the oven to 400°F. Leaving a 1½-inch border on each pastry round, arrange the potato slices in a circle, overlapping them slightly. Season the potatoes lightly with salt and pepper. Divide the onion mixture among the tarts, arranging it in a small mound in the center of the potatoes. Top the onions with a bit of the black olives. Fold the border up and over just to where it meets the potatoes to form a rim; pleat it with your fingers as you go, but don't be too fussy—the tarts should look quite rustic.

WHISK together the egg yolk, crème fraîche, and cream. Season with salt and pepper. Brush the rims of each tart with some of the cream mixture and then drizzle 1½ to 2 tablespoons of the remaining mixture over the top of the olives, onions, and potatoes of each tart. Dot each tart with some feta cheese. Bake until the pastry is golden around the edges and on the bottom, about 25 minutes. Remove from the oven and serve warm or at room temperature.

PORTOBELLO MUSHROOM *and* ROQUEFORT GALETTE

SERVES 6

This galette comes from my love of mushrooms and blue cheese—especially portobellos, whose beefy nature stands up well to the strongly flavored cheese. These are great paired with a salad for a light dinner. Or serve them as a side dish to a perfectly seared steak.

1 recipe Hamersley's Bistro Tart Dough (page 115), divided into 6 equal pieces

Flour, for rolling out dough

4 medium portobello mushrooms (about 14 ounces), wiped clean and stems removed

3 tablespoons unsalted butter

3 medium shallots, thinly sliced

Kosher salt and freshly ground black pepper

¼ cup red wine

¾ cup heavy cream

2 ounces Roquefort cheese, crumbled

1 egg yolk, lightly beaten

LINE a baking sheet(s) pan with parchment paper. On a lightly floured surface, roll each piece of dough out into a round about 7 inches across. Place each round on the baking sheet(s)—they don't need much room between them—and refrigerate until needed.

USE a teaspoon to scrape off the gills on the underside of the mushroom caps. (This will keep the galettes from looking too "muddy.") Slice the mushrooms into ⅛-inch-thick slices.

HEAT the butter in a large sauté pan over medium-high heat until very hot. Add the mushrooms and cook, adding more butter if needed, until the mushrooms are tender and most of the moisture has evaporated from the pan, about 7 minutes. Add the shallots, season with salt and pepper to taste, raise the heat to high, and cook for an additional 2 to 3

minutes. Add the red wine and reduce until almost all the liquid has evaporated. Remove the pan from the heat, add the cream, stir to combine, and cool.

TO ASSEMBLE AND BAKE THE TARTS

Heat the oven to 400°F. Spoon some of the mushrooms onto the center of each pastry round, leaving about a 1½-inch unfilled border. Divide the Roquefort cheese among the tarts, putting it right on top of the mushrooms.

FOLD the border up and over just to where it meets the mushrooms to form a rim; pleat it with your fingers as you go, but don't be too fussy—the tarts should look quite rustic. Brush the rim of each tart with the beaten egg yolk. Bake until the tart crust is golden brown on the sides and bottom, about 25 minutes.

CARAMELIZED ONION, BACON, *and* POTATO TART

Baking the potatoes is a great hands-off way to precook them, and it gives the tart a more appealing texture.

2 russet potatoes

4 ounces good-quality bacon, chopped

2 medium white or Vidalia onions, sliced

3 garlic cloves, finely chopped

¾ cup heavy cream

3 large eggs

Pinch of ground cloves

Pinch of nutmeg, preferably freshly grated

Kosher salt and freshly ground black pepper

1 recipe Hamersley's Bistro Tart Dough (page 115), shaped and blind-baked according to the directions on page 122

HEAT the oven to 350°F. Wash and dry the potatoes and bake them until they are tender when pierced with the tip of a knife, about 1 hour. When cool enough to handle, peel them and slice them into rounds about ¼ inch thick.

COOK the bacon in a large sauté pan over low heat, stirring every few minutes, until the bacon has rendered its fat and begins to crisp. Remove the bacon with a slotted spoon and drain on paper towels.

ADD the onions and garlic to the bacon fat and cook over medium heat, stirring every few minutes, until the onions begin to color. Lower the heat to low and continue to cook until the onions are tender, about 10 minutes.

HEAT the oven to 350°F.

IN a bowl, whisk together the cream and eggs and season with the cloves, nutmeg, salt, and pepper. Spread half of the onions on the bottom of the blind-baked tart shell. Layer the potatoes on top of the onions in overlapping slices; you may not need to use all of the potatoes. Spread the remaining onions on top of the potatoes and sprinkle with the bacon.

CAREFULLY pour the cream mixture into the tart shell, letting it seep in. Put the tart on a baking sheet and bake until the filling has set, about 40 minutes. Let the tart rest for at least 5 minutes before serving.

FRESH GOAT CHEESE, ROASTED BEET, *and* WALNUT TART

As the tart bakes, some of the beet juice will color the custard and the goat cheese, giving each slice a pretty, almost marbleized look. Since the flavors are a riff on the classic beet, walnut, and goat cheese salad, this tart pairs especially well with greens tossed with a bright vinaigrette. A small slice also makes a somewhat unusual but delicious side dish to grilled lamb chops.

2 to 3 small beets

1 tablespoon olive oil

Kosher salt and freshly ground black pepper

1 tablespoon unsalted butter

1 medium onion, thinly sliced

2 tablespoons dry white wine

1 recipe Hamersley's Bistro Tart Dough
(page 115), shaped and blind-baked according
to the directions on page 122

3 large eggs

¾ cup heavy cream

4 ounces fresh goat cheese

1 cup chopped walnuts (about 4 ounces)

1 tablespoon walnut oil (optional)

About 2 tablespoons chopped fresh parsley

HEAT the oven to 350°F. Wash the beets and dry them with a paper towel. Place the beets in a small ovenproof pan, drizzle them with the olive oil, and season with a little salt and pepper. Cover the pan with aluminum foil. Bake until the beets are tender when pierced with a paring knife, about 1 hour.

ALLOW the beets to cool. Peel the beets using a small knife and cut them into a medium dice. (Be careful, as beet juice can stain counters, towels, and even your hands; you may want to wear gloves for this step.)

HEAT the butter in a sauté pan over medium heat. Add the onion, season with a little salt, and cook, stirring every few minutes, until the onion is just tender, about 7 minutes. Add the white wine and cook for another minute, scraping up any browned bits stuck to the bottom of the pan.

HEAT the oven to 350°F. Toss the beets and onion together and put them into the blind-baked tart shell.

WHISK together the eggs and cream, season well with salt and pepper, and carefully pour over the beets and onion, letting the cream seep evenly into

the beets. Dot the goat cheese all over the top of the tart. Put the tart on a baking sheet and bake it for 20 minutes. Sprinkle the chopped walnuts on top of the tart and drizzle the walnut oil over it, if using. Return the tart to the oven and bake until just set, an additional 15 to 20 minutes. Sprinkle the tart with the chopped parsley and let it rest for at least 5 minutes before serving.

LOBSTER, MUSHROOM, *and* SPINACH TART

I have one overriding rule about lobster when featuring it in a dish—don't skimp on it. This makes a great main course for a special-occasion lunch.

1 recipe Hamersley's Bistro Tart Dough (page 115)

Flour for rolling out the dough

Kosher salt

2 or 3 lobsters, to total 3 pounds

2 tablespoons unsalted butter

1 small onion, thinly sliced

5 ounces cremini mushrooms, quartered (about 2 cups)

3 garlic cloves, finely chopped

¼ cup dry sherry

Freshly ground black pepper

12 ounces spinach, well washed, tough stems removed, and roughly chopped

3 large eggs

1 cup heavy cream

½ teaspoon chopped fresh thyme

⅛ teaspoon freshly grated or ground nutmeg

TO SHAPE THE TART

Have a 10-inch tart mold handy. (I use a metal tart pan with a removable bottom.) On a lightly floured surface, roll out the dough so it is slightly larger around than the tart mold and about ⅛ inch thick. If your rolling yielded something unlike a circle, use a knife to trim the raggedy edges, but keep the size of the circle larger than the tart pan. Carefully lift the dough over the tart pan and allow it to fall into the pan, centering it fairly well. Gently ease the dough into where the sides of the pan meet the bottom. If necessary, lift the dough that's hanging over the edge and bring some of the excess down into the pan to ensure that the dough is following the pan's contours. Once the dough covers all of the bottom of the pan, fold the excess dough over into the pan to make thicker walls.

Press the dough into the edges of the pan and build up the wall of dough slightly so that it's a bit higher than the edge of the pan. Refrigerate the dough for at least 30 minutes before baking.

TO BLIND-BAKE THE TART CRUST

Heat the oven to 375°F. Line the mold with aluminum foil, and then fill the foil with baking weights, dried beans, or rice. Bake for 12 minutes. Remove the foil and beans and continue to bake until the crust is well browned. Remove from the oven and let the crust cool a bit before assembling your tart.

TO MAKE THE FILLING

Bring enough water to a boil in a large heavy pot to cover the lobsters. Add 1 tablespoon salt and the lobsters and cook over medium-high heat for 6 to 8 minutes. Remove the lobsters from the water and let them cool on a plate. When you can handle the lobster, remove all the meat from the shells (see Note, page 61). Cut the meat into a large dice, refrigerate, and reserve.

HEAT the butter in a large sauté pan over medium-high heat until hot. Add the onion and cook over medium heat until it is translucent and tender, about 5 minutes. Add the mushrooms and garlic and lower the heat to medium-low. Continue to cook, stirring every few minutes, until the mushrooms and garlic are cooked and there is almost no liquid left in the pan, about 10 minutes. Add the sherry and cook, scraping up the browned bits on the bottom of the pan, until almost all of the sherry has been absorbed or evaporated. Add the lobster to this mixture, season with salt and pepper to taste, and stir to combine the ingredients evenly. Remove from the heat and reserve.

HEAT the oven to 350°F. Bring 1 cup water to a boil in a large sauté pan. Add 1 tablespoon salt and the spinach. Cook until the spinach has turned a vivid green color and is tender, about 2 minutes. Strain the spinach in a colander and run cold water over it to stop its cooking. Squeeze the excess water from the spinach, add it to the lobster mixture, and toss to combine. Spoon the lobster and mushroom mixture into the baked crust.

WHISK together the eggs, cream, thyme, and nutmeg. Season with salt and pepper to taste. Slowly pour this over the top of the lobster-mushroom mixture, letting the cream seep into the rest of the ingredients evenly. The tart mold will be quite full.

PUT the tart mold onto a sheet pan or cookie sheet in case it drips and bake it until the cream has set, 40 to 45 minutes. Let the tart rest for at least 5 minutes before serving it; it's also delicious at room temperature.

CHAPTER
5

Pasta,
RISOTTO, AND
POLENTA

YES, THIS IS
primarily a French cookbook, but pasta,
polenta, and risotto are perfectly suited
to the comforting and casual spirit of
bistro food. I do, however, tend to give
these dishes a French accent: featuring
morels in risotto, adding herbes de Provence
to a carbonara-like pasta, serving a
Provençal-style vegetable ragout with
baked polenta. One thing I really like
about pasta, polenta, and risotto is that they
leave so much room for improvisation—
check out the Thai-inspired pasta
with chicken livers!

YOU MIGHT be used to creating your own pasta dishes based on what's in your fridge and pantry, but you might not think to do that with risotto and polenta, too. Shred that bit of meat left over from your beef Bourguignon and stir it into the basic risotto on page 132; add some of the braising liquid, onions, or mushrooms and you have a great main course. Or reheat roasted vegetables in a little broth and serve them over some creamy polenta for a soothing winter lunch.

I make all three of these kinds of dishes so often that they are like second nature. But as I started paying close attention to what I do as I make them, I noticed a few things that might be helpful to remember.

- Always reserve some of the pasta cooking water in case you need to moisten the pasta and sauce.

- The rice for risotto: Arborio is the most commonly used rice for risotto, and it's available in most supermarkets. Its shortish plump grain can absorb a lot of liquid while still retaining its shape and texture. You can also try other Italian rices, including Carnaroli and Vialone Nano, which will give you slightly different results.

- Buying cornmeal: Sometimes you see it labeled as polenta, but it doesn't have to be; medium-ground cornmeal is what you want. You can also mix some fine-ground cornmeal with the medium-ground for a smoother texture. But for my taste using only finely ground cornmeal makes polenta too much like baby food.

- You don't need to stir risotto and polenta continuously for good results. I think that's why people have come to think of these two dishes as hard to make. Yes, they need attention, and they need time, but you can let them bubble away for a few minutes without stirring while you tend to other things in the kitchen. And for stirring risotto, I like to use a squared-off wooden spoon.

PENNE *with* CLAMS, PANCETTA, *and* SPINACH

Because I don't want to risk overcooking the clams while the pasta finishes cooking, I cook the pasta first and reheat it in the delicious clam sauce. Pancetta, an Italian bacon that's cured but not smoked, is now available at most supermarkets.

½ pound penne

4 tablespoons olive oil

¼ pound pancetta, cut into ¼-inch strips

2 shallots, thinly sliced

4 garlic cloves, thinly sliced

Pinch of red pepper flakes

24 littleneck or countneck clams, washed well in cold water

1 cup dry white wine

3 ounces fresh spinach, washed and coarsely chopped (about 4 cups)

1 tablespoon unsalted butter

Kosher salt and freshly ground black pepper

BRING a large pot of salted water to a boil. Add the penne and cook until al dente, about 8 minutes. Drain and toss with 2 tablespoons of the olive oil.

IN a 12-inch sauté pan or a large Dutch oven, heat the remaining 2 tablespoons olive oil over medium-high heat. Add the pancetta and cook until lightly browned, about 5 minutes. Add the shallots, garlic, and red pepper flakes, and cook until fragrant, about 2 minutes. Add the clams and cook, stirring, for about 3 minutes. Add the

white wine and cover the pan. Cook, stirring occasionally, until the clams open, 5 to 8 minutes. Add the penne and spinach to the pot. Stir to combine. Add the butter and continue stirring until the butter has melted and the penne and spinach are warmed through. Season to taste with salt and pepper.

SPOON the clams, penne, and spinach into bowls and divide the remaining liquid among them.

OVEN-BAKED PENNE *with* ONIONS, WALNUTS, *and* GOAT CHEESE

Walnuts and goat cheese are among my favorite classic pairings, and I feature them together in many of my dishes. The rich, meaty walnuts counter the slightly tangy cheese.

1 pound penne

3 tablespoons olive oil

1 tablespoon unsalted butter

1 small onion, sliced

¼ cup dry white wine

1 teaspoon chopped fresh thyme

Pinch of red pepper flakes

3 ounces chopped walnuts

Kosher salt and freshly ground black pepper

¾ cup heavy cream

5 to 6 ounces fresh goat cheese

2 teaspoons walnut oil

½ cup Parmesan cheese, preferably Parmigiano-Reggiano

About 2 tablespoons chopped fresh parsley

BRING a large pot of salted water to a boil. Add the penne and cook until the pasta is al dente, about 10 minutes. Drain the pasta, put it into a large bowl, and toss it with the olive oil.

HEAT the oven to 350°F. Heat the butter in a medium sauté pan over medium heat. Add the onion and cook, stirring every few minutes, until the onion is tender and golden, about 10 minutes. Add the white wine, bring to a boil, and stir, scraping up any browned bits on the bottom of the pan. Transfer the onion to the bowl with the penne.

Add the thyme, the red pepper flakes, and half of the walnuts, and toss well to combine. Season with salt and pepper to taste.

COMBINE the cream with about 2 ounces of the goat cheese and toss this with the pasta. Pour the pasta into a high-sided baking dish. Dot the top evenly with the remaining goat cheese and sprinkle with the remaining walnuts. Drizzle with the walnut oil and, finally, sprinkle with the Parmesan cheese. Bake for about 15 minutes. Sprinkle with the chopped parsley and serve.

LU LU'S FAVORITE LINGUINE

SERVES 6

No one has worked for Fiona and me at Hamersley's Bistro longer than Luis Flores.
I will never forget the first night he came to the restaurant, straight from the airport,
wet and cold from an early fall snowstorm, to visit his brother, who was washing dishes
for us at the time. Luis had just left the wartorn poverty of El Salvador and was pretty
skinny to prove it. He just started washing dishes that night without being asked.
Fifteen years later, Lu Lu—a name only I call him—is a strapping, not so skinny cook
in our kitchen. This is the pasta dish he loves the most and the one that helped make
him not so skinny.

1 tablespoon vegetable oil

1 onion, sliced

6 ounces thick-cut bacon, cut crosswise
into ¼-inch sticks

¾ cup dry white wine

¼ cup dry sherry

2 teaspoons herbes de Provence (see Bistro
Pantry, page 9)

1½ cups heavy cream

1 bunch very roughly chopped fresh parsley,
washed (about 1 cup, loosely packed)

12 ounces linguine

Kosher salt and freshly ground black pepper

4 to 6 ounces shredded Asiago cheese

HEAT the vegetable oil in a sauté pan over medium-high heat. Add the onion and bacon, lower the heat to medium-low, and cook, stirring every few minutes, until the onion begins to brown and the bacon is crispy, 7 to 9 minutes. Pour off most of the fat from the pan.

ADD the white wine, sherry, and herbes de Provence, and stir with a wooden spoon to release the browned bits from the bottom of the pan. Cook for about 5 minutes over high heat until reduced by about three-quarters. Add the cream

and the chopped parsley and bring to a boil. Lower the heat to medium and cook until the cream has thickened slightly and the parsley is tender, 3 to 4 minutes.

BRING a large pot of salted water to a boil. Add the linguine and cook until al dente. Drain the pasta and then add it to the sauce. Toss to combine. Season with salt and pepper to taste. Add the Asiago and stir to combine and let the cheese melt. Serve in large pasta bowls.

SEARED CHICKEN LIVERS *with* ANGEL HAIR PASTA, PEANUTS, *and* CUCUMBER

This is by no means your traditional bistro dish, but it's one of my favorites, so I had to include it here. (I do, however, use a bistro staple—chicken livers—in this Thai-style dish.) Have all the ingredients ready to go and in front of you before you start cooking; once you turn on the heat, it comes together really fast.

FOR THE PEANUT SAUCE

½ tablespoon vegetable oil

2 tablespoons Thai red curry paste (available in many supermarkets)

¼ teaspoon red pepper flakes

2 tablespoons rice vinegar

2 tablespoons soy sauce

⅓ cup peanut butter

FOR THE PASTA

1 pound chicken livers, trimmed of their fat and sinew and cut in half

1 tablespoon soy sauce

1 tablespoon toasted sesame oil

About 5 tablespoons vegetable oil

1 small red onion, sliced

3 garlic cloves, finely chopped

About a 1-inch piece of fresh ginger, peeled and finely chopped

1 Thai or other hot chile, stemmed and cut into thin rounds

4 cups shredded Napa cabbage (save the nice inner leaves for garnish)

3 scallions, roots trimmed and cut into thin rounds

About 1 tablespoon chopped fresh mint, plus a few whole leaves for garnish

1 bunch watercress, stems trimmed, leaves washed and dried well

2 cucumbers, peeled, cut in half lengthwise, seeds removed, and cut into ¼-inch slices on the diagonal

1 pound angel hair pasta

1 ounce chopped roasted peanuts, preferably lightly salted

TO MAKE THE PEANUT SAUCE

HEAT the vegetable oil in a small saucepan or sauté pan over medium heat. Add the curry paste and the red pepper flakes and cook, stirring constantly, until the curry paste sizzles, about 1 minute. Reduce the heat to low and add the rice vinegar, soy sauce, peanut butter, and ¼ cup water. Cook, stirring, about 3 minutes. Transfer the mixture to a blender and blend until smooth. The sauce should be the consistency of thickened cream; add more water to thin it if necessary.

TO MAKE THE PASTA

BRING a large pot of salted water to a boil. In a small bowl, combine the chicken livers, soy sauce, and sesame oil. Heat 3 tablespoons of the vegetable oil in a large sauté pan over high heat until hot. Add the red onion and cook, stirring, for about 3 minutes. Add the garlic, ginger, chile, cabbage, and scallions, and continue to cook over high heat, tossing the ingredients for even cooking, for about 2 minutes. Add the mint, watercress, and cucumbers, toss to combine, turn off the heat, and reserve.

REMOVE the chicken livers from the marinade and pat them dry. Heat the remaining 2 table-spoons vegetable oil in a sauté pan until very hot. Add the chicken livers and sear over high heat until they are well browned on one side. Turn the livers over and continue cooking until the livers are medium, about another 3 minutes.

MEANWHILE, cook the pasta in the boiling water until al dente. Drain the pasta and put it into a large bowl. Add the warm vegetable mixture and about ½ cup of the peanut sauce and toss until well combined.

DIVIDE the pasta among the plates and arrange the chicken livers on top and around the pasta. Decorate with the reserved Napa cabbage and mint leaves. Sprinkle with the chopped peanuts.

RISOTTO—PLAIN *and* SIMPLE

While this is the most basic preparation of risotto, it is nonetheless delicious. Serve it as a side dish or use it as a springboard for your own, more involved risotto dishes by adding your favorite cooked ingredients to the rice.

About 6 cups chicken broth (see Bistro Pantry, page 10)

1 cup dry white wine

2 tablespoons olive oil

About 5 tablespoons unsalted butter

1 small carrot, chopped into very small cubes

1 small onion, finely chopped

1½ cups Arborio rice

Kosher salt and freshly ground black pepper

About ¼ cup grated Parmesan cheese, preferably Parmigiano-Reggiano

COMBINE the chicken broth and the white wine in a saucepan, bring to a boil, and then keep at a simmer.

IN a large, heavy-based saucepan or Dutch oven, heat the olive oil and 2 tablespoons of the butter over medium heat. Add the carrot and onion and cook until softened but not browned, about 5 minutes. Add the rice and cook, stirring well to coat the rice, for about a minute. Add about 1 cup of the hot broth to the rice and stir gently with long, slow strokes until most of the liquid is absorbed.

Add another cup of broth and cook, stirring, until almost all of that broth has been absorbed. Continue cooking the rice in this way until it plumps up and feels chewy and just slightly firm to the bite, 20 to 30 minutes. Season the rice with salt and pepper to taste toward the end of cooking.

TAKE the rice off the heat. Add the remaining 2 to 3 tablespoons butter and the Parmesan cheese and stir to combine the ingredients. Serve with extra grated cheese, if you like.

LEMON-SCENTED RISOTTO *with* MORELS *and* CHIVES

SERVES 4

While meaty, earthy morels are my first choice for this risotto, other wild mushrooms, such as chanterelles, or even a mix of wild and domestic mushrooms, will also make a delicious risotto.

3 tablespoons unsalted butter

1 pound fresh morels

2 shallots, finely chopped

2 garlic cloves, finely chopped

½ teaspoon chopped fresh thyme

¼ cup dry white wine

Kosher salt and freshly ground black pepper

6 to 8 cups chicken broth or mushroom stock (see Bistro Pantry, page 10)

3 tablespoons olive oil

1 medium onion, finely chopped

1½ cups Arborio rice

½ cup fresh lemon juice (from 3 to 4 lemons)

2 tablespoons finely chopped fresh chives

1 cup grated Parmesan cheese, preferably Parmigiano-Reggiano

HEAT 2 tablespoons of the butter in a medium sauté pan over high heat. Add the morels, lower the heat to medium-high, and cook, tossing occasionally, until tender, about 5 minutes. Add the shallots, garlic, and thyme. Cook, stirring, until aromatic, about another 2 minutes. Add the white wine and cook until most of the wine is gone, about 2 minutes. Season with salt and pepper to taste and reserve.

IN a medium saucepan, bring the chicken broth to a boil and then lower to a gentle simmer.

IN a large, heavy-based saucepan or Dutch oven, heat the olive oil over medium heat. Add the onion and cook until softened but not browned, about 5 minutes. Add the rice and cook, stirring well to coat the rice, for about a minute. Add the

lemon juice and continue to stir until all of the lemon juice has been absorbed.

ADD about 1 cup of the hot broth to the rice and stir gently with long, slow strokes until most of the liquid is absorbed. Add the morels. Add another cup of broth and cook, stirring, until almost all of that broth has been absorbed. Continue cooking the rice in this way until it plumps up and feels chewy and just slightly firm to the bite, 20 to 30 minutes. Season the rice with salt and pepper to taste toward the end of cooking.

TAKE the rice off the heat. Add the remaining 1 tablespoon butter, the chives, and the Parmesan cheese, and stir to combine the ingredients. Serve with extra grated cheese, if you like.

BRAISED WILD MUSHROOMS *with* RED WINE RISOTTO

You can use a mix of fresh and dried mushrooms for this risotto. Soak the dried mushrooms in hot water to soften them before using, and don't forget to add some of this soaking liquid to the broth—just be careful to leave any sediment behind.

5 to 6 cups mushroom stock or chicken broth (see Bistro Pantry, page 10)

1 cup red wine

2 to 3 tablespoons olive oil

4 tablespoons unsalted butter

1 pound mixed wild and domestic mushrooms, trimmed, cleaned, and cut into 2-inch pieces

Kosher salt and freshly ground black pepper

2 garlic cloves, finely chopped

3 shallots, finely chopped

1 teaspoon chopped fresh thyme or marjoram or a mix of both

1½ cups Arborio rice

About ¼ cup grated Asiago cheese

1 tablespoon chopped fresh parsley

IN a saucepan, combine the mushroom stock and the red wine, bring to a boil, and then lower to a simmer.

HEAT the olive oil and 2 tablespoons of the butter in a large, heavy-based saucepan or Dutch oven over medium-high heat until hot. Add the meatiest of your mushrooms, season with salt and a little pepper, and cook until they begin to lose their juices, about 3 minutes. Add the more delicate mushrooms and continue to cook over medium-high heat until these are well browned and have lost some of their juices as well, about 4 minutes more. Add the garlic, shallots, and the thyme or marjoram. Lower the heat and cook, stirring occasionally, until the shallots and the mushrooms are tender, about 5 minutes.

ADD the rice to the mushrooms and cook, stirring well to coat the rice, for about a minute. Add about 1 cup of the hot stock and stir gently with long, slow strokes until most of the liquid is absorbed. Add another cup of stock and cook, stirring, until almost all of that stock has been absorbed. Continue cooking the rice in this way until it plumps up and feels chewy and just slightly firm to the bite, 20 to 30 minutes. Toward the end of the cooking add salt and pepper.

REMOVE the pan from the heat and add the remaining 2 tablespoons butter and the Asiago cheese and stir to combine the ingredients. Divide the risotto among warm bowls and sprinkle with the parsley and more cheese, if you like.

RISOTTO *with* BUTTERNUT SQUASH *and* MAPLE SYRUP

This tastes great with just about any roast bird, including turkey. But I really like to serve it with a crisped leg of Duck Confit (page 193) right on top.

6 cups chicken broth (see Bistro Pantry, page 10)

¼ cup dry sherry

4 tablespoons unsalted butter

1 tablespoon olive oil

1 small onion, finely chopped

½ butternut squash, peeled, seeded, and cut into ½-inch pieces

Kosher salt and freshly ground black pepper

2 garlic cloves, finely chopped

2 tablespoons real maple syrup

1 teaspoon chopped fresh rosemary

3 tablespoons sherry vinegar

1½ cups Arborio rice

3 tablespoons chopped fresh parsley

⅓ to ½ cup Parmesan cheese, preferably Parmigiano-Reggiano

IN a saucepan, combine the chicken broth and the sherry, bring to a boil, and then lower to a simmer.

HEAT 2 tablespoons of the butter and the olive oil in a large, heavy-based saucepan or Dutch oven over medium-high heat until hot. Add the onion and butternut squash, season with salt and pepper to taste, and cook, stirring occasionally, until the onion is tender, about 7 minutes. Add the garlic, maple syrup, rosemary, and sherry vinegar, and cook an additional 2 minutes. Add the rice, stirring to coat it well, and cook for an additional minute. Add about 1 cup of the hot broth and stir gently with long, slow strokes until most of the liquid is absorbed. Add another cup of broth and cook, stirring, until almost all of that broth has been absorbed. Continue cooking the rice in this way until it plumps up and feels chewy and just slightly firm to the bite, 20 to 30 minutes. Season the rice with salt and pepper to taste toward the end of cooking.

REMOVE the pan from the heat and add the remaining 2 tablespoons butter, the parsley, and the Parmesan cheese. Stir to combine. Taste and add additional salt, pepper to taste or even a drop or two of sherry vinegar to taste. Divide the risotto among warm bowls and sprinkle with more parsley and cheese, if you like.

CURRIED ZUCCHINI RISOTTO

SERVES 4 TO 6

This is a dish for curry fans everywhere. I like to serve this risotto as a side dish to sautéed scallops and grilled shrimp.

5 to 6 cups vegetable stock or chicken broth (see Bistro Pantry, page 10)

1 cup dry sherry

Pinch of saffron

3 tablespoons olive oil

4 to 5 tablespoons unsalted butter

1 small onion, finely chopped

1½ tablespoons curry powder

3 to 4 garlic cloves, finely chopped

1½ cups Arborio rice

Kosher salt and freshly ground black pepper

2 medium zucchini, cut into a medium dice

About ¼ cup Parmesan cheese, preferably Parmigiano-Reggiano

2 tablespoons chopped fresh cilantro leaves, plus a few whole leaves for garnish

2 tablespoons chopped fresh mint, plus a few whole leaves for garnish

IN a saucepan, combine the vegetable stock and the sherry. Add the saffron, crumbling it between your fingers and into the pan. Bring the liquid to a boil and then lower to a simmer.

IN a large, heavy-based saucepan or Dutch oven, heat 2 tablespoons of the olive oil and 2 tablespoons of the butter over medium heat. Add the onion and 1 tablespoon of the curry powder and cook, stirring, until the onion is tender, about 7 minutes. Add half of the chopped garlic and cook 1 more minute. Add the rice to the pan and cook, stirring well to coat the rice, for about a minute. Add about 1 cup of the hot stock and stir gently with long, slow strokes until most of the liquid is absorbed. Add another cup of stock and cook, stirring, until almost all of that stock has been absorbed. Continue cooking the rice in this way until you've used about 3 cups of the stock. Season the rice with salt and pepper to taste toward the end of this cooking.

MEANWHILE, in a separate sauté pan, heat the remaining tablespoon of olive oil and 1 tablespoon of the butter over medium heat. Add the zucchini, the remaining garlic, the remaining curry powder, and a good pinch of salt. Cook, stirring occasionally, until the zucchini is just tender, about 7 minutes.

ADD the zucchini to the risotto pan and stir to combine. Add the remaining stock to the pan and cook, stirring gently, until the stock has been absorbed, another 5 to 7 minutes. When the rice is done—it feels chewy and just slightly firm to the bite—remove the pan from the heat. Add another tablespoon or two of butter and the Parmesan cheese and stir to combine. Divide the risotto among warm bowls and sprinkle with the chopped cilantro and mint. Garnish with the whole leaves.

CRABMEAT RISOTTO *with* PEAS *and* MINT

SERVES 6

Sweet crabmeat and sweet peas make a great match in this springlike risotto.

5 to 6 cups vegetable stock (see Bistro Pantry, page 10) or water

1 cup dry white wine

3 to 4 tablespoons unsalted butter

1 small onion, finely chopped

3 garlic cloves, finely chopped

1½ cups Arborio rice

Kosher salt and freshly ground black pepper

3 cups fresh or frozen peas

1 bunch scallions, white parts and 2 inches of the green tops, cut into thin rounds

6 to 8 ounces fresh crabmeat, preferably lump crabmeat

4 to 6 leaves of fresh mint, roughly chopped, plus a few whole leaves for garnish

1 teaspoon grated lemon zest

About ¼ cup Parmesan cheese, preferably Parmigiano-Reggiano

BRING the vegetable stock to a boil. Add the white wine and lower to a simmer.

IN a large, heavy-based saucepan or Dutch oven, heat 2 tablespoons butter over medium-high heat. Add the onion, lower the heat to medium, and cook, stirring occasionally, until tender, about 7 minutes. Add the garlic and cook for another 2 minutes. Add the rice and cook, stirring well to coat the rice, for about a minute. Add about 1 cup of the hot stock and stir gently with long, slow strokes until most of the liquid is absorbed. Add another cup of stock and cook, stirring, until almost all of that stock has been absorbed. Continue cooking the rice in this way until you've used about 3 cups of the stock. Season the rice with salt and pepper to taste at any time during the cooking.

ADD the peas, scallions, and about 1½ cups of the hot stock and continue to cook, stirring, until most of the liquid has been absorbed. Taste the rice. If it is still very hard, add more stock and continue to cook until it is almost but not quite tender. Add the remaining butter, crabmeat, chopped mint, lemon zest, Parmesan cheese, and another cup of liquid. Cook, stirring, until the crabmeat is heated through, most of the liquid is absorbed, and the rice is plump, chewy, and just slightly firm to the bite. Divide the risotto among warm bowls and garnish with mint leaves, if you wish.

BASIC POLENTA

This basic polenta is a wonderful base for almost any braised meat or vegetable dish, especially the Parmesan-Crusted Lamb Shanks on page 226. Served hot off the stove, it has a lovely, soft texture. It thickens as it stands, and when chilled, can be cut into shapes and baked or fried. At the restaurant, we often mix fine- and medium-ground cornmeal for optimum flavor and texture. But if I were to go with just one, it would be the medium.

TO USE IN OTHER RECIPES

2 quarts water

1½ teaspoons kosher salt, or more to taste

2 cups medium-ground cornmeal, or a combination of fine and medium

TO SERVE AS IS, ADD

5 tablespoons softened unsalted butter

½ cup grated Parmesan cheese, preferably Parmigiano-Reggiano

BRING 1 quart of water and the salt to a boil in a large saucepan.

IN a bowl, combine the cornmeal and the remaining 1 quart water and stir to combine. Let the cornmeal absorb some of the water for about 2 minutes.

GRADUALLY whisk the polenta and water from the bowl into the boiling water. Continue to whisk until the polenta begins to thicken, about 5 minutes.

LOWER the heat to low and cook the polenta, stirring well every few minutes, until the polenta begins to pull away from the sides of the pan and has a soft, creamy texture, about 45 minutes. (If the polenta sputters and makes a mess, partially cover the pan.)

IF YOU ARE MAKING BASIC POLENTA FOR ONE OF THE RECIPES THAT FOLLOW

Look at the recipe itself to see how much butter and what kind of cheese and how much of it to add.

IF YOU ARE MAKING BASIC POLENTA TO SERVE AS IS

Add the amounts of butter and cheese in the ingredients list above and stir well to combine. As the polenta sits, it will begin to thicken. If it becomes thicker than you like, add a little more water or some milk and stir to combine.

CREAMY POLENTA *with* SUMMER VEGETABLE RAGOUT

SERVES 6

This is a great dish to turn to after a visit to the farmers' market. Because you don't cook the vegetable ragout for long, the flavor of each vegetable stays pure and unsullied.

1 recipe Basic Polenta (page 139)

About 10 tablespoons unsalted butter, 5 of them softened

½ cup grated Parmesan cheese, preferably Parmigiano-Reggiano, plus 2 tablespoons for serving

2 tablespoons olive oil

About 18 pearl onions, peeled (see Note, page 187)

3 garlic cloves, thinly sliced

1 small fennel bulb, trimmed (reserve some of the feathery top for garnish, if you like), cut in half lengthwise and then thinly sliced crosswise

1 red bell pepper, stemmed, seeded, and cut into a medium dice

1 medium zucchini, cut into a medium dice

About 18 green beans, stemmed and cut into 2-inch pieces

About 18 sugar snap peas

2 ears sweet corn, kernels cut from the cob

1 bunch scallions, trimmed, white parts and about 2 inches of the green tops, thinly sliced

½ cup dry white wine

½ cup chicken broth (see Bistro Pantry, page 10)

Kosher salt and freshly ground black pepper

About 10 fresh basil leaves, washed and dried well and roughly chopped

COOK the Basic Polenta as directed on page 139. Add the 5 tablespoons softened butter and the ½ cup Parmesan cheese and stir to combine.

MEANWHILE, heat the olive oil and 2 tablespoons of the remaining butter in a large sauté pan over medium-high heat. Add the pearl onions and cook, stirring occasionally, until they brown lightly, about 7 minutes. Add the garlic, fennel, and bell pepper, and cook, stirring occasionally, for another 5 to 7 minutes. Add the zucchini, green beans, sugar snap peas, corn, and scallions to the pan, and raise the heat to high. Cook for a few minutes, stirring, and then add the white wine, chicken broth, and salt and pepper to taste, and bring to a boil. Cook over medium-high heat until the beans and sugar snap peas are tender, another 5 to 7 minutes. Turn off the heat and add the basil and the remaining 3 tablespoons butter to the pan and stir to combine.

JUST before serving, thin the polenta with a few tablespoons of water—it should just hold its shape on a plate and not be too thick. Spoon some of the polenta onto warmed rimmed plates. Spoon some of the vegetable ragout over the center of the polenta and let the juices run as they may. Sprinkle with additional grated cheese, and decorate with the reserved fennel tops.

BAKED POLENTA SQUARES *with* PEPERONATA *and* WHITE TRUFFLE OIL

Peperonata—bell peppers cooked in olive oil with tomatoes, onions, and garlic—is a staple of antipasto. Strewn over squares of polenta, peperonata becomes a perfect light dinner to serve on a summer night. You need to cook the polenta ahead, since it has to chill for at least 6 hours before you can cut it into shapes and bake it. You can also make the peperonata ahead, which means that when it's time for dinner, there will be little left to do.

1 recipe Basic Polenta (page 139)

5 tablespoons softened unsalted butter

1½ cups grated Asiago cheese

2 tablespoons olive oil

1 medium onion, thinly sliced

Kosher salt and freshly ground black pepper

2 red bell peppers, stemmed, seeded, and cut into very thin strips

2 yellow bell peppers, stemmed, seeded, and cut into very thin strips

3 garlic cloves, finely chopped

1 cup dry white wine

1 tablespoon tomato paste

About 12 fresh mint leaves, chopped

About 1 tablespoon white truffle oil

COOK the Basic Polenta as directed on page 139. Add the butter and ½ cup of the Asiago cheese and stir to combine. Pour the polenta into a sided baking pan or dish that measures about 13 × 9 × 2 inches and let it cool. Cover and refrigerate for at least 6 hours or overnight.

HEAT the olive oil in a large sauté pan over medium-high heat. Add the onion, season with salt and pepper, and cook, stirring every few minutes, until the onion is tender, about 7 minutes.

Turn the heat down to low and add the bell peppers and garlic. Stir to combine and continue to cook, stirring, until the peppers are tender but not falling apart, 20 to 25 minutes. Add the white wine and tomato paste; let it boil for 1 minute. Add the mint and stir to combine.

HEAT the oven to 350°F. Turn the chilled polenta out onto a cutting board. Cut the polenta into six squares, each about 4 inches. Oil the bottom of a baking sheet large enough to hold the polenta squares without crowding them and put the squares on the sheet. Scatter the peppers on top of the polenta and sprinkle the remaining cheese over the top. Bake until the cheese has melted and the polenta is heated through, about 20 minutes.

TO SERVE

Use a spatula to lift the polenta and peppers out of the baking dish and onto plates. Arrange any peppers left behind in the dish onto the polenta. Spoon the juices from the pan around each piece and drizzle ¼ to ½ teaspoon truffle oil on top.

CRISPY POLENTA TRIANGLES *with* CHANTERELLES *and* ASIAGO

This is a wonderful first course to an elegant meal. The earthy flavors of the chanterelles work their magic with the polenta. The cooked polenta needs to chill for at least 6 hours before you can cut it into shapes and fry it. For hors d'oeuvres or side-dish portions, cut the polenta into smaller pieces.

1 recipe Basic Polenta (page 139)

About 9 tablespoons unsalted butter, 5 of them softened

1 cup shredded Asiago cheese

About ¼ cup vegetable oil

1 pound chanterelles, cleaned and cut into 1-inch pieces

Kosher salt

4 medium shallots, thinly sliced

3 garlic cloves, thinly sliced

1 teaspoon chopped fresh thyme

½ cup dry white wine

½ cup mushroom stock or chicken broth (see Bistro Pantry, page 10)

1 cup heavy cream

1 to 2 tablespoons chopped fresh parsley

Freshly ground black pepper

COOK the Basic Polenta as directed on page 139. Add the 5 tablespoons softened butter and ½ cup of the Asiago cheese and stir to combine. Pour the polenta into a sided baking pan or dish that measures about 13 × 9 × 2 inches and let it cool. Cover and refrigerate for at least 6 hours or overnight.

HEAT the oven to 425°F. Turn the polenta out onto a cutting board and cut it into six 4-inch squares and then in half to form triangles. Heat the vegetable oil in a large, ovenproof sauté pan over high heat. Add the chilled polenta, with the less smooth side down, and sear until browned, about 5 minutes, adjusting the heat to prevent burning. (You may need to do this in two pans or in batches depending on the size of the pan.) Turn the polenta over and put the pan in the oven to cook the polenta until warmed through, 15 to 20 minutes.

MEANWHILE, in a large sauté pan, heat about 4 tablespoons of the butter over medium-high heat until it starts bubbling. Add the chanterelles, season amply with salt, and sear them, without moving them, until well browned on one side, 5 to 7 minutes. Lower the heat to medium. Add the shallots, garlic, and thyme, and cook for a few minutes until fragrant. Add the white wine and stock, stirring to get up any of the browned bits stuck to the bottom of the pan. Let the chanterelles bubble in the liquid until they are tender and much of the liquid has evaporated, about 10 minutes. Add the cream and bring to a boil. Lower the heat and let the cream bubble for 3 to 4 minutes.

Add the chopped parsley and season with more salt, if needed, and some pepper. Divide the mushrooms among six plates and then place the polenta triangles on top.

POLENTA *with* TASSO *and* SWEETBREADS

SERVES 6 TO 8

Tasso, also known as Cajun ham, is a heavily spiced and cured pork shoulder. It's usually chopped and used like a seasoning in such Cajun classics as gumbo and étouf-fée. I use it less traditionally in all sorts of pasta and rice dishes. Its one-of-a-kind flavor makes a wonderful contrast to the richness of sweetbreads (see page 250). You can sub-stitute smoked ham, but the dish will lose a lot of its interest. Even though most super-markets outside of Louisiana don't carry tasso, you can easily mail-order this regional specialty (see Sources). Start this dish earlier in the day you plan to serve it in order to allow the sweetbreads time to soak and chill.

1 cup dry white wine

Pinch of red pepper flakes

¼ teaspoon herbes de Provence (see Bistro Pantry, page 9)

1 bay leaf

Kosher salt

¾ pound sweetbreads, soaked for at least 4 hours in cold water in the refrigerator

1 recipe Basic Polenta (page 139)

About 7 tablespoons unsalted butter, 5 of them softened

½ cup grated Parmesan cheese, preferably Parmigiano-Reggiano

Freshly ground black pepper

About 2 tablespoons vegetable oil, more as needed

¾ pound tasso, thinly sliced

1 large onion, thinly sliced

1 red bell pepper, stemmed, seeded, and thinly sliced

2 tablespoons chili powder

½ cup dry sherry

½ cup chicken broth (see Bistro Pantry, page 10)

1 tablespoon chopped fresh parsley

TO POACH THE SWEETBREADS
In a medium saucepan, combine 4 cups water with the white wine, red pepper flakes, herbes de Provence, bay leaf, and 1 tablespoon salt, and bring to a boil. Lower the heat to a simmer, remove the sweetbreads from the cold water, and add them to the saucepan. Cook the sweetbreads until they are somewhat firm to the touch, about 10 minutes. Remove the sweetbreads from the pot and let cool long enough to be handled. (Discard the poaching

liquid.) While the sweetbreads are still warm, use your fingers to remove the thin outer membrane and any cartilage and fatty white bits from the two lobes of the sweetbreads. Try not to tear the meat when you do this. Let the sweetbreads come to room temperature. Wrap them well in plastic wrap and refrigerate them for a couple of hours.

MEANWHILE, cook the Basic Polenta as directed on page 139. Add the 5 tablespoons softened butter and the ½ cup Parmesan cheese and stir to combine.

SLICE the sweetbreads into pieces about ¼ inch thick. Season with salt and pepper. In a large sauté pan, heat the vegetable oil over medium-high heat. Add the sweetbreads and brown on one side and then the other. Remove them from the pan and reserve. Add the tasso and sear it quickly over high heat. Reserve the tasso with the sweetbreads. Add the onion, red bell pepper, and chili powder. Lower the heat to medium and cook, stirring every few minutes, until the onion and pepper are tender, about 10 minutes. Return the sweetbreads and tasso to the pan and stir to combine. Season with salt and pepper to taste. Add the sherry and chicken broth and cook for about 5 minutes. Add the remaining 2 tablespoons butter to the pan and stir to combine. Thin the polenta with a few tablespoons of water. It should just hold its shape on a plate and not be too thick. Spoon some of the polenta onto the plates. Spoon the sweetbread mixture over the top and serve, sprinkled with some chopped parsley.

FISH
Bistro Style

MY WIFE, FIONA,
makes what to my mind is the quintessential
bistro fish dish. She butters a skillet, puts
some halibut steaks on top of the butter,
sprinkles some sliced shallots, salt, and
pepper over the fish, adds white wine to
the pan, and cooks the fish on the stove
until done. A quick reduction of the liquid
in the pan and a sprinkling of fresh herbs,
and she has a really simple, really good-
tasting dinner. (To tell the truth, I only
recently found out just *how* good, as this
is something she often makes for herself
and our daughter, Sophie, while I'm
cooking at the restaurant.)

FIONA'S APPROACH to fish mirrors mine as well as that of most bistro chefs: When it comes to fish, keep it simple. Let the fish speak for itself. A splash of wine, a pat of butter, a little fresh herb is often enough. That said, there are some fish, especially the more full-flavored varieties such as mackerel and salmon, that cry out for strongly flavored accompaniments to round out their richness.

BEGIN WITH THE BEST FISH. As with all ingredients, but with fish even more so, the quality of the raw ingredient is paramount to the success of the dish. For this reason, try to be flexible when shopping for fish. Have a couple of different recipes in mind and go to the fish market or to the fish counter before you get the rest of the components for your meal. That way, if you had swordfish in mind but it's unavailable or looks suspect, you can either ask the fishmonger to recommend a suitable substitute or switch gears entirely and go with a different recipe to feature the fish that's the best that day.

How do you tell which fish is best? Start by looking at the display. The fish should be on clean ice with some separation between the different kinds of fish. Whole fish is easiest to judge: It should look as close to alive as possible. The eyes of a fresh fish are clear and bright. Its scales should be intact (missing scales can signify improper handling or old age), and its gills, if intact, should be vivid red. Don't just use your eyes to pick a good fish. Ask to touch and smell it. Good fish will feel firm and won't smell "fishy." It will smell fresh, a little sweet, and, in the case of shellfish, of the sea.

Fish that has been cut into steaks or fillets is a little trickier to judge. If you've been to a great sushi bar, have the image of the fish served there in your mind. Does the fish you're about to buy look appetizing in its raw state? Does it look firm and fresh? Avoid any fish that looks bruised; in some fillets this will look like uneven red blotches. Bruised fish may have been crushed in transport; it may have an off flavor and will spoil faster. As with whole fish, fillets and steaks should have a fresh, sweet smell.

I like to buy larger pieces of fish and portion them myself. As opposed to the precut fillets and steaks on display, the larger piece has probably been handled less. And while a good fishmonger will cut the fish so that it looks good (no jagged edges) and will cook evenly, I prefer the control I get by cutting it myself. I also generally remove any pin bones myself. Though a good fish market will do this for you (and do it well), sometimes fillets look quite mangled because someone removed the pin bones with something less than finesse.

If you plan to do more shopping after you buy your fish, ask the fishmonger to pack it on ice. Once you get it home, keep it well refrigerated and use it within a day or so.

FIONA'S EASY HALIBUT *with* WHITE WINE, SHALLOTS, *and* BASIL

SERVES 4

This is the easiest way to cook fish I know of. Halibut is a wonderful, clean-tasting white fish that's caught both here on the East Coast as well as on the West Coast. You can play with the flavors, too. Cook the fish with, say, mushrooms and garlic in the winter or tomatoes and basil in the summer and serve it with Braised Fennel (page 272) and steamed new potatoes.

2 tablespoons unsalted butter, softened at room temperature

4 halibut steaks, 6 to 8 ounces each, about 1 inch thick

1 shallot, very thinly sliced

1 teaspoon kosher salt

1 teaspoon freshly ground white pepper

2 cups dry white wine

6 to 8 fresh basil leaves, washed and dried well and cut into a fine chiffonade (see page 4)

1 teaspoon coarsely chopped fresh parsley

SPREAD the butter evenly over the bottom of a large sauté pan. Put the halibut steaks on top of the butter.

SPRINKLE the shallot slices, salt, and white pepper over the fish. Add the white wine to the pan. Cover the pan and bring to a boil over high heat. Lower the heat to low and cook the fish until done, about 8 minutes. To test for doneness, gently pull the bones away from the meat; they will come away easily when the fish is cooked. Remove these bones, if you like. Lift the halibut out of the pan and keep it warm on the plates.

ADD the basil and parsley to the pan. Bring the juices in the pan to a boil and reduce them until you have a rich sauce. Season with more salt and pepper if needed. Spoon the sauce over the fish.

Wine suggestions: *The possibilities for this very clean but flavorful dish are endless and can vary with the seasons. Some suggestions: a relatively simple white Burgundy, a Saint-Aubin or a Rully; a minerally Sauvignon Blanc from the Loire. A Trimbach Riesling from Alsace would also work well.*

SEARED SEA SCALLOPS *with a* GARLIC, TOMATO, *and* OLIVE COMPOTE

This full-flavored compote also works well with salmon, tuna, swordfish, and even grilled chicken. Serve the scallops with some angel hair pasta tossed with a little of the compote. When buying scallops, look for ones that have not been chemically treated. Often called "dry" scallops, they brown better and have more flavor.

10 garlic cloves, peeled and root ends trimmed off, but cloves left whole

About ¾ cup olive oil

½ cup black olives, such as Kalamata, pitted and coarsely chopped

1 cup sun-dried tomatoes, soaked in warm water until soft, drained, and coarsely chopped

1 shallot, finely chopped

2 tablespoons chopped fresh basil

2 tablespoons balsamic vinegar

Kosher salt and freshly ground black pepper

24 large sea scallops (1 to 1¼ pounds), side muscle removed

1 to 2 tablespoons vegetable oil

2 tablespoons chopped fresh parsley

TO MAKE THE COMPOTE

Put the garlic in a small saucepan. Add enough olive oil to cover the cloves completely; the size of your pan will dictate how much oil you need. Bring the olive oil to a simmer, turn the heat down to low, and cook the garlic until it's very tender, 15 to 20 minutes. Using a slotted spoon, transfer the garlic to a bowl. Add ⅓ cup of the olive oil and reserve the rest in case the compote needs more. (The garlic-infused oil is also great on its own.) Let the garlic cool to room temperature. Add the olives, sun-dried tomatoes, shallot, basil, and balsamic vinegar. Mix the ingredients gently with a rubber spatula so as not to break up the tender garlic. Season with salt, if necessary, and pepper. Allow the flavors of the ingredients to blend for at least 15 minutes before serving. (The compote will taste better if it has more time for the flavors to meld; it will keep in the refrigerator for a few days; allow it to come to room temperature before serving.)

TO COOK THE SCALLOPS

Pat the scallops dry and season them well with salt and pepper. Heat the vegetable oil in a large sauté pan over medium-high heat until very hot. Add the scallops to the pan, leaving space between them. Cook without moving them until well browned on one side, 2 to 3 minutes. With tongs, turn each scallop over and cook for another minute. Remove the pan from the heat and allow the scallops to continue to cook in the pan for another minute.

TO SERVE

Add additional olive oil to the compote if it seems dry. Spoon some of the compote on each plate.

Arrange the seared scallops on top and sprinkle with the parsley.

Wine suggestions: *If it's summer, I'd go for a really good rosé from Provence or a Sancerre or a Chinon rosé from the Loire. Other good options: a Tuscan Sauvignon Blanc or one from New Zealand, specifically the Marlborough area.*

BACON-WRAPPED SCALLOPS *with* BEURRE BLANC

SERVES 4

Try these scallops with the Gratin of Artichoke and Swiss Chard on page 107. When buying scallops, look for ones that have not been chemically treated. Often called "dry" scallops, they brown better and have more flavor.

12 strips of bacon (not thick-cut), cut in half

20 to 24 large sea scallops (1 to 1¼ pounds, depending on size)

About 1 tablespoon vegetable oil

Kosher salt and freshly ground black pepper

1 shallot, finely chopped

1 cup dry white wine

2 tablespoons heavy cream (optional)

3 tablespoons unsalted butter, cut into small pieces

1 tablespoon chopped fresh parsley

4 lemon wedges (optional)

HEAT the oven to 425°F. Wrap the bacon around the scallops and fasten with a toothpick. Heat the vegetable oil over high heat in a large ovenproof sauté pan until very hot. Sprinkle the scallops with salt and pepper and put the scallops in the pan, leaving space between them. Cook the scallops over high heat until well browned on one side, about 2 minutes. Turn the scallops over and place the pan in the oven. Cook until the bacon just begins to crisp and the scallops are cooked, about 5 more minutes. Remove the scallops from the pan, leaving the fat and any juices behind, and keep the scallops warm while you make the pan sauce.

ADD the shallot to the pan and sauté over medium heat for 1 minute. Add the white wine and bring to a boil over high heat, scraping up the browned bits from the pan. Lower the heat to medium-high and reduce the liquid to about 3 tablespoons. Add the heavy cream, if using, and bring to a boil. Reduce the heat to low and whisk in the butter a few pieces at a time until it is completely incorporated and a smooth emulsion forms. Season with salt and pepper to taste. Divide the scallops among four plates, spoon the sauce over the scallops, sprinkle with the parsley, and serve with the lemon wedges, if using, on the side.

Wine suggestions: *There are two ways to go with this dish. Either accentuate the inherent richness of the dish and select a Fumé Blanc from the United States, which is usually low in acid and quite rich, or opt for a crisper white Burgundy (a Pouilly-Fuissé). Better still, choose a Sancerre whose fruity acid and mineral flavors will cut through the richness of the cream.*

GRILLED SALMON *with* PEAS, POTATOES, *and* MINT

SERVES 6

A lemony vinaigrette and bright bites of mint balance the richness of the grilled salmon in this summery dish. To keep the salmon from sticking to the grill, make sure the grill is hot and don't move the salmon until it's well seared on one side.

1½ to 2 cups peas, fresh or frozen

2 tablespoons kosher salt, or more to taste

1 pound new (red) potatoes, washed and cut into ½-inch pieces

⅓ cup fresh lemon juice (from 2 to 3 lemons)

¾ cup extra virgin olive oil, more as needed

2 large shallots, finely chopped

6 salmon fillets, 6 to 7 ounces each

Freshly ground black pepper

About 18 fresh mint leaves, torn into pieces

About 3 cups mixed mild salad greens, such as red leaf, green leaf, Boston, and Bibb, washed and dried well

Lemon wedges (optional)

BRING about 6 cups water to a boil. Have ready a bowl of ice water. Add the peas and 1 tablespoon of the salt to the water and cook the peas until tender, about 3 minutes for fresh peas, 1 minute for frozen. Drain the peas and transfer them to the ice bath.

BRING another 6 cups water to a boil. Add the potatoes and another tablespoon salt and cook until just tender, 5 to 10 minutes. Drain the potatoes and let them cool in a single layer to keep them from overcooking.

WHISK together the lemon juice and olive oil.

HEAT your grill to between medium-high and high. Just before grilling, combine the shallots and potatoes in a large bowl and toss with just enough of the lemon juice and olive oil to coat them well.

RUB the salmon all over with a little olive oil and season amply with salt and pepper. Place the fillets on the grill and cook without moving them for 3 to 4 minutes. Turn the fillets over and continue cooking until the fish feels firm to the touch but is still deep pink in the center, another 3 to 4 minutes.

JUST before serving, toss the peas and mint with the potatoes, adding a little more dressing to coat the peas well. Season with salt and pepper. Add the greens and toss, adding a bit more dressing if necessary.

SPOON some salad onto each plate. Place a salmon fillet on top of each salad. Drizzle with any remaining dressing. Serve with a wedge of lemon, if you like.

Wine suggestions: *This lovely dish has both richness in the salmon and lively flavors in the mint and lemon juice; it can be paired with a white Burgundy or with a California Chardonnay (which I particularly love in summer), or you can even try a relatively lush Pinot Gris from Oregon.*

SALMON WRAPPED *in* LEEKS *with* ANCHOVY BUTTER

SERVES 4

This is a very pretty dish. Don't worry if the edges of the leeks start to brown; it will just add a delicious toasty flavor to the dish. Serve the salmon with some sautéed spinach (page 255) and the lentil salad on page 197.

2 medium leeks, roots cut off and green parts trimmed to leave the leek about 4 inches long

Kosher salt

8 tablespoons unsalted butter, softened at room temperature

4 anchovy fillets, rinsed (or soaked if using salt-packed), patted dry and very finely chopped

1½ teaspoons fresh lemon juice

Freshly ground black pepper

4 salmon fillets, 6 to 7 ounces each

1 tablespoon chopped fresh marjoram or oregano

1 lemon, cut in half and thinly sliced

1 tablespoon olive oil

1 tablespoon chopped fresh parsley (optional)

CUT the leeks in half lengthwise. Trim the ends and separate the "leaves." Soak in water to remove the dirt. Have ready a bowl of ice water. Bring 3 cups water and a pinch of salt to a boil in a saucepan. Add the leeks and boil until tender, about 5 minutes. Drain and plunge the leeks in the ice water to stop the cooking.

IN a small bowl, mash together the butter, anchovies, and lemon juice. Season with a pinch of pepper.

LIGHTLY oil a sided baking sheet.

LAY three or four leek leaves down on your work surface, overlapping them slightly so that they form a rectangle. Pat the leeks dry. Put a salmon fillet on top of the leeks. Spread about one-fourth

of the anchovy butter on top of the fish and sprinkle a little marjoram or oregano over the butter. Wrap the leeks around the salmon, and put the salmon, seam side down, onto the baking sheet. Repeat with the remaining leek leaves and salmon. (You can also do them all at once, assembly-line style, if you have the space.) Place the lemon slices on top of the leeks along the length of the salmon and sprinkle lightly with pepper. Refrigerate for 20 minutes before cooking to firm up the butter so it doesn't ooze out immediately.

HEAT the oven to 425°F. Just before the pan goes into the oven, drizzle the olive oil over the leek-wrapped fish and add 2 to 3 tablespoons water to the pan. Cook the fish until it offers some resistance when poked with your finger, 10 to 15 minutes depending on the thickness of your fillets. You can discreetly check the interior of one of the fillets by making a small cut with a paring knife. Take the fish out of the oven just before it's cooked to your liking; I take mine out when the interior is rosy pink. Transfer the salmon to plates or a serving platter and sprinkle with the chopped parsley, if using.

Wine suggestions: *Anchovies are always a challenge for wine, but a Sancerre would definitely work with this dish. A Schramsberg rosé sparkling wine, which has a remarkable ability to work with lots of different foods including salty anchovies, would also be lovely. A good red wine option would be a Pinot Noir from California's central coast or from Oregon's Willamette Valley.*

OVER-ROASTED SKATE *with* HORSERADISH *and* WALNUT CRUMBS

SERVES 4

This recipe calls for roasting skate on its wing, which I think gives the fish more flavor, and is also a breeze to cook. You may have to special-order a whole skate wing, which has fillets on both sides of a center of cartilage. When eating the meat on the wing, simply start on one side of the cartilage, remove the cartilage, and keep eating. With no bones to fret over, nothing could be easier! The recipe can be adapted to skate fillets and just about any other flaky but firm white fish as well. If using fillets, skip the roasting step and cook both sides on top of the stove until done. Serve the skate with some lemon wedges and a dollop of horseradish-flavored mayonnaise that you've bought or made yourself by adding some prepared horseradish to your favorite mayonnaise. The Gratin of Potatoes and Caramelized Onions on page 103 makes a great side dish.

1 cup fresh bread crumbs (see Bistro Pantry, page 7)

1 shallot, thinly sliced

1 tablespoon chopped fresh thyme

1¼ cups coarsely chopped walnuts

½ cup prepared horseradish, drained and squeezed dry

Grated zest of 1 lemon

1 tablespoon kosher salt

1½ teaspoons freshly ground black pepper

2 eggs, beaten

1 large skate wing, about 2 pounds

About ¼ cup vegetable oil

2 tablespoons unsalted butter

Lemon wedges

Horseradish mayonnaise (optional)

ON a plate, combine the bread crumbs, shallot, thyme, walnuts, prepared horseradish, lemon zest, salt, and pepper. Mix lightly to combine the ingredients.

HEAT the oven to 400°F. Beat the eggs in a large bowl and then dip the skate wing into the eggs to coat it on both sides. Immediately put the skate

wing on the plate with the bread-crumb mixture and coat it on both sides. Press down on the fish to help the crumbs adhere.

HEAT the vegetable oil and butter in a large oven-proof sauté pan over medium heat. Place the skate wing in the pan and cook until the crumbs are browned on one side, about 3 minutes. Carefully turn the skate wing over. Put the pan in the oven and roast the skate wing until done, 18 to 20 minutes. Check for doneness by seeing if the meat pulls away from the cartilage at the thickest part. Transfer the skate wing to a cutting board.

USING a large chef's knife, cut the wing into 4 pieces with the grain, from the top narrow end to the wider end. Serve the skate with the lemon wedges and some horseradish mayonnaise, if you wish.

Wine suggestions: *Try a good premier cru Chablis or Sancerre or one of my perennial favorites: a Riesling from Trimbach in Alsace.*

GRILLED TUNA AU POIVRE *with* RED WINE VINAIGRETTE

Cracked black pepper adds an intense hot bite to the cooking of beefsteaks, as we know from a visit to any bistro in France. It does the same for tuna steaks. The tomato and fennel salad on page 39 is wonderful with this dish and offers a reprieve from the heat of the pepper.

1 teaspoon vegetable oil

1 shallot, finely chopped

1 cup red wine

2 tablespoons red wine vinegar

1 tablespoon Dijon mustard

Kosher salt and freshly ground black pepper

¼ cup olive oil, plus more for rubbing on the tuna

About 2 tablespoons cracked black pepper (see Bistro Pantry, page 9)

4 tuna steaks, 6 to 8 ounces each, preferably 2 inches thick

Lemon wedges

HEAT the vegetable oil in a small saucepan over medium heat. Add the shallot and sauté for 1 minute, being careful not to let it brown. Increase the heat to high, add the red wine and red wine vinegar, and bring it to a boil. Lower the heat to medium and cook until the wine is reduced by a little more than half. Transfer the wine to the bowl of a blender, scraping the shallot from the pan with a rubber spatula, and allow it to cool. Add the mustard to the cooled red wine reduction, season with a pinch of salt and a little freshly ground black pepper, and pulse to combine. With the motor running, add the ¼ cup olive oil in a thin, steady stream.

RUB each tuna steak with about 1 teaspoon olive oil. Put the cracked pepper on a plate or small sheet pan and place the tuna steaks on top. Press the pepper onto the fish. Turn the tuna over and repeat. Using your hands, press any extra peppercorns up onto the sides of the tuna also.

HEAT the grill of your choice to hot. Drizzle a little olive oil over each steak and sprinkle with salt. Cook the tuna for about 3 minutes on the first side. Turn the tuna steaks and continue to cook until medium rare, about another 4 minutes. Use less time for rare and more time for medium, but remember that the tuna will become dry if over-cooked. (You can check for doneness by discreetly cutting into the tuna with a paring knife; take it off the grill just before it's cooked to your liking.)

PLACE the tuna on plates and drizzle the red wine vinaigrette over it. Serve with the lemon wedges.

Wine suggestions: *I especially like a good rosé from Provence or the southwest of France to go with grilled food, but a rich, fruity, somewhat spicy American Syrah would be wonderful with this meaty fish and its peppery coating.*

TROUT *with* LEMON, BROWN BUTTER, *and* PARSLEY

Although there are a million ways to flavor trout, as a fisherman and a bit of a purist, I prefer mine simply with lemon, butter, and parsley. Better known as *à la meunière,* this quick little sauce is also great with any delicate white fish, such as sole or haddock. When the lemon juice hits the hot pan, it makes the butter foam. I like to try to get the plate on the table before the butter stops foaming—or as close as possible.

4 whole trout, about 10 ounces each, scaled and boned but heads and tails intact

1 teaspoon chopped fresh thyme

1 shallot, finely chopped

½ cup all-purpose flour

½ cup cornmeal

Kosher salt and freshly ground black pepper

2 tablespoons vegetable oil

7 tablespoons unsalted butter

2 tablespoons fresh lemon juice

2 teaspoons chopped fresh parsley

OPEN each trout and sprinkle some thyme and shallot over its flesh.

ON a plate, mix together the flour and cornmeal and season with a pinch of salt and pepper. Press both sides of each trout onto the flour and cornmeal and sprinkle them with salt and pepper.

HEAT 1 tablespoon of the vegetable oil and 2 tablespoons of the butter in each of two large sauté pans over medium-high heat. When the butter stops bubbling, put 2 trout in each pan and lower the heat to medium. Cook the trout on the first side for about 7 minutes, adjusting the heat if necessary so that the skin side of the fish gets crispy but does not burn. Turn the trout over and cook them for another 4 to 6 minutes. Transfer the fish to warm plates or a platter while making the sauce.

WIPE out one of the pans with a paper towel and place it on medium heat. Add the remaining 3 tablespoons butter and cook it over high heat until it stops bubbling and turns a nutty brown. Take the pan off the heat and let the butter cool down for 30 seconds. Add the lemon juice, parsley, and a little salt and pepper to the pan, and shake to combine. Tilt the skillet so the butter and lemon juice pool on one side of the pan. The butter should foam. Pour the foaming sauce over the trout.

Wine suggestions: *This is a relatively delicate dish, so I would encourage choosing any number of light white wines to go with it: a Muscadet or a Mâcon-Villages or a white Graves from Bordeaux.*

ORANGE *and* GINGER-GLAZED ROASTED SWORDFISH *with a* CARROT *and* TARRAGON VINAIGRETTE

SERVES 4

Try to find a center-cut piece of swordfish that is at least 1 inch thick. I often cook one or two larger pieces and cut them into serving sizes after cooking. An aromatic rice, such as jasmine rice, or steamed couscous would go nicely with this dish.

3 tablespoons olive oil

1 medium carrot, cut into a very fine dice

1-inch piece of ginger, peeled and finely chopped

1 shallot, finely chopped

2 garlic cloves, finely chopped

2 tablespoons chopped fresh tarragon

1 tablespoon curry powder

2 cups orange juice, preferably fresh squeezed

½ cup rice vinegar

Kosher salt and freshly ground black pepper

2 tablespoons vegetable oil

4 swordfish steaks, 6 to 8 ounces each, preferably 1 inch thick

4 thin slices of orange (optional)

HEAT 1 tablespoon of the olive oil in a small sauté pan over medium-low heat. Add the carrot, ginger, shallot, and garlic, and cook, stirring, until the carrot is just tender, 5 to 8 minutes. Place the carrot mixture in a small bowl, add the chopped tarragon, and allow it to cool.

HEAT the curry powder in a small saucepan over low heat for about 30 seconds. Add the orange juice and the rice vinegar and bring to a boil. Lower the heat and cook until the liquid is reduced by half. Let cool.

RESERVE about ⅓ cup of the reduced orange juice and vinegar in a small separate bowl. Add the carrot-tarragon mixture to the remaining orange juice reduction. Whisk in the remaining 2 tablespoons olive oil and season with salt and pepper.

HEAT the oven to 350°F. Heat the vegetable oil in a large ovenproof sauté pan over medium-high heat. Sprinkle the swordfish with a little salt and pepper. Place the swordfish in the pan and brown it on one side, about 4 minutes. Turn the fish over and brush it with some of the reserved orange juice reduction (the one *without* the carrots). Put the pan in the oven to finish cooking, 5 to 10 minutes. (The cooking time will vary depending on how thick the fish is.) As the fish cooks, baste it with the reduced orange juice a couple more times.

TO serve, divide the swordfish among four plates and spoon some of the orange-carrot vinaigrette over the fish. Arrange the slices of orange, if using, in an attractive way near the fish.

Wine suggestions: *A very full, intense dry Alsace Riesling (a Grand Cru is best) would be great with this spicy and sweet fish. Another option would be a very ripe Chardonnay, one with tropical flavors, preferably from California's central coast.*

SALT COD *with* SPICY TOMATOES, GARLIC, *and* ONIONS

SERVES 4

This Dish features the excellent salt cod that my chef de cuisine, Michael Ehlenfeldt, makes (see page 165). You'll need to soak the salt cod for 2 days before using it. You can also make the dish with fresh cod; it will have a tad less flavor and the fish won't be as firm. If using fresh cod, skip the soaking step and season the fish with salt before searing it.

1½ pounds Homemade Salt Cod (page 165) or store-bought

2 to 3 tablespoons olive oil

2 to 3 tablespoons vegetable oil

½ teaspoon cayenne pepper

6 garlic cloves, cut into slivers

1 medium onion, very thinly sliced

2 russet potatoes, peeled and cut into a small dice

1 slice of bacon, chopped

Kosher salt and freshly ground black pepper

2 plum tomatoes, seeded and coarsely chopped

4 thin slices of lemon

4 sprigs fresh thyme

2 bay leaves

¾ cup dry white wine

SOAK the salt cod in cold water in the refrigerator for 2 days, changing the water two to three times a day. Rinse the fish and pat it dry.

HEAT the oven to 450°F. Heat 1½ tablespoons of the olive oil and 1½ tablespoons of the vegetable oil in a large ovenproof sauté pan over medium-high heat until hot. Sprinkle the cod with half of the cayenne and sear it on one side until well browned, 3 to 5 minutes. Remove the cod from the pan, leaving any oil behind.

ADD more oil to the pan if needed. Add the garlic, onion, potatoes, bacon, and the remaining cayenne

to the pan. Season lightly with salt and pepper. Cook over medium heat, stirring occasionally, until the potatoes are just tender and the onion browns slightly, about 10 minutes.

RETURN the cod to the pan, seared side up, nestling it on and among the potatoes. Arrange the tomatoes, lemon slices, thyme, and bay leaves on and around the fish. Sprinkle the wine over everything, and bake the cod until it flakes and the vegetable mixture is hot, 12 to 15 minutes.

TO serve, break the cod into pieces and spoon some of it, the vegetables, and the pan juices onto plates.

> **Wine suggestions:** *A good sparkling rosé, like one from Schramsberg Vineyards in California, or a Riesling from Alsace, would go well with this dish.*

MICHAEL EHLENFELDT'S HOMEMADE SALT COD

I've never been a big fan of industrially produced salt cod. After complaining for years about the quality of salt cod we were using in various dishes at the restaurant, Michael Ehlenfeldt, Hamersley's Bistro's longtime chef de cuisine, made his own version. Wow! What a huge difference it made. We don't even bother to dry it, as is customary for salt cod, because we use it up so fast. (It does freeze very well if you make more than you need.) Try to use a thicker piece of cod; the results will be better. As you have more experience with making salt cod, you may want to push and pull Mike's recipe around to suit your needs and tastes. Try less salt or more depending on what recipe you are using it for and how thick the cod is. This is easy to make, and the difference in flavor will sell you on the amount of extra effort needed to salt the cod yourself.

8 ounces kosher salt or sea salt

Grated zest of 1 lemon

2 teaspoons chopped fresh thyme

Pinch of red pepper flakes

2½ pounds thick, skinless cod fillets

IN a bowl, combine the salt, lemon zest, thyme, and red pepper flakes. Add the cod and gently toss it in the seasonings, covering all sides of the fish. Put the cod in a nonreactive perforated pan or on a baking rack with a pan or dish underneath to catch the drippings. Pat any excess salt mixture on top of the cod. Let the cod cure in the refrigerator for 4 days. It's best to let air circulate around it, but to keep its smell from affecting other foods (and other foods from affecting it), you can cover it loosely with plastic wrap.

DRAIN the cod of any excess water and brush off any excess salt. At this point the fish can be soaked (as your recipe directs) right away and then cooked, or it can be refrigerated for up to 3 days. It can also be frozen (before soaking). To freeze the cod, wrap the fillets well in plastic wrap and freeze. Defrost them for a day in the fridge before soaking them.

GRILLED MACKEREL *with* BEETS, FENNEL, *and* LIME VINAIGRETTE

SERVES 4

The acid in the lime helps to counter the mackerel's rich flavor, while the natural sweetness of the beets gives the dish balance. Orzo, tossed with a little of the lime vinaigrette, is a good accompaniment.

3 medium beets, trimmed

About 5 tablespoons olive oil

Kosher salt and freshly ground black pepper

2 fennel bulbs, top stalks and any tough outer layers removed (reserve some feathery fronds for serving)

2 tablespoons fresh lime juice

2 teaspoons Dijon mustard

Pinch of red pepper flakes

Pinch of fennel seeds, crushed

1 teaspoon finely chopped shallot

4 mackerel fillets, about 6 ounces each, skin left on, pin bones removed

Vegetable oil for the grill

HEAT the oven to 375°F. Place the beets in a small baking pan and toss with just enough olive oil to coat lightly, about 1 teaspoon. Sprinkle with some salt and pepper and cover with aluminum foil. Cook until tender when pierced with a knife, about 1½ hours. When cool enough to handle, peel the beets with a paring knife and cut them into a medium dice. (Be careful, as beet juice can stain counters, towels, and even your hands; you may want to wear rubber gloves for this step.)

CUT the fennel bulbs into quarters lengthwise and then crosswise into ⅛-inch slices. Season with salt and pepper. Heat 2 tablespoons of the olive oil in a large sauté pan over medium heat. Add the fennel and cook on one side until golden brown. Turn the fennel over and lower the heat. Continue to cook until the fennel is tender, another 5 to 7 minutes.

IN a small bowl, whisk together the lime juice, mustard, red pepper flakes, fennel seeds, and shallot. Whisk in the remaining 3 tablespoons olive oil in a slow, steady stream until an emulsion forms. Add the beets and fennel to the vinaigrette. Toss the vegetables to combine the flavors, taste, and add more salt, pepper, lime juice, or red pepper flakes as needed.

HEAT the grill of your choice to high. Season the mackerel with salt and pepper. Oil the grill and put the fish on it skin side down. Cook until the skin is crisp and the fish begins to turn white around the edges, about 6 minutes. With a spatula, carefully turn the fish over. Continue to cook on the flesh side until the mackerel is just done, about another 2 minutes.

WHILE the fish is cooking, divide the fennel and beet mixture among four plates. Place the mackerel fillets near the beets and drizzle with any remaining vinaigrette.

Wine suggestions: *A tough dish to pair wine with—deep breath—so I suggest a very good, preferrably grand cru Riesling from Alsace, as they have an enormous range and good acid. They have enough fruit to stand up to the oiliness of the fish and some earthiness to go with the beets. Another option: a creamy Russian River Valley Chardonnay with light oak and lots of acid.*

WHOLE RED SNAPPER *with* SHIITAKE MUSHROOMS, WATER CHESTNUTS, *and* SUGAR SNAP PEAS

SERVES 4

I love the look on my guests' faces when I present them with this glorious-looking whole fish. You can now find Chinese five-spice powder at most supermarkets. For a mail-order source, see page 317. This full-flavored dish could use some steamed rice or noodles to help soak up its flavors.

FOR THE COOKING BROTH

1 cup soy sauce

⅓ cup rice vinegar

¼ cup toasted sesame oil

2 tablespoons honey

2 tablespoons Chinese five-spice powder

Pinch of red pepper flakes

½ teaspoon coriander seeds

1 tablespoon chopped fresh ginger

4 garlic cloves, thinly sliced

FOR THE FISH AND VEGETABLES

2 whole red snappers or other similar whole fish, each 1½ to 2 pounds, cleaned and scaled with heads and tails intact

4 ounces dried shiitake mushrooms, softened in warm water for about 15 minutes and cut in half if they are large

4 ounces sliced water chestnuts

4 heads of baby bok choy, cut in half lengthwise and boiled briefly until just tender

1 red bell pepper, stem, seeds, and ribs removed, and sliced very thinly into julienne

2 scallions, roots trimmed and cut into 2-inch lengths

24 sugar snap peas

About 12 leaves of fresh mint

About 12 leaves of cilantro

TO MAKE THE COOKING BROTH

In a medium bowl, whisk together 2 cups water, the soy sauce, vinegar, sesame oil, honey, five-spice powder, red pepper flakes, coriander seeds, ginger, and garlic.

TO COOK THE FISH AND VEGETABLES

Heat the oven to 450°F. Clean and rinse the fish. Remove the gills if still intact. With a sharp knife, slash the flesh of each fish diagonally 2 to 3 times on each side. Put the fish in a baking dish large enough to hold them easily. Scatter the mushrooms, water chestnuts, bok choy, and red bell pepper over and around the fish. Pour the cooking broth over the fish. Cook the fish, basting it occasionally, until its flesh starts to flake, 20 to 25 minutes.

USING two large metal spatulas, lift the fish out of the baking dish and place them on a sided platter. Add the scallions, snap peas, 8 of the mint leaves,

and 8 of the cilantro leaves to the pan. Bring the liquid to a boil and cook over high heat until the peas and scallions are tender, about 3 minutes.

ARRANGE the vegetables around the fish, pour some of the cooking broth over the top of the fish. Decorate with the remaining mint and cilantro leaves.

Wine suggestion: *A light dry white wine is the way to go with this one, perhaps a good Chenin Blanc from Touraine in the Loire Valley.*

LOBSTER *with* CORN, TOMATOES, GREEN BEANS, *and* CITRUS VINAIGRETTE

SERVES 4

This visually stunning dish tastes best when made with tomatoes and corn that are at their peak. A good crusty bread would go well with this main-course salad.

FOR THE VINAIGRETTE

Grated zest of 1 lime

Grated zest of 1 orange

3 tablespoons fresh lime juice

¼ cup fresh orange juice

1 tablespoon fresh lemon juice

1 shallot, finely chopped

Pinch of red pepper flakes

2 teaspoons Dijon mustard

¾ cup extra virgin olive oil

Kosher salt and freshly ground black pepper

FOR THE LOBSTERS AND THE VEGETABLES

4 lobsters, about 1½ pounds each

2 tablespoons kosher salt

8 ounces green beans, stemmed and cut into 2-inch pieces

2 ears corn, shucked

3 scallions, white parts and 2 inches of the green tops, cut into very thin rounds

4 medium tomatoes, cut into wedges

4 large fresh basil leaves, washed, dried, and torn into small pieces

2 cups mixed greens, washed and dried well and torn into 1- to 2-inch pieces

4 tablespoons vegetable oil

1 tablespoon Gordon's "Famous" Spice Mix (page 63) (optional)

Freshly ground black pepper

2 tablespoons unsalted butter

Sprigs fresh parsley for garnish

TO MAKE THE VINAIGRETTE

In a small bowl, whisk together the lime zest, orange zest, lime juice, orange juice, lemon juice, shallot, red pepper flakes, and mustard. Add the olive oil in a slow, steady stream until emulsified. Season with salt and pepper to taste. (The vinaigrette can be made up to 2 days ahead; store, covered, in the refrigerator.)

TO PARCOOK THE LOBSTERS

Bring a pot of water large enough to submerge the 4 lobsters to a boil. Add the lobsters and the salt to the pot. Cover and bring the water back to a boil. Boil the lobsters for 5 minutes. (You are not trying to cook the lobsters completely.) Remove the lobsters from the water and let them cool. Twist off the claws from the bodies and remove the claw meat (see page 61). Cut the lobsters in half lengthwise. Remove the intestinal tract and tomalley, but keep the coral intact if present.

TO COOK THE VEGETABLES

While the lobsters cook and cool, bring a medium pot of water to a boil. Add the beans and cook them until they are just tender, 3 to 4 minutes. Lift the beans out of the water and refresh them under cold running water to stop the cooking and preserve their vivid green color. Shake off any excess water and reserve them in a large bowl.

NEXT add the corn to the boiling water and cook until just tender, about 3 minutes. Remove the corn from the water and refresh under cold running water. Shake off any excess water and cut the corn kernels from the cob. Add the corn to the bowl with the beans. Add the scallions, tomatoes, basil, and greens to the bowl with the beans and corn.

TO FINISH THE DISH

Heat the vegetable oil in one or two large sauté pans over medium-high heat until very hot. (See Note.) Pat the lobster halves dry with a paper towel, season them with a little of the spice mix, if using, or salt and pepper, and place them in the pan, meat side down. Watch out for any splattering from the moisture in the lobsters. Add the butter and cook over high heat until the lobsters brown slightly and the meat is heated through, about 5 minutes. Turn the lobsters over and add the claw meat to the pan. Continue to cook for another 3 minutes. Reserve in a warm place while finishing the salad.

TOSS the beans, corn, scallions, tomatoes, basil, and greens with just enough of the citrus vinaigrette to coat the vegetables and the greens lightly; you will have at least ¼ cup remaining. Taste and season with additional salt and pepper if needed.

PUT two lobster halves on each plate, meat side up, with their bodies aligned. Divide the claw meat among the four plates, placing it on any "white" space on the plate. Divide the salad among the four plates, filling the cavity of each lobster and letting the remaining vegetables spill out onto the plate. Place the parsley sprigs around the lobster. Drizzle with the remaining vinaigrette and serve.

Note: If your pan or pans can't hold all of the lobsters at once, sear them in batches. Place the seared lobster halves on a baking sheet and drizzle with a little olive oil. Just before serving, reheat them briefly in a hot oven.

Wine suggestions: *I do like a California Chardonnay with this because it seems like such a summer wine. But you might want to also consider another quintessential summer wine, which is a good rosé from Provence. A dry Tavel rosé from the Rhône or a grand cru Chablis are other good choices.*

NEW ENGLAND BOUILLABAISSE *with* ROUILLE *and* CROUTONS

Bouillabaisse is a stew that celebrates the local bounty of the sea, which is why my version features haddock and littleneck clams. You should feel free to substitute similar-style fish that's available in your area. I sometimes put small lobsters into my bouillabaisse, which you can do if you are feeling flush, but it isn't necessary to make a really fantastic stew. Instead of using fish stock, I make a flavorful soup base from tomatoes, onion, fennel, leeks, and orange juice. The shellfish and fish are added in stages, the hearty types first and the delicate ones second, just before the stew is to be eaten. You can serve bouillabaisse in the traditional manner—broth separate from the fish—or serve it as a hearty, brothy stew.

FOR THE BROTH

2 to 3 tablespoons olive oil

1 small onion, cut into a medium dice

1 medium leek, roots and all but an inch or so of the green part trimmed, cut into a medium dice, and washed and dried well

1 fennel bulb, top stalks and any tough outer layers removed, cut into a medium dice

2 celery stalks, cut into a large dice

4 garlic cloves, finely chopped

1 teaspoon saffron

Pinch of red pepper flakes

1 teaspoon kosher salt

4 tomatoes, stemmed, seeded, and chopped

2 tablespoons tomato paste

2 cups dry white wine

Juice of 1 orange

FOR THE FISH

12 littleneck clams, washed well in cold water

½ pound monkfish, trimmed and cut into 2-inch chunks

½ pound haddock fillet, skin removed, cut into 2-inch pieces

¼ pound cleaned squid bodies, cut into thin rings

12 mussels, scrubbed

12 small shrimp, shelled and deveined

2 tablespoons Pernod or anisette (optional)

¼ cup extra virgin olive oil

2 tablespoons chopped fresh parsley

½ cup rouille (see Bistro Pantry, page 10)

1 loaf of French bread, sliced into rounds and toasted

(continued)

TO MAKE THE BROTH

Heat the olive oil in a large soup pot over medium-high heat. Add the onion, leek, fennel, celery, garlic, saffron, red pepper flakes, and salt. Cook, stirring occasionally, for about 10 minutes.

ADD the tomatoes and tomato paste and stir to combine. Add 2 quarts water, the white wine, and the orange juice, and bring to a boil. Lower the heat to just bubbling and cook for 30 minutes. (This broth can be made the day ahead, refrigerated, and reheated when needed. It can also be frozen.)

TO COOK AND SERVE THE FISH

Add the clams to the broth and cook them for 6 to 8 minutes. Add the monkfish to the pot and stir gently. Simmer for 5 more minutes. When the clams open and the monkfish is almost cooked, add the haddock, squid, mussels, and shrimp. Add the Pernod, if using. Cook for an additional 5 minutes, or until the haddock is cooked and the mussels open. All the fish should be delicately cooked.

CAREFULLY take the fish out of the broth with a strainer spoon and divide it among large heated bowls. Bring the broth to a boil and whisk in the ¼ cup of olive oil. Ladle the broth over the fish. Sprinkle with the chopped parsley. Serve the bouillabaisse with rouille spread on the croutons.

Wine suggestions: *A good, dry rosé, such as a Tavel from the Rhône or a Bandol from Provence. A white Hermitage from the Rhône would be wonderful as would a Cassis Blanc from Provence.*

BARBECUED BLUEFISH *with* SMOKED SHRIMP BUTTER

SERVES 4

Bluefish, like mackerel, falls into the oily fish category, and has the bum rap of being a "fishy" fish. The trick is to get it very fresh. It's plentiful off the northeast coast in summer, which is the perfect time to enjoy this. Try it with some coleslaw and a cold beer. Look for smoked shrimp near other smoked fish and shellfish in the supermarket or order it by mail (see Sources).

FOR THE SMOKED SHRIMP BUTTER

6 tablespoons unsalted butter, softened at room temperature

3 ounces smoked shrimp, cut into a medium dice (see Sources)

1 shallot, very finely chopped

1 garlic clove, very finely chopped

1 tablespoon chopped fresh parsley

2 tablespoons fresh lemon juice

Kosher salt and freshly ground black pepper

FOR THE SPICE RUB

2 teaspoons cayenne pepper

2 tablespoons paprika

½ teaspoon herbes de Provence (see Bistro Pantry, page 9)

¼ teaspoon kosher salt

½ teaspoon sugar

4 bluefish fillets, 6 to 8 ounces each, skin on but scales removed

Olive oil

TO MAKE THE SHRIMP BUTTER

In a small bowl, mash together the butter, shrimp, shallot, garlic, parsley, and lemon juice. Season with salt and pepper to taste.

TO MAKE THE SPICE RUB

In another small bowl, mix together the cayenne, paprika, herbes de Provence, salt, and sugar.

TO COOK THE FISH

Coat each of the bluefish fillets with a little olive oil and then rub the fillets gently with the spice

mix. Let the fish sit at room temperature for 10 minutes to absorb the flavors of the spice mix.

HEAT the grill of your choice to high. Put the fillets, skin side down, on the grill and cook until the skin is very crisp and the sides of the bluefish turn white, 6 to 8 minutes. Turn the fish over and cook until the fish is done, about another 4 minutes.

PLACE the fish, skin side up, on plates or a large platter and immediately spoon some of the butter on top of each fillet.

Wine suggestions: *An unusual but delicious pairing would be a rich fruity California Pinot Noir. A rosé from Provence would go down nicely with the smokiness of this grilled fish.*

CHICKEN AND *other Winged* THINGS

L'AMI LOUIS,
the famous Paris bistro, is one of my most
favorite places to eat. I first went there with
Fiona years ago, before we opened
Hamersley's Bistro. An unobstructed view
into the kitchen allowed us to watch the chef
as he prepared his roast chicken. I could see
the blue tag that indicated that the birds
were from Bresse, in Burgundy, where the
best chickens in France are raised. The chef
split those birds in half with a big cleaver,
brushed the halves with butter, put them
on metal platters, and slipped them into
a giant wood-burning oven.

I'M GUESSING the temperature was about 600 degrees because those birds took practically no time to roast. Mine came to the table still smoking from the oven, skin slightly blackened, blistered, and crispy, and the meat inside juicy and moist. One bite and I knew that when we opened our own place we would offer a roast chicken like the one served there.

As it turns out, that was not so easy to do. Certainly, I couldn't roast chickens to order, as was done at L'Ami Louis. For one thing, they take much longer to roast in a conventional oven. And while the French think nothing of spending a leisurely few hours at dinner, I knew that many American patrons would not want to wait over an hour for their entrée. Roasting a lot of chickens during service also calls for a lot of space, something sorely lacking at our restaurant's original location.

Instead, Jody Adams (who was my first sous-chef) and I developed a technique that would allow us to roast many chickens hours ahead of time yet deliver a bird that tasted as if it were just roasted. And while there are some restaurant tricks that don't translate well to the home kitchen, this method—roasting a whole chicken and then broiling it in pieces—does. In fact, it's an ideal dish for a dinner party because almost all of the work can be done before the guests even arrive. The chicken can be marinated (it gets liberally coated with a pestolike mix of lemon, mustard, garlic, parsley, and other herbs) in the morning and then roasted later in the day. The bird, once cooled a bit, is easily split into serving pieces and arranged in a roasting pan. The only thing that has to be done right before serving is a quick broiling of the chicken parts to reheat the meat and crisp the skin. Because you add the reserved cooking juices (plus some broth) to the broiling pan, the meat stays incredibly moist while the intense heat of the broiler makes the skin wonderfully crisp. With this technique all of the guesswork ("is it done yet?") has been taken out of roasting a chicken. There's also no last-minute deglazing of the roasting pan and no carving in front of an audience—two tasks that can leave the host harried. While the method for my Roast Chicken with Garlic, Lemon, and Parsley (page 000) will make you very happy, it's the outstanding flavor of this dish—one that's been on the menu since the day we opened—that will make you want to cook it often.

Roast chicken is both a bistro staple and an American favorite, which is why I offer a couple of other takes on it as well. One, dubbed "Walk-Away Roast Chicken" at our house (page 181), is a very simple, very straightforward family-style roast chicken that includes a side dish—roasted onions and potatoes—that cooks right in the roasting pan. By following another technique—cutting out the bird's backbone and then flattening it—you not only get a bird that cooks more quickly than a conventionally roasted chicken, but also one that's easy to cut into serving pieces and has more crispy skin. With this split and roasted chicken (page 184), you can have delicious roast chicken even when you don't have a lot of time.

There are, of course, other ways to cook a chicken. I love to braise it until its meat practically falls from the bone, which is the way it's cooked in classic Coq au Vin (page 186). And although I'm not a huge fan of boneless, skinless chicken breast, I do appreciate how it acts as a canvas for other flavors, such as the bell peppers and sherry vinegar in Chicken Pipérade (page 188), or when coated in crisped bread crumbs (page 190).

Whichever part of the chicken you use, and whether you roast it, braise it, or sauté it, you'll get the best results by starting with a good-quality bird. While you won't happen upon the legendary birds of Bresse at the supermarket, you *can* find great-flavored chicken, usually from smaller producers whose chickens tend to be raised more naturally. But because a label can go only so far in indicating quality, your best bet is to try different brands, including some of the excellent kosher brands, to see which you like best. Some of these producers might have to charge more, but getting a more flavorful bird that has also been raised free of antibiotics and hormone injections seems to me to be worth the price.

TRY DUCK FOR A DELICIOUS CHANGE. Duck, which we Americans tend to think of as reserved for special occasions, is always on the menu at even the most casual French bistro (and is often on the table in French homes, too). Duck, especially boneless duck breast, is very easy to cook. Too often, however, the ample fat between the meat and skin isn't rendered properly, which leaves people with the mistaken notion that duck feels and tastes fatty. When cooked slowly, that layer of fat slowly melts away. The excess fat is discarded and the skin crisped in the oven or on the stove. Perfection.

The duck I like best is called Pekin duck (not to be confused with the Chinese dish called Peking duck). Because Pekin ducks were originally raised almost exclusively on Long Island in New York (some still are), they are often referred to as Long Island or Long Island–style duck. Pekin ducks weigh about 5 pounds and are mild tasting and tender. Pekin or Long Island–style ducks are also the ones you'll most likely find at the supermarket. Muscovy ducks have a much stronger, gamier flavor than Pekin ducks, and are rarely found at supermarkets. Moulard ducks are a cross between a Muscovy and a Pekin, and are bred domestically for foie gras (see Sources). They are larger than the Pekin, have a meatier flavor, and are a bit chewier. When testing the recipes for this book, I used Pekin ducks; if you use a Moulard, you may need to increase the cooking time.

Duck, unlike chicken, is dark meat and can be cooked to medium rare or medium. Duck meat is deeply flavored, holds its own when paired with acidic, even slightly tart, flavors, and stands up to robust seasoning. Though duck is wonderful roasted whole (see page 203), duck legs and duck breast are often cooked separately. Traditionally the legs are salted and slowly cooked in duck fat (see Duck Confit, page 193). There are recipes for using whole legs of duck confit in this chapter, including how to reheat the legs to make the skin irresistibly crisp and what to serve them with—a tangy lentil salad, for example, or a spicy pumpkin-mango chutney. You'll also find suggestions for using duck confit elsewhere in this book; it makes a wonderful addition to a main-course green salad, pasta, and risotto, and it plays a starring role in cassoulet.

SOME LITTLE BIRDS TO CONSIDER. Other birds on my menu which you might want to try cooking at home are quail and squab; they are available at many gourmet grocers and through mail-order (see Sources). Like duck, squab and quail are red-meat poultry. Squab, young domesticated pigeons, weigh in at about 1 pound each. Since they never fly, their meat is extremely tender. Quail, another game bird that's widely farm raised, are smaller still at about ½ pound. They almost always come semiboned for easier cooking and eating and are excellent pan seared or grilled. Both squab and quail cook up extremely tender and have rich, dark meat. Cornish hens are also small birds, but since they're simply a chicken that's bred to be small, they taste exactly like, well, chicken. Weighing in at 1½ to 1¾ pounds, they can be treated the same as a whole chicken, including being stuffed and roasted (although their cooking time will be less). Poussins, which are very young chickens, are not as easy to find as Cornish hens, although some markets do carry them. Poussins are very tender and delicate, and their 1-pound size makes them perfect for single servings.

WALK-AWAY ROAST CHICKEN *with* ONIONS *and* POTATOES

If you want "to double the recipe," don't buy a larger bird; roast two smaller ones in the same pan instead and double the rest of the ingredients. What's good about this dish is that it cooks the main and side dishes at one time. A crisp salad or sautéed greens would brighten up the plate.

2 tablespoons olive oil

2 tablespoons Dijon mustard

1 teaspoon dried thyme

1 teaspoon dried rosemary

Kosher salt and freshly ground black pepper

1 lemon, cut in half

1 whole roasting chicken, 3 to 3½ pounds, rinsed inside and out and patted dry

1 large red onion, cut into thick rounds

4 medium red potatoes, washed but not peeled, sliced in half

½ cup chicken broth (see Bistro Pantry, page 10) or water

HEAT the oven to 375°F. In a small bowl, combine 1 tablespoon of the olive oil, the mustard, thyme, and rosemary, and season with a little salt and pepper. Squeeze one half of the lemon into this mixture; squeeze the other half into a small bowl. Reserve the juice as well as the squeezed lemon halves. Rub the herb mixture over the chicken and inside its cavity. Put the squeezed lemon halves in the cavity as well.

PUT the onion and potatoes in the bottom of the roasting pan and toss with the remaining olive oil and some salt and pepper. Make room for the chicken in the pan and put it in breast side up. Cook until the juices run clear when the thigh is pricked, about 1¼ hours; a meat thermometer inserted into the thigh should register 165° to 170°F.

TRANSFER the vegetables to a serving platter. Pour the juices from inside the chicken's cavity into the roasting pan and transfer the chicken to a cutting board to rest.

DEGREASE the juices in the roasting pan. (See page 211 for more information on degreasing.) Set the pan over medium-high heat. Add the reserved lemon juice and the chicken broth or water. Bring to a boil, stirring with a wooden spoon to scrape up the flavorful browned bits stuck to the pan. Carve the chicken or cut it into pieces and serve it with the potatoes, onions, and some of the pan juices poured over all.

> **Wine suggestions:** *If you're in the mood for white wine, try a Mâcon-Villages, or a Saint-Véran, both from Burgundy. Reds that would go well with this casual meal include Beaujolais (not nouveau) or a Spanish Rioja.*

HAMERSLEY'S ROAST CHICKEN *with* GARLIC, LEMON, *and* PARSLEY

This is a great dish for both restaurant and home kitchens because much of the long work gets done in advance. The chickens can be roasted earlier in the day, allowed to cool, and cut into pieces. Just before serving, the chicken pieces go under the broiler to reheat them and to crisp their skin. At the restaurant, this chicken has ardent fans; once you make it, you'll become one, too. Try serving it with the roasted potatoes and onions on page 181.

FOR THE MARINADE

1 bunch fresh Italian parsley, well washed and coarsely chopped

3 garlic cloves, coarsely chopped

3 shallots, coarsely chopped

1 tablespoon herbes de Provence (see Bistro Pantry, page 9)

1 teaspoon dried rosemary

3 tablespoons Dijon mustard

2 teaspoons kosher salt

2 teaspoons coarsely ground black pepper

6 tablespoons olive oil

Grated zest of 1 lemon

FOR ROASTING THE CHICKENS AND THE GARLIC

2 whole chickens, about 3 pounds each

Kosher salt and freshly ground black pepper

1 whole head of garlic

1 tablespoon olive oil

FOR MAKING THE SAUCE AND SERVING

1½ cups chicken broth (see Bistro Pantry, page 10)

1 lemon, one half sliced into ¼-inch pieces, the other half juiced

1 tablespoon unsalted butter

Kosher salt and freshly ground black pepper

Parsley

TO MAKE THE MARINADE

In the bowl of a food processor, combine the parsley, garlic, shallots, herbes de Provence, rosemary, mustard, salt, and pepper. Pulse the ingredients together until finely chopped. With the motor running, add the olive oil in a drizzle and process until smooth. Fold in the lemon zest.

TO ROAST THE CHICKENS AND THE GARLIC

Remove the giblets from the chickens and rinse the birds inside and out with cold water. Pat them dry with paper towels and put them on a rack in a roasting pan. Rub the marinade all over the chickens, patting it on with your hands, and using all of it for a thick coating. Season with salt and pepper. Cover the chickens with plastic wrap and let sit in the refrigerator for at least 2 hours and up to 4 hours. Or let them stand at room temperature for 1 hour. Heat the oven to 350°F. Roast the chickens until done, about 1¼ hours. The birds are done when the leg bone separates easily when twisted; a meat thermometer inserted into the thigh should register 165° to 170°F.

MEANWHILE, separate the garlic cloves from the head, but do not peel them (but do pull off any loose, papery skins). Put the garlic into a small baking pan in a single layer. Drizzle a little olive oil over the cloves and toss to coat. Sprinkle them with salt and pepper, cover with aluminum foil, and bake in the same oven as the chickens until the cloves are very soft, about 1 hour.

TO MAKE THE SAUCE

Transfer the chickens to a cutting board and let the birds rest for at least a half hour and up to an hour before cutting them into pieces. Pour off the juices from the roasting pan and degrease them. (See page 211 for more information on degreasing.) Add the juices and the chicken broth back to the roasting pan, place the pan over medium-high heat, and deglaze the pan by scraping up the browned bits stuck to it and reserve.

TO SERVE

Carefully remove the chicken breasts from the bone, keeping the wings attached and leaving on as much skin as possible. Use a knife and pull with your hands; the breasts should come off easily.

Carve around each leg bone to remove the leg and thigh in one piece. Arrange the chicken pieces, skin side up, in the roasting pan or in another baking pan shallow enough to fit underneath the broiler. (You can prepare the chickens ahead up to this point. They can remain at room temperature for a half hour before broiling. If you want to make them ahead earlier than that, refrigerate the chickens and bring them back almost to room temperature before broiling them.)

MOVE the oven rack closer to the broiler and heat the broiler. Place the lemon slices on top of the chicken. Pour the reserved pan juices and chicken broth into the pan, but not over the chicken. Set the pan under the broiler and cook until the skin is crisp and the meat has thoroughly heated through, 8 to 10 minutes. Arrange the chicken on a platter or on individual plates, scatter the roasted garlic cloves over the chicken, and keep the chicken warm. Carefully pour the liquid from the roasting pan into a saucepan. Add the lemon juice and cook over high heat until the sauce is reduced by almost half and becomes slightly thickened. Swirl in the butter and season with salt and pepper to taste. Pour the sauce around the chicken, garnish with parsley, and serve immediately.

Wine suggestions: *Virtually any wine, white or red, would go well with this dish: a Sancerre, a Pouilly-Fuissé, or even a simple but decent white Côtes du Rhône. A lush, fruity Barbera d'Asti from Italy would also be delicious.*

SPLIT ROASTED CHICKEN *with* HERBED BUTTER

SERVES 2 TO 4

Flattening chicken before roasting not only makes it cook a little faster, it also gives you more crispy skin, especially around the legs. This version includes the flavor bonus of herbed butter under the bird's skin, but you can use this same roasting technique with another flavored butter or with your favorite spice rub or marinade.

I really like to serve this with the Curried Zucchini Risotto on page 136 or Leeks with Fennel and Cream on page 260.

FOR THE HERBED BUTTER

6 tablespoons unsalted butter, softened at room temperature

2 garlic cloves, finely chopped

¼ teaspoon kosher salt

2 teaspoons chopped fresh thyme

2 teaspoons chopped fresh rosemary

FOR THE CHICKEN

1 whole chicken, 3 to 3½ pounds, rinsed inside and out and patted dry

Kosher salt and freshly ground black pepper

1 shallot, finely chopped

½ cup medium to dry sherry

1 cup chicken broth (see Bistro Pantry, page 10)

IN a small bowl, mash together the butter, garlic, salt, thyme, and rosemary until smooth. Using plastic wrap, roll it into a log, wrap it, and chill it until firm.

HEAT the oven to 425°F.

POSITION the chicken, breast side down, on a cutting board. Using kitchen scissors or poultry shears, cut through the ribs on either side of the backbone and remove the bone, leaving the "wishbone" in place. (Save the backbone—you can freeze it—for making stock.) Turn the chicken over and flatten it by pressing down on the breastbone until you hear it snap.

BEGINNING at the wing end on one side of the breast, insert your fingers between the skin and the breast meat and carefully loosen the skin away from the breast. If you can reach all the way down to the thighs, make a space between the skin and the leg meat as well. Slice the flavored butter into disks and push the butter between the skin and meat where you have made space. You're looking to have a layer of butter between the skin and meat of the chicken breasts and legs.

RUB the skin side with about 1 teaspoon each of salt and pepper. Turn the chicken over and season it with a little salt and pepper as well.

PLACE the chicken, skin side up, on a rack fitted into a roasting pan and roast until the chicken is browned, its juices run clear, and the thigh registers 165° to 170°F on a meat thermometer, 50 to 55 minutes. Remove the chicken from the pan and allow it to rest in a warm place for a few minutes while preparing the sauce.

POUR off the fat that has accumulated in the bottom of the roasting pan. Add the shallot to the roasting pan and cook, stirring, for a minute. Add the sherry and bring it to a boil over high heat, scraping the pan with a wooden spoon to release the flavorful browned bits from the bottom of the pan. Add the chicken broth and bring it to a boil. Lower the heat to medium and reduce the sauce by half, about 10 minutes. Add additional butter, if desired, to make a velvety sauce.

TO serve, cut the chicken in half by cutting right down the breastbone. Cut each half into 2 or 4 pieces and serve with the sauce on the side in order to show off the crisp skin.

Wine suggestions: *I do love red wine with roast chicken: a reasonably priced Burgundy, such as those from Givry or Marsannay. A lively Sancerre Rouge from the Loire would also be a hit. If you go for white, a simple white Côtes du Rhône or a Pouilly-Fuissé would do the trick.*

COQ AU VIN

SERVES 4

Braising chicken makes it unbelievably tender. Instead of sautéing the mushrooms separately and adding them at the end of cooking, I add them at the beginning so that their juices get released right into the dish. Rice or potatoes would go well with this stewlike dish while some soft polenta (page 139) makes a less traditional but delicious side.

2 to 3 tablespoons vegetable oil

4 ounces (about 4 slices) bacon, cut crosswise into ¼-inch pieces

1 carrot, cut into a small dice

12 pearl onions, peeled (see Note)

4 garlic cloves, thinly sliced

4 whole chicken legs, legs and thighs attached and skin on (about 2½ pounds), excess skin and fat removed

Kosher salt and freshly ground black pepper

2 tablespoons all-purpose flour

1¾ cups hearty red wine

½ cup chicken broth (see Bistro Pantry, page 10)

1 bay leaf

About 2 teaspoons chopped fresh thyme

12 cremini mushrooms (about 4 ounces), halved

2 tablespoons chopped fresh parsley

IN a large high-sided ovenproof sauté pan, heat 1 tablespoon of the vegetable oil over medium heat. Add the bacon and cook, stirring, until most of the fat has rendered and the bacon is just lightly browned in places, about 5 minutes. Use a slotted spoon to remove the bacon from the pan, leaving the bacon fat in the pan. Reserve the bacon.

ADD the carrot and onions to the sauté pan with the bacon fat and cook over medium heat, stirring occasionally, until the onions brown in spots, about

5 minutes. Add the garlic and cook for an additional 2 minutes. Take the vegetables out of the pan and reserve them with the bacon.

HEAT the oven to 325°F. Add enough vegetable oil to the bacon fat in the pan to coat the bottom by about ¼ inch and heat the pan over medium-high heat. Season the chicken pieces all over with a little salt and ample pepper. Add the chicken to the pan, skin side down, in one layer and brown well on that side, about 5 minutes. (If the pieces don't fit in one layer, brown them in batches.) Turn the chicken pieces over and brown on the other side. Transfer the chicken pieces to a rimmed plate.

RETURN the bacon, onions, carrot, and garlic to the pan. Add the flour, lower the heat to medium-low, and cook, stirring well so that the flour doesn't burn, for 3 minutes.

PUT the chicken and any accumulated juices back into the pan. Add the red wine, chicken broth, bay leaf, thyme, and mushrooms. Bring to a boil on top of the stove. Cover the pan with a lid or aluminum foil, put it in the oven, and cook for 40 minutes.

Uncover the pan and continue to cook for an additional 15 to 20 minutes. (If the liquid is boiling, reduce the oven temperature to 300°F.) Check that the chicken is cooked through by cutting into a piece; it should be extremely tender.

TRANSFER the chicken to a sided platter and cover to keep warm. Degrease the cooking liquid. (See page 211 for more information on degreasing.) Bring the liquid to a boil and cook until reduced slightly. Spoon some mushrooms, onions, and sauce over the chicken legs, sprinkle with parsley, and serve.

Note: To peel pearl onions easily, blanch them first by boiling them for about 2 minutes and then plunging them in ice water.

Wine suggestions: *I would drink a lighter red than the one the chicken was cooked in, perhaps a Mercurey or a Côte de Beaune from Burgundy.*

CHICKEN PIPÉRADE

SERVES 4

This Basque dish, a favorite of French bistros, has many variations. I like to add watercress to give the stew's sweet sauce a peppery note. It's great with either soft polenta (page 139) or with plain risotto (page 132).

4 tablespoons sherry vinegar

About 1½ pounds boneless, skinless chicken breasts, cut crosswise into 1-inch strips

1 tablespoon vegetable oil

1 tablespoon unsalted butter

Kosher salt and freshly ground black pepper

1 medium onion, thinly sliced

1½ red bell peppers, stemmed, seeded, and cut into very thin strips

3 garlic cloves, thinly sliced

¼ teaspoon cayenne pepper

8 cherry or grape tomatoes, stemmed and cut in half

3 ounces smoked ham or Canadian bacon, thinly sliced or julienned

5 ounces watercress, leaves and 1 inch of stems washed and dried well, roughly chopped (about ½ cup)

PUT 2 tablespoons of the sherry vinegar on a rimmed plate. Put the chicken on top of the vinegar, turning it to coat, and allow the chicken to marinate for about 15 minutes at room temperature.

HEAT the oil and butter in a large sauté pan over medium-high heat until very hot. Pat the chicken dry and season it well with salt and pepper. Brown the chicken well on both sides. Remove the chicken from the pan and reserve it on a rimmed plate. Add the onion to the pan and lower the heat to medium-low. Allow the onion to cook slowly for about 10 minutes, stirring occasionally. Add the red bell peppers, garlic, and cayenne. Cover the pan and lower the heat to low. Cook until the peppers are very tender, another 15 to 20 minutes. Add the chicken pieces, tomatoes, ham, and remaining sherry vinegar to the pan. Cover the pan and continue to cook until the chicken is cooked through, another 5 to 7 minutes. There should be a very flavorful juice in the pan. Add the chopped watercress to the pan and let it melt into the sauce. Give everything a stir and serve the chicken with the sauce.

Wine suggestions: *A Sancerre Rouge from the Loire, a juicy ripe American Pinot Noir, or a Dolcetto d'Alba from Italy would all work well with the sweetness of the peppers and onions and the smoky ham.*

CRISPY CHICKEN BREASTS

SERVES 4

A few easy additions make this version of breaded chicken a standout: chopped garlic, sliced shallot, herbes de Provence, and hot paprika in the crumb mixture and some Dijon mustard mixed in with the egg. If your chicken breasts are very thick, you might want to flatten them a bit to help them cook through more speedily. Place them one at a time between sheets of wax paper or plastic wrap (before dipping them in the egg mixture) and pound them gently with a mallet. This full-flavored chicken dish does just fine on its own, but a flavored homemade mayonnaise, such as a garlicky aïoli (see Bistro Pantry, page 16) or spicy rouille (see Bistro Pantry, page 17), on the side makes a great accompaniment. The tian on page 108; the mashed potato cake on page 264; or the salad with peas, cucumbers, and radishes (page 46) would all make good side dishes to this crispy chicken.

2 cups fresh bread crumbs (see Bistro Pantry, page 7)

1 garlic clove, finely chopped

1 shallot, very thinly sliced

1 teaspoon herbes de Provence (see Bistro Pantry, page 9)

¼ teaspoon kosher salt

½ teaspoon freshly ground black pepper

About ½ teaspoon hot paprika

1 egg

1 tablespoon Dijon mustard

4 boneless, skinless chicken breast halves, about 1½ pounds

¼ cup vegetable oil

2 tablespoons unsalted butter

ON a plate, combine the bread crumbs, garlic, shallot, herbes de Provence, salt, pepper, and ¼ teaspoon of the paprika.

IN a bowl, whisk together the egg and the mustard. Sprinkle the chicken breasts with salt and about another ¼ teaspoon paprika. Dip the breasts

completely into the egg mixture and then into the bread crumbs, patting the crumbs onto both sides of the chicken with your hands.

HEAT the vegetable oil and the butter in a large sauté pan over medium heat. Test the pan with a bit of bread crumb to be sure it's hot; the bread crumb should immediately sizzle. Add the chicken breasts to the pan, leaving space around each. Brown the chicken well on one side, adjusting the temperature so the bread crumbs do not brown too fast, about 7 minutes. Turn the chicken breasts over and cook until they feel firm to the touch and the meat is cooked through, another 7 to 12 minutes depending on size.

Wine suggestions: *If you're serving the aïoli or rouille with the chicken, then pair the dish with a good chilled rosé, such as a Bandol or a Tavel. If not, you have more wine choices. Try a Savennières from the Loire for fun, or a white Burgundy in any price range as long as it's good, such as an Aligoté. You can also go with red wine because of the bold flavored crumb coating: a Beaujolais (not nouveau), a Pinot Noir, or a good Chianti would all go well.*

CHICKEN PAILLARDS *with* LEMON *and* CAPERS

SERVES 2

I have to be honest: Boneless chicken breast is not a favorite of mine. Even with the best sauce, it can taste bland. The solution? Pounding the breasts until they're about a quarter inch thick. With these thin paillards, there's more surface area to brown, which adds a lot of flavor. The sauce will also better permeate each bite of a thinner breast. If you want to double this recipe, you'll find it easiest to get two skillets going, since the flattened breasts take up a lot of room. Serve it with the Roasted Asparagus with Pancetta and Shaved Asiago on page 261, or simply with steamed asparagus.

2 boneless, skinless, chicken breast halves

About ¼ cup all-purpose flour, for dusting

1 tablespoon vegetable oil

1 tablespoon unsalted butter

Kosher salt and freshly ground black pepper

1 shallot, finely chopped

1 tablespoon capers, drained and rinsed

2 tablespoons fresh lemon juice

¼ cup chicken broth (see Bistro Pantry, page 10)

2 teaspoons chopped fresh parsley

PLACE each chicken breast half between 2 pieces of plastic wrap on a work surface. Leave some room for the breasts to increase in size by about half again. Using the flat side of a kitchen mallet or a meat mallet, pound the chicken until it's about ¼ inch thick.

PUT the flour on a plate near the stove. Heat the oil and about ½ tablespoon of the butter in a large sauté pan until very hot. Sprinkle the chicken breasts with salt and pepper. Coat both sides of the breasts with the flour, shake off any excess flour, and immediately put the chicken in the hot pan.

Cook the chicken for about 2 minutes, increasing the heat if necessary to brown it nicely. Turn the chicken over and cook until done, about another minute or two. Transfer the chicken to serving plates and keep it warm.

ADD the shallot to the pan and cook it for about 1 minute. Add the capers, lemon juice, and chicken broth. Cook over high heat until slightly thickened. Add the other ½ tablespoon butter for a slightly richer sauce. Add the chopped parsley to the sauce and pour the sauce over the chicken breasts.

Wine suggestions: *The capers in this dish cry out for a white wine with good acidity. A crisp Sauvignon Blanc from New Zealand, a Fumé Blanc from Friuli, or a Riesling from Alsace are all good possibilities.*

DUCK CONFIT

Before refrigeration, ducks were salted and cooked slowly in their own
fat and then stored in the cooled fat as a way to preserve them for months without
spoiling. Nowadays we make duck confit not for safe storage, but for the deliciously
intense flavor and succulent texture this technically obsolete method creates. Making
duck confit is a bit of a project. It takes some time (although most of it is unattended),
and you may need to special-order the duck legs or the duck fat. But despite what we
chefs might want you to think, duck confit is easy to make. Best of all, having duck
confit in the fridge is like having a secret cooking weapon. It transforms the most
humble salad, soup, or pasta into something extraordinary. It's also fabulous on its
own, simply warmed in a sauté pan until its skin achieves crispy perfection (see pages
196–199). Duck confit is also an important component of cassoulet (see page 238).

There are different approaches to making duck confit. I use just duck legs,
because duck breasts can easily overcook and become stringy. But some recipes will
suggest you buy a whole bird, render the duck fat yourself, and confit both the legs
and the breast. That's great, but my feeling is that if you're going to make duck
confit, you might as well make a lot of it, which means you'll need a lot of duck
fat. That's why I recommend buying fresh duck fat, which is available from some
butchers, at some gourmet grocery stores, and through mail-order from the Sources
listed on page 317.

By the way, if you don't already own Paula Wolfert's *The Cooking of South-
West France,* go get it. In this book, she details many of the classic recipes from the
region, including duck confit. When I first opened Hamersley's, I based my confit
on her method. Duck confit can be used right away, but it's better if you wait at least
a couple of weeks before using it. As the duck confit ages, it develops "the big taste,"
as Paula would say. If you plan to use the confit within a week, use the lesser amount
of salt listed.

(continued)

5 pounds duck legs with thighs attached (see Note)

2 to 3 tablespoons kosher salt

1 tablespoon pickling spices

1 head of garlic, cut in half crosswise

1 white onion, sliced

4 sprigs fresh thyme

4 to 5 pounds rendered duck or goose fat or fresh pork lard

PUT the duck legs into a large container (a large, heavy-duty zip-top plastic bag works well) and add the salt, pickling spices, garlic, onion, and thyme. Mix together thoroughly, making sure each leg is coated with the salt. Cover with plastic wrap (if not using the bag) and refrigerate for at least 18 hours and up to 2 days.

IN a very large Dutch oven or other large heavy-based pot, melt most of the fat slowly over low heat. Remove the duck legs from the refrigerator. Remove the garlic, rinse the salt off it, and pat it dry. Rinse each duck leg well under cold running water. Dry each duck leg well with paper towels.

HEAT the oven to 200°F.

SLIP the legs and the garlic into the pot of warm fat. The fat should cover the duck completely. If not, add more fat. Cook the legs over medium heat until the temperature of the fat reaches 190°F on a candy/frying thermometer. Then carefully move the pot into the oven. Allow the legs to cook at a temperature between 190° and 200°F (you may need to raise the oven temperature) until the legs are fork-tender, about 3 hours.

REMOVE the pot from the oven and allow the duck legs to cool in the fat for about a half hour. Have ready one or more clean containers to hold the duck legs and the fat (see the Note about containers). Use a slotted spoon to transfer the legs to the containers. Remove the garlic from the pot, but don't add it to the duck legs; when you have a minute, press the garlic through a mesh strainer for the best garlic purée known to man or woman.

ALLOW the duck fat to cool. Strain the fat through a fine-mesh strainer onto the legs. Use only the clear fat, leaving behind any debris and juices from the duck legs, which will have sunk to the bottom of the pot. Make sure that the legs are completely covered and tap the container lightly on the counter to help remove any air bubbles. Reserve any clear strained duck fat in the refrigerator. Refrigerate the confit until the fat hardens fully. When the fat is hard, add another ½-inch layer of melted duck fat (or fresh pork lard or peanut oil) to ensure that the legs are completely sealed in fat. Refrigerate the confit and allow the legs to "mellow" and develop flavor for at least a few days or up to 1 month before using.

TO use the confit, let the fat in the container soften at room temperature. Or set the container in a pan of warm water. Take out as many pieces as you plan to use. Cover the remaining pieces with more melted fat or peanut oil. (The confit becomes more perishable once the seal is broken, so use the rest within a week or so.) Scrape away the fat clinging to the confit and use the confit as you like or as directed in a recipe.

A note about ducks: At the restaurant, I use Pekin ducks, also called Long Island ducks, for making the confit. The main reason is that I often serve a whole duck leg confit, and I think the smaller legs look better on a single serving of cassoulet or on an appetizer plate. (Of course, the flavor is great, too!) Moulard ducks, which are a cross between the very large Muscovy ducks and Pekin ducks, also make excellent confit. Five pounds equals about 6 Moulard legs and about 10 Pekin legs.

A note about storage containers: Depending on what you plan to do with your confit, it might make the most sense to divide the duck legs among a few containers for a couple of reasons. To hold all of the duck legs, you will need a very large container that will take up a lot of room in your refrigerator. Also, by dividing the legs, you won't have to disturb the others (making them more perishable) when you want just one or two legs. Glass, stainless-steel, or glazed stoneware are the best materials for containers. A crock that is taller than it is wide will need less fat to cover the duck (see Sources). Whatever container you use be sure that it's clean (either straight from the dishwasher or rinsed with boiling water) and don't crowd the pieces into it.

CRISPED DUCK CONFIT
(and three ways to serve it)

A crisped leg of duck confit is one of my most favorite things to eat. From its long, slow cooking, the meat is incredibly tender and full of flavor. But the skin, ah, the skin: It cooks to an incredible crispness. The following technique for searing legs of duck confit works well whether you have made the confit yourself (page 193) or bought it (see Sources). Duck confit is so delicious, it can probably be eaten on its own, but since a lone leg would look lost on the plate, I offer some suggested accompaniments on pages 197–199. Each goes really well with the duck, but their personalities are very different. You'll just have to try all three!

4 legs of Duck Confit (page 193), skin left on, but any excess skin removed

Freshly ground black pepper (or cracked black pepper, if directed)

About 1 tablespoon duck fat or vegetable oil

HEAT the oven to 400°F. Season the duck legs with pepper to taste. Heat the duck fat or vegetable oil in a large ovenproof sauté pan over high heat until the oil is hot. Put the duck legs in the pan, skin side down. Sear them for about 5 minutes, lowering the heat a little if necessary. Pour off the fat that accumulates in the pan. Put the pan in the oven and cook until the meat is heated through, about 5 minutes. (Do not turn the legs over.) Remove the duck from the oven, pour off any fat, turn the legs over, and allow them to rest for a minute before serving. (If the skin is not as crispy as you would like, turn the duck legs again and cook, skin side down, for another couple of minutes over medium-high heat.)

DUCK CONFIT *with* FRENCH LENTIL SALAD *and* CLASSIC BISTRO VINAIGRETTE

SERVES 4 AS AN APPETIZER OR A LIGHT MEAL

The amount of vinaigrette you will use for this dish can vary. For example, you might want to serve some greens on the side. In that case, you can use some of the vinaigrette to lightly dress them. Also, the lentils will absorb varying amounts of the vinaigrette. They might also need a little more mixed in just before serving, especially if you have made them ahead of time. Finally, I like to drizzle a little vinaigrette over the crisped duck confit just before serving.

2 teaspoons olive oil

1 medium carrot,
cut into a small dice

1 medium leek, cut into a small dice
and washed well

4 garlic cloves, finely chopped

1 teaspoon chopped fresh marjoram

1 cup lentils du Puy (see Bistro Pantry, page 9)

3 cups chicken broth (see Bistro Pantry, page 10)

½ to ⅔ cup Classic Bistro Vinaigrette
(page 29)

Kosher salt and freshly ground black pepper

4 duck confit legs, crisped according to the
directions on page 196

HEAT the olive oil in a small saucepan over medium heat. Add the carrot, leek, garlic, and marjoram. Cook, stirring, for about 2 minutes. Add the lentils and stir to combine. Add the chicken broth and bring to a boil. Lower the heat and simmer until the lentils are tender, 35 to 40 minutes. Allow the lentils to cool and then drain off any excess liquid. Toss them gently with enough of the vinaigrette to moisten them well and season with salt and pepper. Serve a large spoonful of the lentils with each crisped duck leg as well as a handful of lightly dressed greens, if you like.

Wine suggestions: *Strangely enough a Los Vascos Cabernet Sauvignon Reserva from Chile—lots of ripe, velvety fruit—works really well with this. Another great pairing is at the other end of the spectrum: a creamy, lemony, oak-aged California Sauvignon Blanc. Odd, but true.*

DUCK CONFIT *with* ROASTED SHALLOTS *and* BALSAMIC VINEGAR

The heat of the cracked black pepper counters the sweetness of the roasted shallots.

12 whole shallots, unpeeled

1 tablespoon olive oil

½ teaspoon dried thyme

Pinch of kosher salt

Pinch of coarsely ground black pepper

½ cup balsamic vinegar

1 cup chicken broth (see Bistro Pantry, page 10)

2 tablespoons unsalted butter

1 tablespoon duck fat or vegetable oil

4 duck confit legs, crisped according to the directions on page 196, but with 1 tablespoon cracked black pepper (see Bistro Pantry, page 9) replacing the freshly ground black pepper in that recipe

HEAT the oven to 350°F. In a small pan, toss the shallots with the olive oil, thyme, salt, and ground pepper. Cover the pan with aluminum foil, put the pan in the oven, and cook the shallots until tender, about 1½ hours. Let the shallots cool and set 4 of them aside whole and unpeeled. Remove the skins from the remaining shallots by nipping off the root ends and pressing the insides out into a sauté pan. Add the vinegar and chicken broth; bring to a boil, lower the heat to a simmer, and cook the sauce until it reduces by three-quarters and becomes thicker. Whisk the butter into the sauce a little at a time, and season with additional salt and pepper if needed.

DIVIDE the shallot sauce among four plates. Place a crisped duck leg on the sauce and add one of the whole shallots to each plate.

Wine suggestions: *With lots of black pepper, try a very lush, fruity Shiraz with little tannin or a smooth California or Washington State Merlot.*

DUCK CONFIT *with* SPICY
PUMPKIN-MANGO CHUTNEY

Be warned, this chutney has a bit of a kick. If that doesn't suit you, you can cut back a little on the jalapeño. As an appetizer, the chutney and the duck are ample. If you want to serve this as a main dish, some aromatic rice would go well with it.

1 tablespoon vegetable oil

1½ cups peeled and diced pumpkin, acorn, or butternut squash

½ small onion, cut into a medium dice

1 jalapeño pepper, stemmed, seeded, and cut into thin slices

2 garlic cloves, sliced

Pinch of red pepper flakes

1 teaspoon coriander seeds

1 cinnamon stick

1 bay leaf

¾ cup red wine vinegar

¼ cup sugar

1 ripe mango, peeled and cut into a large dice

8 fresh mint leaves, chopped

4 duck confit legs, crisped according to the directions on page 193

HEAT the vegetable oil in a large sauté pan over medium-high heat. Add the pumpkin and onion and sear over high heat for about 5 minutes; the pumpkin should be cooked about halfway. Lower the heat and add the jalapeño, garlic, red pepper flakes, coriander seeds, cinnamon stick, and bay leaf. Stir to combine. Add the vinegar and sugar. Cook over medium heat until the pumpkin is tender, about 10 minutes. (Much of the liquid will evaporate during this time, but watch that the pan does not become completely dry. Lower the heat if that seems to be the case.) Let the pumpkin mixture cool and then add the mango and mint leaves. Remove the cinnamon stick and bay leaf. Let the chutney mellow for at least a half hour before serving. (It will keep up to 3 days in the refrigerator.) Taste the chutney before serving and add additional salt, pepper, red wine vinegar, or mint as needed. Serve crisped duck legs with some chutney on the side.

Wine suggestion: *A California Riesling would be lovely.*

SEARED DUCK BREAST *with* PLUMS *and* PORT

SERVES 4

The Garlicky Mashed Potato Cakes on page 264 and some lightly dressed greens would round out this dish nicely.

2 tablespoons soy sauce

1¼ cups port

1 shallot, thinly sliced

1 tablespoon finely chopped fresh ginger

Pinch of red pepper flakes

¼ teaspoon ground cumin

Pinch of coarsely ground black pepper

4 boneless duck breast halves

1 tablespoon unsalted butter

2 ripe plums, pits removed, cut into quarters or sixths, depending on size

Kosher salt and freshly ground black pepper

1½ cups veal stock or chicken broth (see Bistro Pantry, page 10)

About 1 teaspoon vegetable oil

IN a small bowl, combine the soy sauce, ¼ cup of the port, the shallot, ginger, red pepper flakes, cumin, and pepper. Stir to combine.

TRIM away the silverskin from the meat side of the duck breasts and trim away any excess skin and fat along the edges. Score the skin by making diagonal cuts just through the skin at ⅛-inch intervals. Put the duck breasts, skin side up, on a large rimmed plate and pour the marinade over them. Marinate, turning the breasts over once or twice during the process, for 1 hour at room temperature.

TO COOK THE PLUMS AND MAKE THE SAUCE

Heat the butter in a small sauté pan over medium-high heat until hot. Season the plums with salt and pepper and cook, tossing them occasionally, until they are browned, about 5 minutes. Using a flexible spatula, transfer the plums and most of the butter to a plate. To the pan the plums cooked in, add the remaining 1 cup port and the veal stock. Remove the duck breasts from the marinade and pour the marinade into the pan as well. Bring the liquid to a boil, reduce to a simmer, and cook until reduced by almost half. Add the browned plums to the sauce and continue to cook until the plums are tender. (The time it takes for all of this to happen is about the same as it takes for the duck to cook.)

TO COOK THE DUCK

Pat the duck breasts dry with paper towels. Heat enough vegetable oil to coat the bottom of a large sauté pan over medium heat. Add the duck, skin side down. As the meat cooks, fat will render. Pour this fat off, using a large spatula or a plate to hold the breasts in place. Keep pouring off the fat

(continued)

as the duck cooks, adjusting the heat if the skin begins to burn. (Use your nose to detect any burning, as the sugar in the port as well as the soy sauce will blacken the skin.) While the duck cooks, check on the sauce; if it seems to be reducing too much, turn down the heat.

TURN the duck over when almost all of the fat in the skin has melted away and the skin is dark and crispy, about 12 minutes. Cook an additional 2 minutes on the flesh side. Take the pan off the heat and let the duck rest in the pan off the heat for at least 5 minutes before slicing it.

TO SERVE
Remove the duck breasts to a cutting board skin side up. Pour any juices (but not the fat) from the sauté pan into the pan with the plums. Slice the breasts across the grain into thin pieces, about 6 slices per breast. Place the duck slices neatly on each plate. Spoon some sauce and plums onto each plate.

Wine suggestions: *A few options come to mind with this one: a medium-bodied American Zinfandel, a Syrah from the Rhône, or a Shiraz from Australia.*

ROAST DUCK *with* GRAPEFRUIT, GARLIC, *and* TARRAGON *with* WILTED GREENS

SERVES 2 TO 3

Simmering the duck before roasting it removes much of the fat between the skin and the meat. Serve some roasted potatoes with the duck or toss the greens with some cooked penne for a more substantial side.

1 whole Pekin duck (also called Long Island duck), neck and giblets removed, rinsed inside and out, and patted dry

2 cups soy sauce

4 grapefruits

3 tablespoons chopped garlic

1 cup dry sherry

½ cup honey

1 teaspoon red pepper flakes

About 5 tablespoons chopped fresh tarragon

1 small onion, sliced

2 red chiles, coarsely chopped

Vegetable oil for sautéing

2 cups chicken broth (see Bistro Pantry, page 10)

½ red onion, very thinly sliced

About 4 cups mixed bitter greens (such as watercress, mustard greens, escarole, frisée), trimmed, washed and dried well, and torn into pieces

Kosher salt and freshly ground black pepper

REMOVE any excess fat in the duck's cavity and neck opening. Cut the wing tips off at the joint. (You can freeze them and use them in stock.) Prick the skin of the duck with the tip of a small knife about 20 times, concentrating around the thicker wing area. (Try not to poke the meat beneath as you do this.)

FILL a large pot or heavy-based Dutch oven with enough water to cover the duck completely (about 6 quarts). Add 1 cup of the soy sauce, bring to a boil, and then carefully add the duck. Lower the heat enough to cook the duck at a steady simmer for 1 hour.

MEANWHILE, you'll need to zest one grapefruit, section another, and get 2 cups of grapefruit juice.

To obtain the zest, peel one of the grapefruits with a sharp paring knife or vegetable peeler, striving for only the colored part of the skin and as little of the white pith as possible. A good way to do this is to make a sawing motion as you draw the knife or peeler down the side of the fruit. Reserve the zest. Squeeze the juice from the zested grapefruit into a bowl. Over the same bowl, section another grapefruit (see page 36 for how to section an orange and do it the same way). Reserve the sections separate from the juice and zest. Finally, squeeze one or both of the remaining grapefruits to get 2 cups juice total.

COMBINE the grapefruit juice, 1 tablespoon of the chopped garlic, the remaining 1 cup soy sauce, the

(continued)

sherry, honey, red pepper flakes, and about 3 table-spoons of the chopped tarragon. Set 1 cup of this mixture aside to make the sauce and use what remains for basting the bird.

HEAT the oven to 350°F.

HAVE ready a roasting pan with a rack in it. Carefully lift the poached duck out of the water, letting any excess water drip back into the pot. Place the duck, breast side up, on the rack in the roasting pan.

STUFF the duck's cavity with 1 tablespoon of the chopped garlic, the grapefruit zest, the sliced onion, the remaining 2 tablespoons chopped tarragon, and the chiles. Fill the roasting pan to about ¼ inch with water. Roast the duck, basting it frequently with the grapefruit juice mixture, until a meat thermometer inserted into the thigh registers 190°F, about 2 hours. Transfer the duck to a cutting board and let the duck rest while you make the sauce.

TO MAKE THE SAUCE

Heat about 1 teaspoon vegetable oil in a saucepan over medium-high heat. Add the remaining garlic and cook, stirring, for about 1 minute. Add the reserved 1 cup marinade and the chicken broth. Bring to a boil, lower to a simmer, and cook until about 1 cup of liquid remains. Add the reserved grapefruit sections and keep the sauce warm until ready to serve.

TO SERVE

When the duck is cool enough to handle, carefully cut it into 6 to 8 pieces. Start by cutting away the duck breasts, keeping the wings attached and leaving on as much skin as possible. Use a knife and pull with your hands; the breasts should come off easily. Carve around each leg bone to remove the leg and thigh in one piece. Cut the breasts in half to make 6 pieces. (You can prepare the duck ahead up to this point. The pieces can remain at room temperature for a half hour before they get their final crisping. If you want to make it even further ahead, refrigerate the duck and bring it back to close to room temperature before crisping it.)

HEAT about 1 tablespoon vegetable oil in a large nonstick sauté pan over medium-high heat until hot. Add the duck pieces, skin side down, and cook until the pieces are nicely browned and crispy, lowering the heat to medium, if necessary. Remove the duck from the pan and keep it warm. Increase the heat to high, add the red onion and the greens to the pan, season with salt and pepper, and toss until the greens just begin to wilt, 45 seconds to a minute. Place the greens mixture on a platter or divide it among plates. Arrange the duck pieces around the greens and spoon the sauce around all.

Wine suggestions: *For a white wine, try a good Gewürztraminer from Alsace, or for an even sweeter, richer version of that varietal, one from Germany. For a red wine, choose something very fruity: a rich cool-climate Pinot Noir from California's central coast or a medium-bodied young Zinfandel with lots of zip.*

SEARED QUAIL *with* LEEKS *and* STAR ANISE

Sweet, tender quail are a tasty little treat. And I mean little; if you're serving quail to hungry folks for dinner, add some aromatic rice to the plate, give them two birds each, and encourage them to eat with their fingers. Quail are usually sold partially boned, which means the backbone and breastbone have been removed, but the tiny leg and wing bones remain. For the best flavor, cook the birds to medium rare or medium; the meat is light pink when cooked. The marinade also tastes great with chicken, duck, pork, and even salmon.

FOR THE MARINADE AND THE VINAIGRETTE

¼ teaspoon Chinese five-spice powder

4 whole star anise

2 tablespoons soy sauce

2 tablespoons dry sherry

1 teaspoon chopped fresh ginger

1 teaspoon chopped garlic

½ teaspoon coriander seeds

¼ teaspoon cracked black pepper
(see Bistro Pantry, page 9)

1 teaspoon sesame oil

¼ cup fresh orange juice

4 partially boned quail

1 teaspoon Dijon mustard

¼ cup olive oil

Kosher salt and freshly ground black pepper

FOR THE LEEKS

2 medium leeks

1 tablespoon vegetable oil

About 2 teaspoons unsalted butter

½ cup vermouth

½ cup chicken broth (see Bistro Pantry, page 10)

Kosher salt and freshly ground black pepper

FOR COOKING AND SERVING QUAIL

2 tablespoons vegetable oil

About 2 handfuls mixed greens, washed and dried well

TO MAKE THE MARINADE

In a small bowl, combine the five-spice powder, star anise, soy sauce, sherry, ginger, garlic, coriander seeds, pepper, sesame oil, and orange juice. Let the flavors blend for 15 minutes. Place the quail, breast side down, on a sided platter or baking sheet. Reserve 2 tablespoons of the marinade in a small bowl and pour the rest of it over the quail.

Let the quail marinate at room temperature for 30 minutes, turning once. Whisk the mustard and olive oil into the reserved marinade. Season with salt and pepper to taste and reserve.

TO COOK THE LEEKS

Cut off all but 1 inch of the green tops. Trim the roots, but leave enough of the bottom of the leek so it will hold together when cut lengthwise. Cut the leeks in half lengthwise. Soak them in warm water to remove the dirt. (Depending on how dirty they are, you may need to use a couple of changes of water.) Drain and pat dry.

HEAT the vegetable oil and butter in a large sauté pan over medium-high heat. Add the leeks, cut side down, and lower the heat to medium. Cook until the leeks are brown, about 5 minutes. Turn the leeks over and add the vermouth and the chicken broth and season with salt and pepper to taste. Cover the pan, bring the liquid to a boil, lower to a simmer, and cook until the leeks are just tender, about 8 minutes. Uncover the pan, bring to a boil, and cook until the liquid in the pan reduces to about 3 tablespoons, about 5 minutes. Reserve.

TO COOK THE QUAIL

Heat the vegetable oil in a large sauté pan over high heat until very hot. Pat the quail dry and add them, breast side down, to the sauté pan. Lower the heat to medium-high and cook the quail until well browned on one side, about 5 minutes. Turn the birds over and cook until medium rare to medium, or another 5 minutes. (The juices from a pierced thigh will still be slightly pink.) As the quail cook, you might need to press down gently on the legs so that they cook through. Remove the birds from the pan and let them rest in a warm place. Pour the fat out of the pan, add about 2 tablespoons water to the pan, put the pan back on the heat, and scrape up the flavorful browned bits with a wooden spoon.

TO SERVE

Place a leek and quail on each plate. Drizzle the deglazed pan juices and a little of the vinaigrette over and around each quail. Toss the greens with enough of the remaining vinaigrette to coat them lightly. Place the greens next to the quail and serve immediately.

Wine suggestions: *For a great pairing, try a delicate, soft, fruity red Burgundy from the Côte de Beaune, perhaps one from Pommard or Aloxe-Corton.*

MEAT—
Braised, Roasted,
SEARED,
AND GRILLED

TAKE A MINUTE
to imagine you are eating at a little bistro in
Paris. You have had your appetizer, perhaps
a bowl of mussels or a crisp salad, and you
are now awaiting your main course.
The waiter approaches and puts a plate
down in front of you. The aroma is so
wonderful that you pause to enjoy it before
taking that first bite. "This," you think,
"is what bistro dining is all about."

WHAT DID YOU imagine you were eating? I'll bet it was something braised. Lamb shanks or short ribs. Meat that's full of flavor from long, slow cooking surrounded by wine and broth and those flavorings—garlic, onion, sage, thyme, rosemary—that make you sit back and sigh contentedly. Meat so tender it falls away from the bone with the touch of your fork and then practically melts in your mouth. Maybe you imagined another bistro classic: steak frites, a perfectly seared piece of beef topped with garlicky butter and accompanied by a pile of impossibly thin, golden-brown fries. Or perhaps you pictured breaking through the crisp bread-crumb topping of a piping hot cassoulet to reveal creamy white beans, succulent chunks of pork, and silken duck confit.

Although I love fish, and a favorite bistro experience of mine centered on a simply amazing roast chicken, it's these hearty, homey meat dishes—braises and roasts that cook for hours, filling the kitchen with warmth and mouthwatering aromas—that seem to me to be the most characteristic of bistro foods.

As you plan your bistro-inspired meals, keep in mind the time investment of the various cooking methods as described in the beginning of the book (see Bistro Techniques). If you want something that will cook quickly, look for those dishes that are seared, grilled, or sear-roasted, such as the rib steak with garlic butter (page 212), the burger stuffed with blue cheese (page 216), the veal chops with capers and cornichons (page 223), the lamb racks with a curry and date coating (page 232), or the pork tenderloin with a spicy watermelon salad (page 246).

Braises and roasts, while they don't require a lot of active work, do need time in the oven, which is why they're perfect for relaxed weekend cooking. I especially like making a braise one day and serving it the next. Storing the meat in its cooking liquid allows it to absorb even more flavor. And chilling the braising liquid lets you degrease it more efficiently, resulting in a sauce with better flavor and texture. Making a braise ahead of time also gives you more control if you are entertaining. And because smelling your braise cook all day can make you feel like you've had your fill of it without even taking a bite, you might actually be hungrier for it the next day.

Whichever cooking technique you use, the following points bear repeating:

LET COOKED MEATS REST BEFORE SERVING. When meat cooks, the exterior juices are pulled in toward the meat's center. When you rest the meat this allows the juices to redistribute. Without resting, the meat will taste dry. A quick sauté needs just a couple of minutes, but bigger cuts need at least 10 to 15 minutes before carving. Covering a large piece of meat with aluminum foil will keep it warm enough for serving, but you might want to put smaller cuts in a warm—not hot—oven while they rest so that they don't get cold.

DEGREASE THE PAN JUICES OR COOKING LIQUID. Certainly a little fat adds flavor to a sauce but too much obscures it. You usually pour off the fat from a roast or sauté, which is easy enough to do. Getting rid of the fat that floats on the top of braising liquid can be a little trickier. There are a few ways to do this. At the restaurant, we dip a three-ounce ladle into the braising liquid so that the bottom half of the bowl is submerged but not the edges. We slowly move the ladle in circles, starting with small circles in the middle of the pot and gradually increasing the size of the circles until the ladle reaches the edge of the pot. This movement pushes the fat toward the edge, making it easier to collect. To gather the fat, simply allow the ladle bowl to just break the surface of the liquid so that what flows into it is mainly the clear fat. Throw that fat away and repeat the process until you have removed much of the fat. You can also pour the liquid into a gravy separator—a glass or plastic pitcher with a spout on the bottom; pour the juices back into the pan, stopping when the fat on top begins to enter the spout. Both of these methods require a little work and some patience. The easiest and most effective way to remove the fat takes time but no effort: Chill the braising liquid completely. The fat on top will solidify and come off easily with a spoon.

REDUCE COOKING LIQUIDS FOR BETTER FLAVOR AND MORE BODY. The transformation that results from simply cooking a sauce until its volume is reduced is nothing short of magical. As the sauce cooks, it becomes thicker and more deeply flavored; the more it reduces, the thicker and more intensely flavored it will be. This can take some time, but usually no more than the time the meat needs to rest anyway. If you are in a rush and have a lot of liquid, don't reduce all of it; pour just half of it into a skillet to reduce it more quickly. Season the sauce with additional salt and pepper only after it has reduced.

SEAR-ROASTED RIB STEAK
with GARLIC BUTTER

Here's the secret of those delicious bistro steaks: a little garlicky butter slathered on while searing. Serve the steak with Pommes Frites (page 266) and wallow in your happiness.

3 garlic cloves

Kosher salt

8 tablespoons unsalted butter, softened

1 teaspoon dried thyme

Ample pinch of coarsely ground black pepper

2 tablespoons vegetable oil

Two large (16 to 20 ounces) or four small (8 to 10 ounces) bone-in rib steaks or boneless rib-eye steaks

CHOP the garlic finely. Sprinkle 1 tablespoon salt over the garlic and continue to chop it, occasionally smashing and smearing the garlic with the flat side of a knife, until the garlic becomes pastelike. (Alternatively, mash the garlic and salt together in a mortar and pestle.) Put the garlic paste, butter, thyme, and pepper in a small bowl. Fold the softened butter over and onto the garlic and thyme, mashing it down with the back of the spoon or spatula. Use a sheet of plastic wrap to help shape the butter into a log, wrap the log well with the plastic wrap, and refrigerate until ready to use. (The garlic butter can be made up to 3 days ahead; it can also be frozen, well wrapped, for a couple of months.)

MELT half of the garlic-butter mixture in a small pan over medium heat. (Rewrap and save the other half for future use; it's great stuffed under the skin of a chicken before roasting or tossed into the broth of steamed mussels.)

HEAT the oven to 425°F. In a large ovenproof sauté pan, heat the vegetable oil over high heat until very hot. Season the steaks with a little salt and pepper. Add the steaks to the pan and brown them well on one side, about 5 minutes. Turn the steaks and brush them liberally with the garlic butter. Finish cooking the steaks in the oven, brushing them occasionally with more garlic butter, until done, about another 5 minutes. (The time will vary depending on how you like your steaks cooked and how thick they are.) Remove the steaks from the oven and allow them to rest for 5 minutes before serving. Serve smaller steaks whole or sliced thinly across the grain. Cut larger steaks into 2 servings or into thin slices. Spoon any meat juices from the pan onto the meat as well.

Wine suggestions: *The choices are almost endless with this classic steak. A big bold Bandol, a Côte-Rôtie if you're feeling flush, a Napa Valley Cabernet Sauvignon, a big Italian Barbaresco, or a Brunello di Montepulciano, but lots of other reds will work, too. Drink what you love.*

GRILLED FLANK STEAK *with* COFFEE *and* BLACK PEPPER MARINADE

SERVES 4

At first bite, the flavor of the marinade seems almost too subtle. Then you realize that the flank steak itself tastes better than ever—richer with a slight sweetness that complements rather than drowns out the flavor of the meat. The sugar may cause the meat to char somewhat, but this just adds flavor. To give regular coffee some added punch, dissolve a teaspoon of instant espresso powder into it. As long as you have the grill going, try serving the steak with some grilled zucchini and eggplant.

1 cup strong brewed black coffee or espresso

1½ tablespoons Dijon mustard

2 garlic cloves, finely chopped

1 shallot, finely chopped

2 tablespoons balsamic vinegar

About 1 tablespoon vegetable oil, plus a little more for rubbing on the steak

2 tablespoons dark brown sugar

½ teaspoon kosher salt

¾ teaspoon coarsely ground black pepper

1½ to 2 pounds flank steak, trimmed of fat

COMBINE the coffee, mustard, garlic, shallot, balsamic vinegar, the 1 tablespoon vegetable oil, the brown sugar, salt, and pepper in a large dish or zip-top bag. Remove and reserve ¼ cup. Add the flank steak, refrigerate the meat, and marinate it for at least 2 hours and up to 24 hours, turning the meat every so often.

HEAT the grill of your choice to medium-high. Remove the meat from the marinade, reserving the liquid. Pat the steak dry with paper towels, rub it all over with a little oil, and season with a little more salt. Grill, basting with the coffee marinade frequently, until cooked rare to medium rare, 3 to 6 minutes per side, depending on thickness. (You don't want to overcook flank steak, so take it off the grill when it's slightly less done than you would like.) Let the meat rest at least 5 minutes before slicing it thinly across the grain. Combine any juices that have collected with the reserved marinade, over and around the beef and serve immediately.

Wine suggestion: *A peppery Syrah from California or Australia with lots of big fruit would go nicely with the subtle coffee flavor here.*

BEEF SHORT RIBS BRAISED *in* DARK BEER *with* BACON *and* RED ONIONS

SERVES 6

Mashed potatoes are a must with this dish, which is why I've included a version of them here. At the restaurant, we put the mashed potatoes right on top of the ribs so that you get some meat, potatoes, and sauce in every bite.

FOR THE RIBS

6 to 8 pounds bone-in beef short ribs (see Note)

Kosher salt and freshly ground black pepper

About 3 tablespoons vegetable oil

½ pound bacon, cut into 1-inch pieces

2 medium red onions, cut crosswise into ½-inch rounds

2 tablespoons tomato paste

2 bottles stout beer, such as Guinness

¼ cup red wine vinegar

2 cups beef stock or a combination of beef stock and chicken broth (see Bistro Pantry, page 10)

FOR THE POTATOES

5 large russet potatoes, peeled and cut lengthwise into quarters

2 garlic cloves

2 scallions, trimmed and cut into very thin rounds

½ cup milk

3 tablespoons unsalted butter

Kosher salt and freshly ground black pepper

TO COOK THE RIBS

Heat the oven to 350°F. Trim the excess fat off the ribs and season them on all sides with salt and pepper. In a large, heavy-based, ovenproof pot, heat 3 tablespoons vegetable oil until very hot. Working in batches if necessary so as not to crowd the pan, brown the ribs well on all sides, adding more oil if needed. Remove the ribs from the pan. Pour off the rendered fat, but don't clean the pot. Add the bacon and cook until most of its fat has rendered, about 5 minutes. Add the onions and cook until lightly browned, about 6 minutes. Add the tomato paste and cook, stirring, for another 2 minutes. Add the

beer, vinegar, and beef stock. Put the short ribs back into the pot. Bring the liquid to a boil. Cover the pot and cook the ribs in the oven until they are fork-tender, about 2 hours and 15 minutes. (Begin checking at 2 hours.) Take the lid off the pot and continue cooking the ribs for an additional 15 minutes, uncovered. (If you want to prepare this dish a day or two ahead, stop here. Cool the ribs and their cooking liquid as quickly as possible and refrigerate the ribs in the liquid. On the day you plan to serve the dish, remove any cooled fat from the cooking liquid, reheat the ribs in the oven in their cooking liquid, and then continue with the recipe.)

VERY carefully, so as not to break apart the meat, transfer the ribs and the onions to a rimmed platter or sheet pan and keep them warm. Degrease the cooking liquid, if necessary. (See page 211 for more information on degreasing.) Bring the liquid to a boil and cook until reduced by at least a third.

TO COOK THE POTATOES

In a large pot, cover the potatoes and garlic with salted water. Bring to a boil and cook until the potatoes are tender, about 20 minutes. Drain the potatoes and garlic and return them to the same pot they were cooked in. Cook the potatoes over very low heat, stirring with a wooden spoon, until dry, about 3 minutes. Add the scallions, milk, and butter. Mash with a potato masher or fork until just mashed. Season with salt and pepper.

TO SERVE

Divide the ribs and onions among six plates. Top with a large spoonful of the mashed potatoes and pour some of the cooking liquid over the top.

Note: Short ribs, the meaty tail ends of beef ribs, come in various sizes depending mainly on the whims of the butcher. I prefer two-bone-cut short ribs, which are about 1½ inches thick and weigh about 8 ounces each. At the restaurant, we serve two of these ribs per person, which is a very hearty portion. Try to get these bigger, meatier ribs. For one thing, there are fewer pieces to turn while browning. More important, they cook to a better flavor and texture than the short ribs you typically see cut into small squares. If you can only find smaller-cut short ribs, keep in mind that they may take less time to cook, so begin checking on them at about 1½ hours.

Wine suggestions: *Go with a big red Italian Barolo, a Malbec from Argentina, or a Châteauneuf-du-Pape from France.*

WOLFGANG'S BLUE CHEESE—STUFFED BURGER *with a* PORT *and* GREEN PEPPERCORN SAUCE

Forget the bun. As you cut into this burger (inspired by one we used to serve at Ma Maison), the cheese oozes out and mixes deliciously with the deeply flavored sauce. Peppery arugula, dressed very lightly with a balsamic vinaigrette, goes extremely well with these flavors.

4 ounces blue cheese, such as Gorgonzola or Roquefort

1½ pounds ground beef

Kosher salt and freshly ground black pepper

1 tablespoon vegetable oil

1 medium shallot, finely chopped

1 teaspoon green peppercorns, very finely chopped (see Note)

2 teaspoons brine from the green peppercorns

⅓ cup port

⅓ cup beef stock (see Bistro Pantry)

3 tablespoons heavy cream

DIVIDE the blue cheese into 4 equal pieces and shape them into balls. Divide the meat into 4 equal portions. Wrap one portion of meat around each piece of cheese. Flatten the meat and cheese to form patties. Sprinkle with salt and pepper.

HEAT the vegetable oil in a large sauté pan until it is very hot. Add the hamburgers and cook over high heat until well browned on one side. Turn the burgers over and lower the heat to medium-high. (Don't worry if some of the cheese oozes out; it will just add flavor to the sauce.) Continue cooking until the burgers are done to your liking, 10 to 12 minutes total cooking time. Remove the burgers from the pan and let them rest in a warm place.

POUR the excess grease from the pan. Add the shallot and cook, stirring, for 1 minute. Add the green peppercorns, peppercorn brine, and port. Bring to a boil and cook until the liquid is reduced by half. Add the beef stock and continue to cook until the sauce has reduced by half again. Add the cream and bring to a boil.

PLACE the burgers on plates and spoon the sauce over them.

Note: Don't look for green peppercorns on the spice shelf at your supermarket. These unripe peppercorns most often come jarred in brine, and can usually be found near the pickles and capers.

Wine suggestion: *A Petite Syrah would be great.*

SKILLET-COOKED SKIRT STEAK *with* BLUE CHEESE BUTTER

SERVES 2

Skirt steak is a long narrow steak that's available in most supermarkets and has great flavor. It's similar in spirit to that classic bistro offering, hanger steak, which is also delicious, but almost impossible to find retail. The key to keeping both cuts tender is to cook them quickly over high heat and serve them rare. Serve the steak with Pommes Anna on page 265 and the broiled tomatoes on page 270.

2 tablespoons blue cheese, such as Roquefort or Gorgonzola

2 tablespoons unsalted butter, softened at room temperature

1 shallot, finely chopped

1 tablespoon chopped fresh parsley

Kosher salt and freshly ground black pepper

2 to 4 tablespoons vegetable oil

About 1 pound skirt steak, cut into 2 pieces

IN a small bowl, mash together the blue cheese, butter, shallot, and parsley. Season with salt and pepper to taste.

HEAT the vegetable oil in a large, heavy sauté pan or cast-iron skillet until very hot. Season the steak well with salt and pepper. Put the steak in the pan and reduce the heat to medium-high. Cook until done, about 3 minutes on each side, depending on the thickness of the steaks. Let the meat rest a couple of minutes and then thinly slice the steak across the grain. Serve with a tablespoon or so of the flavored butter placed right on top.

Wine suggestions: *The blue cheese needs a wine with lots of ripe fruit: an Australian Cabernet Sauvignon or a Cabernet-Shiraz blend from the Coonawarra region.*

BEEF BRAISED *in* RED WINE *with* MUSHROOMS *and* SMOKY BACON À LA BOURGUIGNONNE

As the name suggests, this classic French beef stew is traditionally made with wine from the Burgundy region of France. Of course, only you, the cook, will know where your wine came from, and you can certainly use a wine from California (or Australia or Spain or wherever). What matters more than the origin of the wine is its style: full flavored, moderately tannic, with a slight earthiness. Don't use an expensive wine for the stew; the recipe calls for almost two bottles and the subtle nuances of flavor in an expensive wine would be obscured in the cooking anyway. But do use a wine that you would drink without grimacing. Serve the stew with Spätzle (page 243) for a deliciously classic presentation, or with buttered egg noodles or steamed potatoes.

FOR THE MARINADE

3½ cups (about 1 bottle) red wine

1 onion, coarsely chopped

2 carrots, coarsely chopped

1 head of garlic, cut in half crosswise

3 bay leaves

3 sprigs fresh thyme

12 black peppercorns

3 to 4 pounds beef chuck, large pieces of fat removed and cut into 2-inch cubes

FOR THE STEW

About 2 tablespoons vegetable oil

½ pound bacon, cut into ¼-inch strips

Kosher salt and freshly ground black pepper

24 pearl onions, peeled (see page 187)

2 carrots, cut into a ½-inch dice

¼ cup all-purpose flour

3 cups red wine (about 1 bottle plus a glass for you)

3 cups beef stock (see Bistro Pantry, page 10)

1 tablespoon tomato paste

FOR THE GARNISH

1 tablespoon vegetable oil

1 pound cremini mushrooms, cleaned, stems trimmed, and cut into quarters

1 teaspoon finely chopped garlic

Kosher salt and freshly ground black pepper

1 bunch watercress, washed and dried well (optional)

TO MARINATE THE MEAT

Combine all of the marinade ingredients, including the meat. Refrigerate, tossing the meat occasionally, for 12 hours. Drain the wine from the meat. Retrieve just the meat and pat it dry with paper towels. (This drying will allow the meat to brown without steaming.) Discard the rest of the marinade ingredients.

TO MAKE THE STEW

In a large, heavy-based, ovenproof pot, heat about 1 tablespoon of the vegetable oil over medium heat. Add the bacon and cook until much of its fat has rendered but it has not browned, about 5 minutes. Remove the bacon from the pot with a slotted spoon and reserve.

SEASON the beef lightly with salt and liberally with pepper. Working in batches, add the meat to the pot and brown well on all sides. Remove the meat from the pot and reserve.

HEAT the oven to 275°F.

ADD the pearl onions and carrots to the pot and cook, stirring occasionally, until they take on a little color, about 5 minutes. (Add additional oil, if needed.)

LOWER the heat to medium-low. Add the flour and continue to cook, stirring continuously, for another 5 minutes. Add the bacon and the beef back to the pot and toss them well with the flour and vegetables. Add the red wine, beef stock, and tomato paste. Season with a little salt and some pepper and stir to combine. Bring to a boil, cover

the pot, and put it in the oven. Cook until the meat is fork-tender, about 3 hours. Remove the cover and cook for an additional 15 minutes. (If you want to prepare this dish a day or two ahead, stop here. Cool the stew as quickly as possible and refrigerate it. On the day you plan to serve the stew, remove any cooled fat from it, reheat it in the oven, and then continue with the recipe.)

DEGREASE the braising liquid, if necessary. (See page 211 for more information on degreasing.)

FOR THE GARNISH

Just before serving, heat the oil in a large sauté pan over high heat. When the oil is very hot, add the mushrooms and cook without stirring until they're well browned on one side. Stir and continue cooking until the juices from the mushrooms have released and evaporated and the mushrooms are tender, about 8 minutes. Add the garlic, season with salt and pepper, and cook for another 2 minutes. Reserve.

WHEN the beef is done, add the mushrooms to the stew pot and stir briefly to combine.

SERVE in large bowls with steamed potatoes, buttered egg noodles, or spätzle. Garnish with watercress sprigs, if you like.

Wine suggestions: *Big reds like Châteauneuf-du-Pape from the Rhône or a Provençal red from Bandol, or a dark Cornas would work really well. For a luxury dinner: a beautiful Burgundy, such as a Gevrey-Chambertin!*

VEAL BREAST STUFFED *with* SPINACH, MUSHROOMS, *and* GARLIC

SERVES 4 TO 6

This is a great dish for a dinner party. It looks fancy and tastes fabulous, but it's not difficult to make. A simple side of buttered penne sprinkled with grated Asiago, and a salad before or after, are all you need to complete the meal. And there's a bonus: The flavored oil that results from simmering the garlic cloves is great for brushing on steaks, for making a robust vinaigrette for salad, or for simply dipping bread into.

About ¾ cup olive oil

6 whole peeled garlic cloves

1 tablespoon unsalted butter

1 small onion, thinly sliced

2 portobello mushrooms or about 4 ounces cremini mushrooms, cleaned, stemmed, and cut into ½-inch pieces

4 medium oyster mushrooms, cut into ½-inch pieces

Kosher salt and freshly ground black pepper

1 teaspoon dried thyme

5 ounces spinach, well washed and stemmed, about 5 cups

One 4- to 4½-pound piece of boneless veal breast, excess fat removed

3 tablespoons Dijon mustard

2 cups dry sherry

2 cups veal stock or chicken broth (see Bistro Pantry, page 10)

1 tablespoon tomato paste

2 tablespoons unsalted butter

HEAT the olive oil and garlic cloves in a small saucepan over medium-low heat and simmer until the garlic is very tender, about 20 minutes. (If the garlic is not submerged, add more oil.) The cloves may brown slightly, but keep the heat low enough so that they don't brown too much. Allow the garlic to cool in the oil. Remove the garlic cloves and reserve both the garlic and the oil.

HEAT 3 tablespoons of the reserved garlic oil and the butter in a large sauté pan over medium heat. Add the onion and cook until translucent, about 5 minutes. Raise the heat to high and add the mushrooms.

Add a good amount of salt—at least ½ teaspoon—and some pepper to taste. Cook the mushrooms, without stirring, until they brown well on one side. Give them a stir and continue to cook, adding additional butter or oil as necessary, until the mushrooms release their juices, the juices evaporate, and the mushrooms become tender, about 10 minutes. Add the thyme and the reserved garlic cloves and cook another minute. Cool and reserve.

IN another pan, heat about ½ cup water over medium-high heat. Add about ½ teaspoon salt and the spinach and cook until the spinach is wilted.

Drain the spinach and run it under cold tap water to stop the cooking. Squeeze the spinach dry in a fine-mesh strainer or in a clean kitchen towel. Add the spinach to the mushrooms and garlic.

Mix thoroughly so the spinach is evenly distributed through the mushrooms. Allow the mushroom mixture to cool.

(continued)

LAY the veal breast out on a cutting board, with the fattier side facing up. Using a rubber spatula, spread the mustard all over the side facing up. Spread the mushroom and spinach mixture on top of the mustard, leaving a 2-inch border around the outside edge of the meat. Season with salt and pepper. Working with the grain—at the end of cooking, you want to slice the meat against the grain—roll the veal up and around the filling into a roll that's as tight as you can make it. Tie the veal breast at 1-inch intervals (see Note).

HEAT the oven to 300°F.

IN a large, heavy-based, ovenproof pot large enough to hold the veal, heat another 3 table-spoons of the reserved garlic oil over high heat. Season the outside of the rolled veal amply with salt and pepper. Brown the veal well on all sides; this should take at least 10 minutes. Allow the pan to cool slightly and then stir in the sherry, veal stock or chicken broth, and the tomato paste. Cover the pot and cook the veal in the oven until tender, about 3¼ hours. Remove the lid from the pot and cook it for another 15 minutes, basting the meat occasionally, to brown the top a little.

TRANSFER the veal to a cutting board, cover it loosely with aluminum foil, and allow it to rest in a warm place. Degrease the cooking liquid. (See page 211 for more information on degreasing.) Bring the liquid to a boil and cook until reduced by half. Add the butter to the liquid and whisk until the butter has been incorporated.

CUT the string from the veal and slice the veal into 1-inch rounds. Place a slice or two on a rimmed plate and spoon the sauce over and around the meat.

Note: The best way to keep the filling inside the roast is to tie it the way butchers do, so that the twine wraps around both ends. Begin with a piece of butcher twine at least twice as long as your outstretched arms. Tie a loop at the end of the rolled roast nearest to you, leaving one end of the twine very long. With the end of the twine closest to the roast, make a loop that will fit around the roast. Twist the loop on itself once, and then use this loop to "lasso" the rolled roast. Shimmy the loop down the length of the roast to within an inch or so of the first loop. Pull on the long end of the twine to snug the loop against the meat (but don't pull it too tightly) and repeat the process until you have loops of twine down the length of the roast. When you reach the end of the roast, turn it over. Bring the twine up and over the open end of the roast to help keep the filling in. Tuck the twine over and then under the first loop on the new side. Then bring the twine down the length of the roast, tucking it over and under each loop as you go. When you reach the other end of the roast, use what's left of the twine to wrap around the other open end, turn the roast over, and tie the twine off near the first knot.

Wine suggestions: *Go with a medium-bodied Merlot, one that's not too flabby, meaning it has some acidity but also plenty of berry fruit. A Cabernet Franc from Washington State or California would be another good choice.*

SEAR-ROASTED VEAL CHOPS *with* CAPERS *and* CORNICHONS

SERVES 2

A thick chop, ideally 1½ to 2 inches, allows you to brown the chop well—an important flavor step—without overcooking it. Although this dish tastes good when made with chicken broth, veal stock gives it much more richness and depth. An individual new potato galette (page 105) would look great on the plate. I also like to serve this with the braised red onions on page 262 or the sweet-and-sour cabbage on page 263.

2 tablespoons sherry vinegar

1 tablespoon extra virgin olive oil

1 teaspoon herbes de Provence (see Bistro Pantry, page 9)

2 thick, bone-in veal chops

Kosher salt and freshly ground black pepper

1 to 2 tablespoons vegetable oil

1 medium shallot, finely chopped

1 tablespoon drained and chopped capers

1 tablespoon drained and chopped sour cornichons

½ cup dry sherry

½ cup veal stock or chicken broth (see Bistro Pantry, page 10)

1 tablespoon unsalted butter, cut into pieces

1 tablespoon finely chopped fresh parsley

ABOUT 30 minutes before cooking, combine the sherry vinegar, olive oil, and herbes de Provence in a sided dish large enough to hold the veal chops in one layer. Season the chops well on both sides with salt and pepper and lay them in the marinade. Let them absorb the marinade at room temperature, turning once, for about 30 minutes total.

HEAT the oven to 425°F.

HEAT the vegetable oil in a large, ovenproof sauté pan over high heat until very hot. Add the chops to the pan and cook them without moving them

until very well browned on one side, about 2 minutes. Turn the chops over and put the pan in the oven. Cook the chops to medium rare, 7 to 10 minutes. (Smaller chops will take less time.) The chops should feel almost firm when pressed with your finger and should register 130°F on a meat thermometer.

TAKE the meat out of the pan and let it rest, covered loosely in aluminum foil, in a warm place while you prepare the sauce. Pour off the excess fat from the pan. Add the shallot and cook, stirring, for 1 minute. Add the capers and cornichons and

(continued)

cook for another minute. Add the sherry, bring to a boil, and let it boil for a minute or two to cook off some of the alcohol. Add the veal stock or chicken broth and bring it to a boil, stirring with a wooden spoon to scrape up the browned bits from the bottom of the pan. Cook over medium-high heat (you want a gentle boil) until the liquid is reduced by half. Whisk in the butter, piece by piece, until incorporated. Add the parsley and stir. Taste and season with salt and pepper, if needed.

PUT the chops and any juices that have accumulated around them into the pan briefly to warm them, if necessary. Put the veal chops on plates and pour the sauce over them, being sure to get some of the capers and cornichons onto the chops.

Wine suggestions: *To counter the cornichons and capers, choose a wine with earthiness, body, and acidity, such as a Vino Nobile di Montepulciano from Italy or a good Beaujolais cru like Moulin-à-Vent. If you want a little fruitier wine, try a Beaujolais like Fleurie or Brouilly.*

GRILLED BUTTERFLIED LEG *of* LAMB *with* GARLIC *and* ROSEMARY

SERVES 8

For me, the only way to cook lamb in the summer is outside on a grill, preferably over a wood-fueled fire. A butterflied leg of lamb has varying and odd sections. This actually works for the cook; the different thicknesses cook to different doneness, which means everyone will get some lamb cooked to their liking. When slicing the lamb, you'll see that the grain changes from section to section; for the most tender slices, carve against the grain. I like to serve this grilled lamb with the tomato and fennel salad on page 39.

8 garlic cloves

1 teaspoon kosher salt

1 tablespoon chopped fresh rosemary

1 boneless butterflied leg of lamb, 4 to 5 pounds

About 1 tablespoon extra virgin olive oil

2 teaspoons coarsely ground black pepper

CHOP the garlic. Sprinkle the salt over the chopped garlic and mince it with a chef's knife, occasionally smearing it with the flat side of the knife, until it becomes pastelike. (Or mash the garlic and salt together in a mortar and pestle.) Add the rosemary and continue to pound or mince to release the rosemary's flavor.

LAY the lamb out flat and moisten it with some olive oil. Spread the garlic and rosemary paste on both sides. Allow the flavor of the paste to penetrate for at least 1 hour at room temperature or up to 24 hours, covered in plastic wrap and refriger-

ated. Prepare the grill of your choice to medium-high. Sprinkle the lamb on both sides with the black pepper.

GRILL the lamb on one side for about 10 minutes, watching for flare-ups. Turn the meat over and cook until a thermometer inserted in the thickest part of the meat registers 125° to 130°F for medium rare, another 15 minutes or so. Transfer the meat to a cutting board and let it rest, loosely covered in aluminum foil, for 10 minutes. Carve the meat across the grain into thin slices.

Wine suggestions: *I love to drink Domaine Trevallon from Aix-en-Provence with this sumptuous lamb because it reminds me of being in Provence. A red Bordeaux from Saint-Émilion would also taste great.*

PARMESAN-CRUSTED LAMB SHANKS

SERVES 6

As you get closer to Italy along the Mediterranean coast, the food of France takes on a decidedly Italian flavor. We once ate at a little bistro in Nice that served a daube of lamb with a crisp crust. Here is my version of that dish using lamb shanks, which I love because they taste great, are practically no-fail, and don't cost a lot. Serve the lamb like they did at that bistro: over some soft polenta (page 139).

FOR THE LAMB SHANKS

6 lamb shanks, about 1 pound each, trimmed of excess fat

Kosher salt and freshly ground black pepper

6 tablespoons vegetable oil

1 medium onion, coarsely chopped

1 carrot, cut into 2-inch lengths

2 tablespoons tomato paste

1 tablespoon dried rosemary

12 garlic cloves, coarsely chopped

3 cups dry white wine

3 cups chicken broth (see Bistro Pantry, page 10)

FOR THE CRUST

¾ cup coarse fresh bread crumbs
(see Bistro Pantry, page 7)

2 shallots, very thinly sliced

2 garlic cloves, finely chopped

½ cup grated Parmesan cheese, preferably Parmigiano-Reggiano

Kosher salt and freshly ground black pepper

TO BRAISE THE LAMB SHANKS

Heat the oven to 350°F. Season the lamb shanks liberally all over with salt and pepper. In a large, heavy-based, ovenproof pot or Dutch oven, heat about 4 tablespoons of the vegetable oil over medium-high heat. Brown the shanks on all sides, about 5 minutes per side. (You may need to do this in batches.) Transfer the shanks to a platter and pour off the excess oil. Add another 2 tablespoons oil to the pot. Add the onion, carrot, tomato paste, rosemary, and garlic. Cook, stirring and scraping up the browned bits on the bottom of the pot, until they begin to color, 8 to 10 minutes. Return the lamb shanks to the pot. Add the white wine and chicken broth. Bring to a boil, cover, and cook in the oven until the lamb is very tender, about 2 hours. Remove the cover and let the lamb cook an additional 15 minutes; the lamb should be fork-tender but still on the bone. (If you want to prepare this dish a day or two ahead, stop here. Refrigerate the lamb in its cooking liquid. On the day you plan to serve it, remove any cooled fat from the sauce, reheat the lamb in its cooking liquid, and continue with the recipe.)

TRANSFER the lamb shanks to a clean roasting pan or sheet pan. Strain the sauce for a more refined dish or leave the vegetables in. Degrease the cooking liquid. (See page 211 for more information on degreasing.) Bring the liquid to a boil and cook until reduced by at least half.

TO MAKE THE CRUST

In a small bowl, toss together the bread crumbs, shallots, garlic, and Parmesan cheese. Season with salt and pepper to taste.

TO SERVE

Heat the oven to 400°F. Moisten the lamb shanks with a little cooking liquid and pat on a coating of the bread-crumb mixture, about 2 tablespoons per lamb shank. Bake until the crumbs have browned, about 10 minutes. Serve immediately with the remaining cooking liquid on the side.

Wine suggestions: *A good-quality Chianti Riserva would go well with the Italian feel of this dish, especially if you're serving the lamb with polenta. Or choose a California Rhône varietal, such as Edmunds St. John or Bonny Doon.*

SPICY LAMB SHANKS *with* COUSCOUS *and* PRESERVED LEMONS

SERVES 6

The aromatic spices and the unique tangy-salty flavor of preserved lemons give this dish a decidedly Moroccan flavor. *Ras el hanout* is a Moroccan spice blend that can have more than twenty-five spices in it. Here is a streamlined version that includes spices you are likely to have on hand. You can also buy *ras el hanout* already mixed from spice merchants (see Sources), but because every mixture differs, your recipe will be slightly different but still delicious. You can also buy preserved lemons instead of making them yourself. Look for them in Middle Eastern grocery stores and in gourmet stores as well as by mail-order (see Sources). If you make the lemons yourself, you'll need to prepare them about one week ahead.

6 lamb shanks, about 1 pound each, trimmed of fat

About 4 tablespoons *ras el hanout* (recipe follows)

Kosher salt and freshly ground black pepper

About 3 tablespoons vegetable oil

1 medium onion, chopped

2 medium carrots, chopped

6 garlic cloves, chopped

1 tablespoon coriander seeds

3 tablespoons tomato paste

2 cups dry white wine

6 cups veal stock or a mix of chicken broth and beef stock (see Bistro Pantry, page 10)

1 tablespoon dried mint

2 preserved lemons (recipe follows), pulp removed and rind cut into thin strips

2 cups couscous

1 bunch fresh mint, about 8 sprigs reserved for garnish, the rest of the leaves chopped

6 to 8 sprigs fresh cilantro, chopped

RUB each lamb shank with about 1 teaspoon of the ras el hanout. Season them with salt and pepper. Heat the vegetable oil in a large, heavy-based, ovenproof pot. Brown the lamb shanks well on all sides. Add the onion, carrots, garlic, coriander seeds, tomato paste, and 1 tablespoon of the ras el hanout. Stir well to distribute the spices.

HEAT the oven to 350°F.

ADD the white wine, veal stock or broth mix, and dried mint. Bring to a boil and skim off any foam that comes to the surface. Cover the pot and cook the lamb shanks in the oven until just tender, about 2 hours. Remove the cover from the pot, add the preserved lemons, and cook for an additional 20 minutes. (If you want to prepare this dish a day or two ahead, stop here. Cool the lamb in its cooking liquid as quickly as possible and refrigerate the lamb in the cooking liquid. On the day you plan to serve it, remove any cooled fat from the dish, reheat the lamb in the oven in its cooking liquid, and then continue with the recipe.)

DEGREASE the cooking liquid, if necessary. (See page 211 for more information on degreasing.)

WHILE the meat is cooking, pour the couscous and 1½ teaspoons of the ras el hanout into a large, flat container, such as a baking dish. Add 1¾ cups boiling water and stir to combine. Cover with a lid or aluminum foil and allow the couscous to soak for about 10 minutes. When the liquid has been absorbed, scoop up some of the couscous and rub the grains lightly in the palms of your hands, letting them fall back into a clean, dry bowl. Continue doing this until all the grains are separated and no lumps remain.

ABOUT 25 minutes before serving, place the couscous into a large, fine-mesh strainer. Choose a sauce pot that will hold the strainer without it touching the bottom of the pot (like a double boiler). Add 2 cups of the lamb shank cooking liquid to the pot. Bring to a boil and then lower the heat to a simmer. Place the strainer onto the sauce pot. Cover the strainer with aluminum foil and steam the couscous over low heat for 25 minutes.

LIFT the lamb shanks out of their juices and place each on a rimmed plate. Use a slotted spoon to scoop out some of the vegetables and preserved lemons and put them over the lamb. Spoon some of the steamed couscous next to the lamb and sprinkle some chopped mint and chopped cilantro onto each plate. Serve with some of the cooking liquid on the side and decorate each plate with a reserved mint sprig.

Wine suggestions: *To complement the beguiling flavors in this dish, I would reach for one of my all-time favorites, a well-chilled rosé, such as one from Domaine Tempier. A fruity Cabernet Franc or even a good, fruity Beaujolais cru or an equally fruity, rich California Pinot Noir from the Central Coast would also be nice. Yes, fruit is the name of the game here!*

This streamlined version of *ras el hanout* is based on a recipe by Paula Wolfert. The ingredients list does look long, but all you're really doing is measuring out spices.

¼ teaspoon ground cardamom

¼ teaspoon ground mace

½ teaspoon ground nutmeg

½ teaspoon ground cinnamon

1 teaspoon ground white pepper

¼ teaspoon ground cloves

½ teaspoon turmeric

½ teaspoon ground ginger

¼ teaspoon dried lavender (optional)

½ teaspoon fennel seeds, lightly crushed

½ teaspoon ground allspice

½ teaspoon cayenne pepper

2 to 3 dried rosebuds (optional)

MIX the spices together and pack in an airtight container.

QUICK PRESERVED LEMONS

Whole, preserved lemons need about a month of shelf time to reach their peak flavor. By cutting the lemons into thinner wedges, Paula Wolfert speeds up the curing time without any loss of flavor. You generally scoop out and discard the pulp (though it adds an intriguing flavor to salad dressings and sauces) and use just the rind, which has become quite soft. Preserved lemons can be used in other Moroccan-style dishes. They're also great as an accompaniment to grilled and roasted meat and poultry, and are a wonderful addition to salad.

4 large lemons, preferably thick skinned, scrubbed well

⅔ cup kosher salt

2 tablespoons pickling spices (optional)

1 cup fresh lemon juice (from about 5 lemons)

CUT the lemons into 8 wedges. Toss the lemons with the salt and the pickling spices, if using, and transfer them to a clean glass jar with a tight-fitting lid. Add enough lemon juice to completely cover the lemons. Cover the jar and let stand at room temperature for 7 days, shaking the jar each day to redistribute the salt. You can use them after 7 days or store them in the refrigerator for months.

SEAR-ROASTED RACK *of* LAMB *with a* CURRY, DATE, CHILE, *and* ALMOND CRUST

SERVES 4

I use ancho chiles often in my cooking to add a rich, sweet, slightly smoky flavor without much heat. Anchos are increasingly available in the supermarket, but you can also order them by mail (see Sources). The paste can be made a day ahead and kept refrigerated. Mashed potato cakes (page 264) and braised red onions (page 262) are great side dishes with this lamb.

1 ancho chile, stem and seeds removed

5 tablespoons vegetable oil

1 medium onion, chopped

2 tablespoons curry powder

12 dates, pitted and chopped

4 tablespoons sherry vinegar

¼ cup slivered almonds, toasted (see page 4) and chopped

3 tablespoons chopped fresh mint, plus whole mint leaves for garnish

Kosher salt and freshly ground black pepper

Two 7- or 8-bone lamb racks, frenched

1½ cups chicken broth (see Bistro Pantry, page 10)

SOAK the chile in hot water until softened, about 15 minutes. Chop the chile coarsely. Heat about 3 tablespoons of the vegetable oil in a sauté pan over medium heat. Add the onion and cook until soft, about 10 minutes. Lower the heat to medium-low and add the curry powder. Continue to cook, stirring frequently, until the onion has browned, about 20 minutes.

PUT the onion, ancho chile, dates, and sherry vinegar in the bowl of a food processor and process until a paste forms. Transfer the paste to a bowl, mix in the almonds and the chopped mint, and season with salt and pepper to taste.

HEAT the oven to 425°F. Season the lamb all over with salt and pepper. Heat the remaining 2 tablespoons oil in a large sauté pan over high heat.

Brown the lamb, one rack at a time, meat side first. Turn and brown the other sides. Remove the lamb from the pan, but don't clean the pan.

ALLOW the lamb to cool for a few minutes. Set aside ¼ cup of the chile-date mixture. Using a rubber spatula or your fingers, spread a thin layer of the remaining chile-date mixture on the meat side of each lamb rack.

ARRANGE the lamb in a roasting pan, preferably one with a rack, with the chile-date mixture facing up. Roast the lamb until it registers about 125°F on a thermometer for rare; 130°F for medium rare, 15 to 20 minutes (begin checking at 15 minutes). Remove the lamb to a cutting board, cover loosely with aluminum foil, and allow the meat to rest for at least 5 minutes.

POUR off any excess fat from the sauté pan. Add the chicken broth to the pan and cook over high heat, scraping up the browned bits on the bottom of the pan, until the broth is reduced by half. Add the reserved ¼ cup chile-date mixture to the sauce and whisk to combine. Season with salt and pepper.

SLICE the lamb rack into one- or two-bone chops, and serve 3 to 4 chops per person. As you cut the chops apart, be careful not to let too much of the date crust fall off the meat. Spoon some of the sauce around the chops and decorate the plate with whole mint leaves.

Wine suggestion: *With the slight heat and full flavors of this lamb, I would choose a young, medium-bodied, fruity Zinfandel.*

SLOW-ROASTED LEG *of* LAMB *with* WHITE BEANS *and* ESCAROLE

SERVES 6

If the anchovies in this dish give you pause, let me assure you that during the long cooking they melt away, leaving a slightly salty, full-but-not-fishy flavor behind. The longer the roast spends in the marinade, the more flavorful it will be; if you have time, get it started the day before you plan to serve it. Because beans vary so much in their cooking time, you might want to do them a day ahead, too.

FOR THE LAMB

4 garlic cloves

½ teaspoon kosher salt

4 to 6 anchovies, drained, rinsed (or soaked if salt-packed), and finely chopped

2 tablespoons chopped fresh thyme

2 teaspoons cracked black pepper (see Bistro Pantry, page 9)

3 tablespoons Dijon mustard

2 tablespoons olive oil

1 bone-in leg of lamb, prepared by the butcher for roasting (hip bone removed), 6 to 8 pounds

FOR THE BEANS

1 pound large white beans, soaked overnight in water

1 small onion, chopped

4 garlic cloves, chopped

1 tablespoon kosher salt

1 head of escarole, any bruised outer leaves removed, washed well and torn into 3-inch pieces

1 cup dry white wine

1 cup chicken broth (see Bistro Pantry, page 10)

TO PREPARE THE LAMB

Chop the garlic. Sprinkle ½ teaspoon salt over the chopped garlic and mince it with a chef's knife, occasionally smearing it with the flat side of the knife, until it becomes pastelike. (Or mash the garlic and salt together in a mortar and pestle.) Put the garlic paste in a small bowl and add the anchovies, thyme, pepper, mustard, and olive oil. Stir to combine. Using a rubber spatula or your hands, coat the lamb with the garlic-anchovy mix-

ture. Cover the lamb with plastic wrap and place it on a rack in a roasting pan. Allow the lamb to marinate at room temperature for 2 hours or in the refrigerator for up to 24 hours.

TO PREPARE THE BEANS

Drain the beans, place them in a large pot, and cover them with water by 3 inches. Bring the beans to a boil and cook for 20 minutes. Drain the beans and rinse them under cold running water.

Put the beans back in the same pot and add the onion, chopped garlic, and salt. Add enough water to cover by 4 inches. Bring to a boil, lower the heat to medium-low, and continue to cook until the beans are very tender, 1 to 1½ hours. (If you are making the beans ahead, stop here, and refrigerate the beans in their cooking liquid; reheat the beans before continuing.)

RESERVE 1 cup of the bean cooking liquid.

WHEN the beans are fully cooked, add the escarole and cook over low heat until the escarole is tender, about 10 minutes.

TO ROAST THE LAMB

Heat the oven to 325°F. Remove the plastic wrap from the lamb and roast the lamb until its internal temperature is 125° to 130°F for medium rare, about 1¼ hours. Remove the lamb to a cutting board, cover loosely with aluminum foil, and let it rest for at least 15 minutes.

WHILE the lamb rests, pour off the excess fat from the roasting pan. Place the pan on the stove over a low flame. Add the white wine and chicken broth. Bring the liquid to a boil, stirring to loosen the browned bits on the bottom of the pan. Transfer this liquid to a small saucepan and bring to a boil. Add the reserved bean cooking liquid. Bring the liquid to a boil and cook until reduced by about half.

CARVE the lamb leg on a diagonal across the grain into thin slices. The outside pieces will be on the medium-well-done side and the inner pieces will be a perfect rare to medium rare. Place the lamb slices on plates. Serve the white beans and escarole using a slotted spoon and serve the sauce on the side.

Wine suggestions: *A Southern Rhône wine such as Gigondas, a red Hermitage, or a Dāo Reserva from Portugal would all stand up well to this hearty roasted lamb.*

RABBIT BRAISED *in* RED WINE *with* BACON, PEARL ONIONS, *and* CHANTERELLES

SERVES 6

A lot of Americans think rabbits are too cute to eat. The French don't, and they do wonderful things with the delicate, slightly sweet meat. The legs are meant for braising, but the loin is too tender for long cooking. In order to include both in this dish, I add the loin at the very end of cooking. You can also add a few handfuls of well-washed and stemmed spinach or kale at the end, too, if you want some greens with your rabbit. Serve with boiled potatoes or egg noodles topped with some of the braising liquid.

1 tablespoon vegetable oil

6 ounces bacon, cut into ¼-inch strips

2 rabbits, cut into pieces, loin removed from the bone and cut into 2-inch pieces

Kosher salt and freshly ground black pepper

30 pearl onions, peeled (see page 187)

About 10 chanterelles

3 cups red wine

2 cups chicken broth (see Bistro Pantry, page 10)

2 sprigs fresh marjoram

IN a large, heavy-based, ovenproof pot, heat the vegetable oil over medium heat. Add the bacon and cook until the bacon renders most of its fat but does not brown. Remove the bacon from the pan with a slotted spoon, leaving the fat behind in the pan, and reserve.

SEASON the legs and shoulder pieces of the rabbit with salt and pepper. (Reserve the loin pieces to cook later.) Heat the bacon fat over medium heat. Working in batches if necessary, brown the legs and shoulder pieces on both sides in the bacon fat.

Do this slowly over medium heat to avoid over-cooking them. Remove the rabbit pieces from the pot and reserve them on a platter. Add the pearl onions to the pot and cook them for about 5 minutes. Add the mushrooms and continue to cook, stirring, about another 5 minutes. Transfer the onions and mushrooms to the plate with the rabbit.

HEAT the oven to 300°F.

ADD the red wine, chicken broth, and marjoram to the pot, and bring to a boil. Cook over high heat until the liquid is reduced by half. Put the browned rabbit pieces, the bacon, onions, and mushrooms back into the pot. Cover and cook in the oven until the rabbit is tender, about 1 hour. Just before you are ready to serve, add the loin pieces to the pot. Simmer until just cooked through, about 5 minutes.

SEASON the sauce with salt and pepper as needed. If the sauce is thin, remove the meat and vegetables with a slotted spoon and cook the sauce over medium-high heat until the sauce has thickened. Place the rabbit and vegetables back in the sauce to reheat and serve.

Wine suggestions: *These classic bistro flavors would be delicious with a good Beaujolais cru. Or try an older Burgundy, a premier cru from Chambolle-Musigny, maybe, or aged Rioja Reserva from Spain.*

HAMERSLEY'S CASSOULET *with* PORK, DUCK CONFIT, *and* SAUSAGE

Cassoulet, that most famous of all bean and meat dishes, is rife with tradition. But the traditions differ from region to region and person to person. Strong feelings on the subject abound. While your friends and family will just be delighted that you have cooked them something so wonderful, paying customers are allowed to act on their notion of what (and what doesn't) makes for a great cassoulet. I remember a man who returned his cassoulet one night because he felt it was too soupy. Okay, a matter of taste. Another guy insisted that what I served wasn't real cassoulet because it was served in a soup bowl and not in a proper crock. Whatever. But we did have a good laugh the time a guy returned his cassoulet because nobody told him it had all those damned beans in it!

2 pounds flageolet, Great Northern, or cannellini beans, soaked overnight and drained

1 to 1½ pounds boneless pork butt (shoulder), cut into pieces about 2 inches square

1 teaspoon freshly ground black pepper

4 tablespoons duck fat or vegetable oil

1 medium onion, cut into a medium dice

8 to 10 whole garlic cloves

1 carrot, cut into a medium dice

½ pound sliced bacon, cut into ½-inch pieces

1 teaspoon chopped fresh thyme

1 teaspoon chopped fresh marjoram

One 14.5-ounce can diced tomatoes, drained (about 1½ cups)

2 cups dry white wine

6 cups veal stock or chicken broth (see Bistro Pantry, page 10)

1 to 1½ pounds sweet Italian sausages

1 tablespoon kosher salt

4 duck confit legs, cut at the joint between the thigh and drumstick, skin and excess fat removed (see page 193 for confit recipe or page 317 for confit sources)

2 cups coarse bread crumbs (see Bistro Pantry, page 7)

PUT the beans in a large pot and add enough water to cover by about 3 inches. Bring to a boil. Lower the heat to a simmer and cook the beans, skimming off any foam that comes to the surface, for 30 minutes. Drain in a colander and rinse under cold running water. (The beans will not be cooked through at this point.)

HEAT the oven to 300°F.

SEASON the pork with the pepper. Heat the duck fat or vegetable oil in a very large (at least 6½ quarts), heavy-based, ovenproof pot over medium-high heat. Add the pork and brown it well on all sides, about 10 minutes total.

ADD the onion, garlic, carrot, and bacon, and cook, stirring, until the bacon has rendered some of its fat but has not colored, about 5 minutes. Add the thyme, marjoram, drained beans, tomatoes, white wine, and veal stock. Bring to a boil, cover, and cook in the oven for 1½ hours.

WHILE the cassoulet is cooking, put the sausage in a high-sided sauté pan and cover with water. Bring to a boil and then lower the heat to a simmer. Cook until the meat is cooked through, 6 to 8 minutes. Allow the sausage to cool and then cut it into 1-inch pieces. Refrigerate until ready to use.

AFTER 1½ hours, uncover the cassoulet; it should still look quite soupy. Add the salt. Continue to cook, uncovered, until the pork and beans are very tender, another 30 to 45 minutes. The cassoulet should appear drier and you should see mostly beans, vegetables, and meat. If you plan to serve the cassoulet on the same day that you've made it, and there is still a lot of liquid left, bring the cassoulet to a boil on the stove and let it boil for a few minutes. This is important; if the cassoulet is too wet, the bread-crumb topping will not get crisp. However, if you are making the cassoulet ahead, it's good to have some excess liquid, as the beans will have more time to absorb it and the extra liquid will keep everything moist. *If you are making the cassoulet ahead of time, stop now and see the Notes.*

IF you are serving the cassoulet on the same day you make it, add the duck legs and sausage to the pot and stir gently with a wooden spoon so as not to break up the beans and meat. Allow the cassoulet to cool for a half hour. (This cooling will allow a thin skin to form on the surface of the cassoulet, which will help keep the bread crumbs afloat.) Sprinkle the top of the cassoulet with a thin layer of bread crumbs. Raise the oven temperature to 375°F and cook the cassoulet, uncovered, until the sausage and duck heat through and the bread crumbs form a golden brown crust, 20 to 30 minutes.

Wine suggestions: *An earthy red from Cahors in the southwest of France holds up its end of the bargain with this very hearty meal. A big red Bandol or a robust Gigondas would also work really well.*

(continued)

Notes: You can make most of the cassoulet a day or two ahead of when you plan to serve it. Cook the cassoulet until the beans and the pork are tender, but do not add the sausage, duck legs, or bread crumbs. Allow the pork and beans to cool and then refrigerate them. The following day, take the cassoulet out of the fridge a couple of hours before you plan to serve it to speed the reheating time. Heat the oven to 350°F. Add a little water or broth to the beans and meat if they seem dry, and warm them in the oven for about 30 minutes. Give the pot a stir to check that it's warmed throughout. Then add the sausage, duck legs, and bread crumbs as directed in the recipe.

In the restaurant, we portion individual servings of cassoulet by putting some of the beans and meat and a ladleful of stock into a small (8 inches) sauté pan. We add a sausage and a duck leg to the pan, top it with a sprinkle of bread crumbs, and place the pan into a 450°F oven. When the cassoulet is bubbling, crisp, and hot all the way through, we slide it carefully (keeping the crumbs on top) into a large soup bowl to serve. This works very well, is very controlled, and lets you enjoy the cassoulet over a number of days without reheating the whole amount every time. You can do similarly in larger portions, by transferring, say, half of the cassoulet to a large sauté pan, adding half of the sausage and duck legs, sprinkling on half of the bread crumbs, and heating it through.

ROAST PORK *with* APPLES, ONIONS, *and* SAGE

SERVES 6

Brining, which is really just a soak in a salty bath, keeps lean pork from drying out while it cooks. It also makes the pork more flavorful. But you have to soak it at least 24 hours, so you'll need to start the day before you plan to serve it. Another benefit of brining: Any leftover slices of pork make a great sandwich. Try serving the pork with some spätzle (recipe follows) and the braised red cabbage on page 263.

FOR THE BRINE

1 cup kosher salt

½ cup sugar

¾ cup maple syrup

12 juniper berries

3 cloves

2 bay leaves

3 to 4 sprigs fresh sage

FOR THE PORK ROAST

1 pork loin roast, center cut, bone in and notched through the chine bone at 2-inch intervals, 5 to 7 pounds

1 cup plus ⅓ cup real maple syrup

½ teaspoon cracked black pepper (see Bistro Pantry, page 9)

1 tablespoon vegetable oil

About 1 teaspoon unsalted butter

1 medium onion, chopped

4 Granny Smith apples, peeled, cored, and cut into quarters

1½ cups Calvados or other apple brandy

2 cups chicken broth (see Bistro Pantry, page 10)

8 to 10 fresh sage leaves, chopped

Spätzle (recipe follows)

PUT about 1 gallon water in a pot large enough to hold the pork loin. Add all of the brine ingredients and bring to a boil. Allow to cool completely.

IMMERSE the pork loin completely in the brine and refrigerate for at least 24 hours and up to 72 hours. Place a small plate on top of it to make sure the entire roast is under water.

ABOUT 1 hour before you plan to roast the pork, remove it from the brine and pat it dry with paper towels. Put the pork, meat side up, on a rack that will fit into the roasting pan, and then put the rack on a plate or sheet pan to catch any excess liquid or syrup. Allow the pork to come to room temperature.

(continued)

HEAT the oven to 350°F. Pour the maple syrup over the pork, and sprinkle the pepper evenly over it. Place the pork in the roasting pan, and roast the pork until it registers 140°F on a meat thermometer at its thickest point, 1¼ to 1½ hours.

ABOUT 20 minutes before the meat finishes roasting, heat the oil and butter in a large sauté pan over medium-high heat. Add the onion and apples and cook, stirring occasionally, until they begin to brown. Take the pan off the heat and carefully add the Calvados. Be careful as the Calvados may ignite, which is actually a good thing as it burns off the alcohol and concentrates flavors. (Go ahead and ignite the Calvados yourself if you're comfortable with flambéing foods.) If it does ignite, just leave it alone until the flames die out, which will happen quickly. Then add the chicken broth, bring it all to a boil, reduce the heat to medium, and let it bubble away until reduced and flavorful, 7 to 9 minutes.

WHEN the pork is finished cooking, transfer it to a large platter or cutting board and let it rest for at least 15 minutes (see Note). Pour off the fat in the bottom of the roasting pan. Add the sage leaves to the apple and onion mixture and add the mixture to the roasting pan. Bring to a boil and then lower the heat to low. Let the juices bubble on the stove over low heat for another 5 minutes or so to develop the flavor of the sauce. Cut the loin off the bone in one piece and then slice the meat thinly. Spoon the apple and onion mixture over and around the pork. Serve with spätzle.

> **Note:** I usually turn the oven off, cover the roast with aluminum foil, and place the platter or cutting board in the oven while I cook or finish the other dishes I am serving with the pork.
>
> **Wine suggestions:** *This begs for a really good Riesling fom Alsace (a grand cru if you're splurging) or a lush, rich Pinot Gris from Alsace.*

Spätzle, egg dumplings from Alsace, are a nice change of pace from mashed potatoes, rice, and pasta, and they're great with this dish as well as with any braise or stew. I use cream in mine, which makes the spätzle richer and a little more dense than those made with milk or water. Here I brown them, but you can also drop the boiled dumplings right into a stew or braise without the browning step.

2 large eggs

¾ cup light cream

Pinch of kosher salt

Pinch of freshly ground black pepper

Pinch of nutmeg, preferably
freshly grated

1 tablespoon chopped fresh parsley

1½ to 2 cups all-purpose flour

2 tablespoons olive oil

2 to 4 tablespoons unsalted butter

IN a medium bowl, whisk together the eggs, cream, salt, pepper, nutmeg, and parsley. Add 1½ cups flour and beat with a wooden spoon or in a mixer until well combined and somewhat elastic. If the dough is very wet, add more flour, a tablespoon at a time. Let rest for 20 minutes.

BRING a pot of salted water to a boil. Have ready a bowl of ice water. In batches, press the spätzle through a colander, letting the irregularly shaped dumplings drop into the boiling water. (You can also pour some of the dough onto a cutting board and scrape little bits of dough off it into the water with the tip of a knife.) The spätzle are cooked when they float to the top. Lift the first batch of spätzle out of the hot water with a slotted spoon and put them right into the bowl of ice water to stop the cooking. Then lift them out of the cold water, put them on a large plate, and drizzle them with a little olive oil to keep them from sticking to each other. Repeat until you have used up all of the dough. Refrigerate the spätzle until you are ready to brown them.

JUST before serving, heat the butter in a sauté pan over medium-high heat. Add the spätzle and cook them for a couple of minutes, until golden brown. Season with a little more salt and serve.

POT-ROASTED PORK *with* PRUNES, ARMAGNAC, *and* WALNUTS

SERVES 6

Pork, prunes, Armagnac, and walnuts are exalted flavors in the southwest of France, especially when combined. I love how the dried fruit gets transformed in this dish, plumping up and becoming glossy and meltingly soft. Serve the pork over couscous, soft polenta (page 139), or with some crusty bread—anything to further enjoy the deeply flavored sauce this braise creates.

2 cups Armagnac or other brandy

24 to 30 pitted prunes, cut in half if large

1 boneless or bone-in pork shoulder, 4 to 6 pounds (look for cuts labeled "butt" or "Boston butt"), trimmed of excess fat

Kosher salt and freshly ground black pepper

¼ cup vegetable oil

3 red onions, cut into thick rounds

1½ cups dry white wine

1½ cups chicken broth (see Bistro Pantry, page 10)

Pinch of red pepper flakes

8 whole fresh sage leaves, plus 1 tablespoon chopped fresh sage

1 tablespoon tomato paste

¼ cup honey

About 2 tablespoons chopped fresh parsley

½ cup chopped toasted walnuts (see page 4)

BRING ½ cup of the Armagnac to a boil. (Be careful, as the Armagnac may ignite, which is actually a good thing as it burns off the alcohol and concentrates flavors. If it does ignite, just leave it alone until the flames die out, which will happen quickly.) Remove from the heat and toss in the prunes. Reserve.

HEAT the oven to 325°F. Season the pork liberally all over with salt and pepper. Heat the vegetable oil in a large, heavy-based, ovenproof pan over medium-high heat. Add the pork and brown on all sides, about 12 minutes total. Remove the pork.

ADD the onions to the pan and lower the heat to medium. Cook the onions, stirring occasionally, until lightly browned, about 10 minutes. Add the white wine, the remaining 1½ cups Armagnac, the chicken broth, red pepper flakes, whole sage leaves, tomato paste, and honey. Bring to a boil. Put the pork back in the pan, cover tightly with a lid or aluminum foil, and cook in the oven until the pork is very tender, about 2 hours. Add the prunes, the Armagnac they were soaking in, and the chopped sage to the pot. Leave the pot uncovered and cook for an additional 20 minutes. (If you want to prepare this dish a day or two ahead, stop here. Cool the pork and its cooking liquid as quickly as possible and refrigerate the pork in its cooking liquid. On the day you plan to serve it, remove any cooled fat from the dish, reheat the pork in the oven in its cooking liquid, and then continue with the recipe.)

TRANSFER the pork to a cutting board and tent with foil. Strain the cooking liquid into a saucepan and reserve the onions and prunes. Degrease the cooking liquid, if necessary. (See page 211 for more information on degreasing.) Bring the liquid to a boil and cook until reduced by half. Return the prunes and onions to the pot to warm them. Slice the pork and arrange the slices on a platter. Top with the onions and the prunes and pour some of the sauce over the top to moisten everything. Sprinkle with parsley and the toasted walnuts and serve with the remaining sauce on the side.

Wine suggestion: *Try a massive Italian Amarone — its sensuous sweetness feels just right with this dish.*

GRILLED PORK TENDERLOIN *with* SPICY WATERMELON SALAD

SERVES 4

Right now you're saying, "Watermelon?" It does seem a little bizarre, but it's delicious, especially on a hot day in the summer. Don't be too precise when cutting the watermelon; irregular shapes make the salad more visually appealing. As long as you have the grill going, try grilling some small new potatoes or chilled polenta squares (page 142), brushed with a little olive oil, to go with the pork.

½ cup balsamic vinegar

2 tablespoons Dijon mustard

½ teaspoon fennel seeds

¼ teaspoon red pepper flakes

1 teaspoon ground cumin

¼ teaspoon cayenne pepper

½ teaspoon kosher salt

½ teaspoon freshly ground black pepper

¼ cup olive oil

1 tablespoon sesame oil

2 pork tenderloins, trimmed of fat and silverskin

About 1 pound watermelon, rind removed, seeded, and chopped into ½-inch pieces, about 2 cups total

½ large red onion, very thinly sliced

2 bunches watercress, washed and dried well, tough stems removed

1 to 2 teaspoons toasted sesame seeds (optional)

IN a small bowl, combine the balsamic vinegar, mustard, fennel seeds, red pepper flakes, cumin, cayenne, salt, and pepper. Whisk in the olive oil in a steady stream until it is incorporated and forms an emulsion. Add the sesame oil in the same manner.

TOSS the pork tenderloins with ¾ cup of the marinade and allow them to marinate for an hour at room temperature or up to 8 hours in the refrigerator. Reserve the remaining marinade.

HEAT the grill of your choice to medium-high. Remove the pork from the marinade and sprinkle it with more salt and pepper. Grill the pork, turning it occasionally, until cooked through, 10 to 15 minutes. (The pork should register 145° to 150°F on a meat thermometer.) Remove the pork from the grill and allow it to rest for 5 minutes on a cutting board while you make the salad.

TOSS the watermelon, red onion, and watercress with enough of the reserved marinade to coat it lightly. Season with salt and pepper. When ready to serve, place the watermelon salad on each plate and sprinkle with sesame seeds, if you're using them. Slice the pork thinly and place the slices next to the salad. Top with the juices that have collected on the cutting board and serve immediately.

Wine suggestions: *Here again a Riesling from Alsace will save the day—make it one with weight, a grand cru, or try a rich Pinot Gris also from Alsace.*

CALF'S LIVER *with a* SPINACH *and* BACON SALAD *and* WARM MUSTARD DRESSING

In many supermarkets, calf's liver comes already sliced. If you buy a whole liver, remove any exposed connective tissue and veins with a very sharp knife. To keep liver tender, do not overcook it; you want the center of the liver to look pink. All this needs is some good crusty bread to go with it.

½ to ¾ pound calf's liver, sliced into
2 pieces about ½ inch thick

¼ cup milk

4 slices of bacon, cut crosswise into
¼-inch pieces

1 tablespoon Dijon mustard

1 tablespoon red wine vinegar

1 shallot, finely chopped

Kosher salt and freshly ground black pepper

2 tablespoons extra virgin olive oil

¼ cup heavy cream

4 ounces spinach, washed and dried well
and tough stems removed (about 4 cups)

½ medium red onion, very thinly sliced

2 teaspoons mustard seeds

3 tablespoons vegetable oil

PUT the slices of liver on a rimmed plate and pour the milk over them. Let the liver soak for 30 minutes, turning once, to draw out any excess blood.

IN a small sauté pan, cook the bacon over low heat until it renders most of its fat and has begun to brown lightly. Reserve 1 tablespoon of the rendered bacon fat. Remove the bacon from the pan and reserve it in a warm place.

IN a small bowl, combine the mustard, vinegar, and shallot. Combine with a whisk and season with salt and pepper. Whisk in the reserved bacon fat and the olive oil. Measure 2 tablespoons of the vinaigrette into a small saucepan and reserve the

rest. Add the cream to the vinaigrette in the pan and whisk to combine.

TOSS the spinach, onion, and bacon together in a bowl.

DRAIN the liver and pat it dry. Make ⅛-inch cuts at 1-inch intervals around the outside of the slices to help keep the liver from curling as it's cooked. Press the mustard seeds into both sides of the liver slices and season them with salt and pepper. Heat the vegetable oil in a large sauté pan over medium-high heat. Add the liver to the pan and cook over medium to medium-high heat for 3 minutes. (The pan needs to be hot but not so hot that the mustard seeds burn.) Turn the liver over and continue to cook until the liver is done, about another 3 minutes for medium rare. Remove the liver from the pan and keep it warm while you assemble the rest of the dish.

BRING the creamy vinaigrette in the pan to a boil over high heat and cook it until it thickens slightly, about 2 minutes. Meanwhile, toss the spinach salad with enough of the vinaigrette (the reserved portion without the cream) to coat the leaves lightly.

TO serve, divide the spinach salad among the plates. Put a slice of liver on each plate next to the spinach. Season the warm creamy vinaigrette with salt and pepper and drizzle some over both the liver and the spinach salad. Serve immediately.

Wine suggestions: *I like a Chianti Classico or a good Beaujolais cru with this.*

CARAMELIZED SWEETBREADS *with* LEMON *and* WILTED GREENS

SERVES 4

Sweetbreads—thymus glands, usually from veal—are woefully underused despite their being so flavorful and versatile. They do need a little special handling before their eventual quick sauté. Poaching them first makes removing any membrane or connective tissues easier, firms up the sweetbreads, and, with some aromatics in the poaching liquid, adds flavor. A mustardy marinade also adds flavor and the balsamic vinegar in it helps the outside of the sweetbreads to crisp and caramelize beautifully while the interior stays soft and tender. I like to serve mashed potatoes with this dish.

FOR POACHING THE SWEETBREADS

1 pound sweetbreads, soaked for at least 4 hours in cold water in the refrigerator

1 cup dry white wine

1 carrot, cut into a small dice

½ medium onion, thinly sliced (reserve the rest to use in the marinade)

¼ teaspoon kosher salt

1 bay leaf

6 whole peppercorns

1 sprig fresh thyme or ¼ teaspoon dried thyme

FOR MARINATING THE SWEETBREADS

3 tablespoons Dijon mustard

¼ medium onion, thinly sliced

3 tablespoons balsamic vinegar

¼ teaspoon fennel seeds

¼ teaspoon red pepper flakes

½ teaspoon coarsely ground black pepper

FOR SERVING

2 tablespoons vegetable oil

2 tablespoons unsalted butter

Kosher salt

4 cups hearty mixed greens, such as escarole, watercress, and endive, washed and dried well

Juice of ½ lemon

Freshly ground black pepper

TO POACH THE SWEETBREADS

In a medium saucepan, bring the white wine, 3 cups water, the carrot, onion slices, salt, bay leaf, peppercorns, and thyme to a boil. Remove the sweetbreads from the cold water, add them to the saucepan, and immediately lower the heat to a simmer. Cook the sweetbreads for about 12 minutes. Remove the sweetbreads from the pot and let cool long enough to be handled but still be warm, about 10 minutes. (Discard the poaching liquid.)

WHILE the sweetbreads are still warm, use your fingers to remove the thin outer membrane and any fatty white bits from the two lobes of the sweetbreads. Try not to tear the meat when you do this. Cut the sweetbreads diagonally into pieces about ½ inch wide.

TO MARINATE THE SWEETBREADS

In a medium bowl, combine the mustard, onion slices, balsamic vinegar, fennel seeds, red pepper flakes, and pepper. Whisk to combine. Add the sweetbreads to the bowl and toss gently to coat them well. Cover the bowl with plastic wrap and let the sweetbreads marinate for 45 minutes at room temperature or for 2 hours refrigerated.

TO SERVE THE SWEETBREADS

Heat the oil and butter in a large sauté pan over medium-high heat. Sprinkle the sweetbreads with salt and put them in the pan. Lower the heat to medium and brown the sweetbreads well on all sides, occasionally spooning the butter and oil over them, 8 to 10 minutes. Remove the sweetbreads from the pan, put them on a warm plate, and reserve. Add the greens to the pan. Season with salt and toss the greens until they just begin to wilt. Add the lemon juice and more salt and pepper to taste.

PLACE the greens on plates, place the sweetbreads on top, and squeeze another few drops of lemon juice over all. Serve immediately.

Wine suggestions: *Try a white Rhône varietal with these crispy sweetbreads. A California Viognier or an Hermitage from the Rhône would be a luscious choice.*

CHAPTER

9

Vegetables

ON THE SIDE

HOW OFTEN DO YOU
order a main course off a menu primarily
because of what it's being served with? A lot
of people do that, which is why at the
restaurant we provide side dishes that folks
can order à la carte just in case they have
their hearts set on the roast chicken, but they
also want the creamy mashed potato cake
that's served with the grilled rib steak.

AT HOME, vegetables often get short shrift compared to the attention paid to the main course. And while there's nothing wrong with occasionally enjoying unadorned steamed asparagus or plain sautéed spinach, it's amazing how a quick addition of garlic, cheese, a bit of ham, some spices, a little wine, or broth or cream can transform those same vegetables into something that would catch your eye on a menu. In the recipes that follow, I try to keep things simple yet delicious. There are no towering napoleons or glistening terrines, just a lot of great flavors. One thing I do often is braise vegetables: slowly cook them in some flavorful liquid. This simple technique works surprisingly well for such vegetables as fennel, red onion, and endive, which we tend to think of as crisp additions to a dish. When braised, their texture becomes meltingly tender and their flavor sweetens.

SAUTÉED SPINACH *with* GARLIC, LEMON, *and* OLIVE OIL

SERVES 4

This method of cooking spinach gives it a great texture and adds just enough other flavors to enhance the spinach without overwhelming it. You can use this method with other greens, too, such as Swiss chard and young kale. Cook the greens at as high a heat as you can without burning the leaves. The natural moisture in the leaves and the excess water from washing them will help steam the greens. As the moisture evaporates, the flavors become concentrated.

4 tablespoons olive oil

1 pound spinach, large stems removed, washed well and drained of most of the excess water

3 garlic cloves, finely chopped

Pinch of nutmeg, preferably freshly grated

1 to 1½ tablespoons fresh lemon juice

Kosher salt and freshly ground black pepper

HEAT 2 tablespoons of the olive oil in a large sauté pan over medium-high heat. Add the spinach and cook over high heat, stirring and tossing until the leaves begin to throw off their water and wilt, 3 to 4 minutes. Strain the spinach in a fine-mesh strainer, pressing most of the water out of it.

PUT the pan back on the stove over medium heat. Add the remaining 2 tablespoons olive oil, the garlic, and the nutmeg, and cook for 30 seconds. Add the spinach and 1 tablespoon of the lemon juice and continue to cook for 2 to 3 more minutes. Season with salt and pepper and add more lemon juice to taste.

ROASTED ARTICHOKES *with* GARLIC *and* PANCETTA BREAD CRUMBS

SERVES 4

Jody Adams introduced me to the wonderful flavor of roasted artichokes. This version with garlic and pancetta crumbs works best as a first course or light lunch.

4 large artichokes

Juice of 1 lemon

Kosher salt

2 ounces pancetta, finely chopped

1 shallot, thinly sliced

2 garlic cloves, finely chopped

1 cup fresh bread crumbs (see Bistro Pantry, page 7)

2 tablespoons chopped fresh parsley

Freshly ground black pepper

About 4 tablespoons extra virgin olive oil

SNAP the stems from the bottoms of the artichokes and trim the bottoms with a paring knife so that the artichokes will sit up on a plate. Bring about 2 quarts water to a boil in a large pot. Add the artichokes, 2 tablespoons of the lemon juice, and 1 tablespoon salt to the pot. Lower the heat to a rapid simmer and cook until the artichoke leaves can just be pulled away and are tender, 12 to 15 minutes. Remove the artichokes from the water and let them cool and drain.

WHEN they are cool enough to handle, spread the leaves out and remove the inner leaf clump. Using a small teaspoon, scrape out the inner choke and discard.

IN a small sauté pan over medium-high heat, sauté the pancetta until it just begins to crisp. Combine the pancetta, shallot, garlic, bread crumbs, and parsley in a small bowl. Toss lightly to combine. Season with salt and pepper.

HEAT the oven to 375°F.

PUT the artichokes into a shallow, sided baking dish so they sit with the leaves facing up. Lightly fill the cavity of each artichoke with about 1 tablespoon of the bread-crumb filling. Spread the leaves out slightly and sprinkle the remaining filling in between the leaves. Drizzle each artichoke with about 1 tablespoon olive oil and the remaining lemon juice. Add ¼ cup water to the bottom of the dish. Bake the artichokes until they are warmed through and the top layer of bread crumbs is golden brown, 15 to 20 minutes. Serve hot from the oven as a first course, as a side dish, or even as a light lunch.

ROASTED POTATOES *and* ONIONS

This recipe is so very simple, but it's also so very good with all kinds of main dishes. We *always* serve it with our Roast Chicken with Garlic, Lemon, and Parsley (page 182). Its simplicity also works well with the veal chops on page 223, or the blue cheese–stuffed burger on page 216. You can cook the vegetables ahead of serving them and then reheat them when you're ready to eat.

2 or 3 russet potatoes

1 or 2 large onions

1 to 2 tablespoons olive oil

Kosher salt and freshly ground black pepper

PUT a rimmed baking sheet in the oven and heat the oven to 350°F. Wash the potatoes well, cut away any eyes or dark spots, and cut the potatoes lengthwise into quarters. Leave the skin on the onion. Cut the onions in quarters through the root. When the baking pan is hot, carefully pour the olive oil onto the pan and arrange the potatoes and onions on the hot pan, cut sides down. Season amply with salt and pepper. Roast until the vegetables are well browned and tender, about 1 hour. (The onions may cook faster; if so, remove them from the pan and set them aside.) Remove the outer skin of the onions. Serve immediately or set aside at room temperature and reheat briefly before serving.

BRAISED LEEKS *with* CORIANDER *and* ORANGE VINAIGRETTE

This leek dish is lighter and slightly more exotic than the following one. Try these leeks with the bacon-wrapped scallops on page 154, or the grilled leg of lamb on page 225.

4 medium leeks

1 orange

1 tablespoon vegetable oil

1 tablespoon unsalted butter

½ cup dry vermouth

¾ cup chicken broth (see Bistro Pantry, page 10)

½ teaspoon coriander seeds

Pinch of red pepper flakes

Kosher salt

2 teaspoons rice vinegar or white wine vinegar

1 teaspoon Dijon mustard

¼ cup extra virgin olive oil

1 tablespoon chopped fresh parsley

Freshly ground black pepper

TRIM the tops of the leeks, leaving 1 inch of the green part. Trim the root end of the leeks, but leave the leeks intact. Pull off any tough outer layers of the leeks and cut the leeks lengthwise. Soak in plenty of warm water. You may need to do this in two or three changes of water if the leeks are very dirty. Open up the "leaves" of each leek a little to check if they are clean. Lift the leeks out of the water, drain, and pat dry.

ZEST the orange and then juice it; reserve the zest and juice separately.

HEAT the vegetable oil and butter in a large sauté pan over medium-high heat until the butter is very hot. Add the leeks, cut side down, and cook until well browned. Sometimes the leeks will expand and bend while they are browning, but try to keep the leeks intact. Turn the leeks over and add the vermouth, chicken broth, coriander seeds, red pepper flakes, and 2 tablespoons of the orange juice to the pan. Season with a little salt. Bring to a boil and then lower the heat to low. Cover the pan and cook the leeks until they are quite tender, 30 to 40 minutes. (Check by piercing the root ends with the tip of a small knife.)

REMOVE the leeks from the pan with a metal spatula and keep them warm. Turn up the heat in the pan to medium and carefully reduce the cooking liquid until only about 2 tablespoons remain.

Scrape these juices into a small bowl and let cool for a couple of minutes. Add 1 tablespoon of the remaining orange juice, the zest, vinegar, and mustard, and combine. Whisk in the olive oil in a steady stream until it's all incorporated and an emulsion forms. Add the chopped parsley. Taste and season with salt and pepper and add additional vinegar or orange juice, if needed. To serve: Spoon some of the vinaigrette over the top of the leeks.

LEEKS *with* FENNEL *and* CREAM

SERVES 4

I love leeks and often feature them as side dishes. This is your classic, creamy version, which would be great as a side to Split Roasted Chicken (page 184). You can also use it, saucelike, to dress up baked salmon or a sear-roasted veal chop.

2 tablespoons unsalted butter

5 medium leeks, roots trimmed, white and pale green parts cut into thin rounds and well washed

Kosher salt

¼ teaspoon fennel seeds, lightly crushed

1 teaspoon fresh marjoram or ½ teaspoon dried marjoram

Pinch of red pepper flakes

⅓ cup dry white wine

1 cup heavy cream

1 tablespoon chopped fresh parsley

About 1 tablespoon fresh lemon juice

Freshly ground black pepper

IN a large sauté pan, heat the butter over medium-high heat. Add the leeks and cook, stirring, for about 3 minutes. Add about 1 teaspoon salt, the fennel seeds, marjoram, and red pepper flakes. Stir to combine. Add the white wine and bring to a boil. Cook the leeks over high heat until the wine is reduced by about half. Add the cream and bring to a boil. Lower the heat and let the cream bubble until the leeks are tender and the cream has thickened slightly, 8 to 10 minutes. Add the parsley and season to taste with the lemon juice, additional salt, and pepper. Stir to combine and serve.

ROASTED ASPARAGUS *with* PANCETTA *and* SHAVED ASIAGO

SERVES 4 TO 6

These tasty asparagus under their blanket of cheese work really well as part of an antipasto-like assortment of hors d'oeuvres or as a side dish to accompany the chicken paillards on page 192. Use a vegetable peeler or the slicing side of a box grater to create paper-thin slices of cheese.

30 to 40 medium asparagus (about 2 bunches), tough woody ends snapped off

2 ounces pancetta, finely chopped

2 shallots, sliced

1 tablespoon fresh lemon juice

Kosher salt and freshly ground black pepper

About 1 ounce Asiago cheese

1 teaspoon grated lemon zest

HEAT the oven to 450°F. On a small, rimmed baking sheet or in a gratin dish, toss the asparagus with the pancetta and shallots. Sprinkle with the lemon juice and season with a pinch of salt and pepper. Roast the asparagus, tossing them once or twice during cooking, until tender, 8 to 10 minutes depending on size.

REMOVE the pan from the oven and heat the broiler.

IF necessary, rearrange the asparagus so they are all facing in the same direction and are in an even layer on the bottom of the pan. Spoon any shallots and pancetta that have fallen to the side over the asparagus. Top the asparagus with the Asiago cheese, preferably in one covering layer. Broil the asparagus until the cheese melts, about 1 minute. Transfer the asparagus, with the shallots and pancetta, to plates or a large platter. Sprinkle with the grated lemon zest and serve.

RED ONIONS BRAISED *in* RED WINE *with* GARLIC *and* THYME

SERVES 4

This Dish bakes for a long time, but it's mostly unattended ("walk-away") time. We make these onions by the score at the restaurant because they are so versatile. They are a great side dish—fabulous with the blue cheese–stuffed burger on page 216—but they also work well as the featured item in a green salad or as a component of an all-vegetable meal.

2 medium to large red onions

Kosher salt and freshly ground black pepper

1 tablespoon vegetable oil

2 tablespoons unsalted butter

2 garlic cloves, finely chopped

4 sprigs fresh thyme

1 cup red wine

2 cups chicken broth (see Bistro Pantry, page 10)

HEAT the oven to 325°F.

MAKE a tiny slice on the top and bottom of each onion so that when it is cut in half, each half will stand without rolling. Cut the onions in half and remove the papery outer skin. Season the onions with salt and pepper.

HEAT the vegetable oil and 1 tablespoon of the butter in a large ovenproof sauté pan over medium-high heat. Add the onions, cut side down, and lower the heat to medium. Cook until the cut side is well browned, about 4 minutes. Turn the onions over. Sprinkle each onion half with the chopped garlic and thyme and season

with additional salt and pepper. Add the red wine and chicken broth and bring to a boil. Put the pan in the oven and cook the onions, basting every 20 minutes or so, until the onions are very tender, about 1½ hours. (If the liquid evaporates before the onions are tender, add more broth to the pan.)

TRANSFER the onions to a serving platter or plates. You should have about 1 cup liquid remaining in the pan. Strain the liquid into a small saucepan, bring it to a boil, then lower to a simmer. Add the remaining tablespoon of butter and whisk until combined. Pour over the top of the onions and serve.

SWEET-AND-SOUR RED CABBAGE

A terrific fall dish, especially when served with the pork roast on page 241 or the veal chops on page 223.

1 tablespoon vegetable oil

2 slices of bacon, cut into ¼-inch strips

1 head of red cabbage, trimmed of its tough outer leaves, cored, and shredded

1 medium white onion, cut into a medium dice

½ teaspoon caraway seeds

1 tablespoon sugar

1 tablespoon kosher salt

½ teaspoon freshly ground black pepper

1 cup red wine

½ cup balsamic vinegar

1½ cups chicken broth (see Bistro Pantry, page 10)

1 tablespoon chopped fresh parsley

HEAT the oven to 350°F.

IN a high-sided, ovenproof sauté pan or Dutch oven, heat the vegetable oil over medium-high heat. Add the bacon and cook for about 2 minutes. Add the cabbage, onion, caraway seeds, sugar, salt, and pepper. Cook, stirring occasionally, until the cabbage begins to wilt, about 8 minutes.

ADD the red wine, vinegar, and chicken broth. Bring to a boil and put the pan in the oven. Cook, stirring every 15 minutes or so, until the cabbage is tender, about 1 hour. Remove from the oven, add the parsley, and serve.

GARLICKY MASHED POTATO CAKES

This is the most popular side dish served at our restaurant. Soft on the inside with a thin golden brown crust outside, these potato cakes are perfect with just about everything. You'll get the best results if you chill the cakes completely before browning them, so plan to mash the potatoes and form the cakes either earlier in the day or even the day before. Then all they need is to be quickly browned and heated through before serving.

3 russet potatoes, peeled and quartered lengthwise

Kosher salt

2 tablespoons unsalted butter

Freshly ground black pepper

3 garlic cloves, finely chopped

¾ to 1 cup heavy cream

2 tablespoons vegetable oil

PUT the potatoes and about 1 tablespoon salt in a pot and cover by 2 inches with cold water. Bring to a boil and cook the potatoes until tender, about 20 minutes. Drain them well, return them to their cooking pot, and dry them over low heat for a couple of minutes.

WHILE the potatoes are cooking, heat the butter in a small saucepan. Add the garlic and cook over medium-low heat until the garlic softens and turns a nutty brown, 5 to 7 minutes. Add the cream and bring it to a boil. Take the cream off the heat and let it sit for 5 minutes so the garlic can infuse the cream with its flavor.

ADD ¼ cup of the cream and the garlic to the potatoes and mash them with a potato masher or a fork until they're just barely mashed. Add more liquid only if the potatoes seem dry; you don't want them to be too loose or they won't keep their shape when browned. Season with ample salt and pep-

per. Allow the mashed potatoes to cool. (Spreading them on a sheet pan makes them cool more quickly and evenly.) Using your hands, form the potatoes into 4 large or 6 smaller cakes, about an inch or so thick. Chill the cakes in the refrigerator for at least 2 hours and up to a day.

HEAT the oven to 375°F.

HEAT the vegetable oil in a large, ovenproof, nonstick sauté pan or a well-seasoned cast-iron skillet over medium-high heat until very hot. (Check the heat by adding a tiny bit of potato; it should sizzle immediately.) Add the cakes and cook on the stove for 1 to 2 minutes. Put the pan in the oven and cook until the bottom side is well browned, 6 to 8 minutes. Using a spatula, carefully flip over each cake. Continue to cook the cakes in the oven until hot throughout, about 4 more minutes. You can check the cakes by inserting a metal skewer into them, pulling it out, and feeling the tip to see if it's hot.

POMMES ANNA

This potato dish can be flavored with anything from wild mushrooms and garlic to black truffles. Truly perfect to serve at a party, the potatoes can be made a couple of hours in advance, left in their baking pan, and reheated for about 10 minutes in a 350°F oven.

½ pound unsalted butter

3 russet potatoes, peeled and sliced ⅛ inch thick

2 shallots, finely chopped

Kosher salt and freshly ground black pepper

HEAT the oven to 350°F.

SMEAR about 1 tablespoon of the butter onto the bottom and sides of an 8-inch cast-iron skillet or other heavy-based ovenproof pan. Arrange a layer of potatoes neatly on the bottom of the pan. (This becomes the top layer when the dish is inverted.) Start in the middle of the pan and work your way out from there, overlapping the potatoes a bit until you get to the outside edge. Sprinkle some of the shallots on top of the potatoes and dot some of the butter on as well. Sprinkle lightly with salt and pepper. Continue to make layers of potatoes, giving each layer a sprinkle of shallots, dots of butter (use a couple of tablespoons per layer), and seasoning it with salt and pepper until all of the potatoes have been used. The pan should be completely filled with potatoes.

COVER the potatoes with a lid that fits just inside the pan or with aluminum foil. Press down on the lid and cook the potatoes in the oven for about 20 minutes. Carefully remove the lid and continue to cook until the potatoes are very tender when pierced with the tip of a knife. The potatoes should be browned slightly around the edges. Carefully invert the potatoes onto a large plate or cutting board while still hot. Cut into wedges and serve.

POMMES FRITES

Serve these with the rib-eye steak on page 212 for the quintessential bistro meal. Frying the potatoes twice, the first time at a lower temperature, ensures they'll be cooked through and tender on the inside. A thermometer and a Chinese slotted spoon (the wire basket kind) make frying less fearsome.

4 large russet potatoes, skins left on, washed well, any eyes or dark spots cut out

2 quarts vegetable oil for frying

Kosher salt

CUT the potatoes lengthwise into ¼-inch slices. You can use a mandoline for this, or if using a knife, slice a bit off the bottom of the potato to keep it from rolling. Stack the slices, and then cut the slices into ¼-inch-thick sticks.

SOAK the fries in room-temperature water for at least 10 minutes; longer is fine. Drain them and then dry them well. (Drying the potatoes keeps them from splattering when adding them to the hot oil; it also helps keep the oil temperature from dropping too much.)

LINE a cooling rack or baking sheet with paper towels. Pour the vegetable oil into a heavy-based, high-sided pot, being sure that the oil is at least 2½ inches deep and that the pot is less than halfway full to prevent the oil from bubbling over during frying. Heat the oil until it reads 325°F on a frying thermometer (also called a candy thermometer; see Bistro Tools, page 6). Carefully fry the potatoes in batches, being careful of the oil splashing and splattering. Adjust the heat as needed to keep the tem-

perature at 325°F. Fry the potatoes until cooked through but not colored, 4 to 6 minutes. Lift the potatoes out of the oil, using a slotted spoon or a Chinese skimmer, and drain them in a single layer on the paper towel–lined cooling rack. The fries will be light colored and limp, which is fine. Allow them to cool. Reserve the oil in the pot for the second frying. (This blanching can be done 1 to 2 hours in advance with the potatoes left at room temperature. Refrigerate the fries if you intend to keep them longer before the final fry and allow them to come to room temperature before frying.)

TO SERVE THE FRIES

Heat the same oil to 375°F. Fry the potatoes in batches, stirring them gently, until they are golden brown. (For best results, crank up the heat after adding the cold fries, as they will bring the temperature of the oil down.) When they are done, lift the potatoes out of the oil and drain them on paper towels. Season with salt and serve immediately for the best texture or keep in a warm oven.

JAPANESE EGGPLANT *with* CORIANDER, MINT, *and* GINGER

SERVES 4 TO 6

I love Asian food and this dish, paired with simply grilled chicken, salmon, or beef, is an easy way to add some great flavors to your meal. You could even serve the eggplant as a light main dish by heaping it on a bed of rice or tossing it with some soba noodles. Plus it's as good—maybe even better—at room temperature.

4 to 6 tablespoons vegetable oil

4 Japanese eggplants, sliced into ¼-inch rounds

1 medium Vidalia or other sweet onion, thinly sliced

3 garlic cloves, thinly sliced

2 tablespoons finely chopped fresh ginger (from about a 2-inch piece)

½ tablespoon coriander seeds

½ teaspoon Chinese five-spice powder

¼ to ½ teaspoon red pepper flakes

1 teaspoon tomato paste (optional)

¾ cup chicken broth (see Bistro Pantry, page 10)

¼ cup fresh orange juice

2 tablespoons soy sauce

2 tablespoons mirin (sweet rice wine)

2 tablespoons chopped fresh mint

2 tablespoons sesame oil

HEAT 2 tablespoons of the vegetable oil in a large sauté pan over medium-high heat. Working in batches so as not to crowd the pan and adding more oil as necessary, sear the slices of eggplant until well browned on both sides. Drain the eggplant on paper towels and reserve.

ADD the onion to the same pan and cook over medium heat, stirring every few minutes until tender, about 7 minutes. Return the eggplant to the pan and add the garlic, ginger, coriander seeds, five-spice powder, red pepper flakes, and tomato paste, if using. Stir to combine, lower the heat to medium, and cook for about 3 minutes.

ADD the chicken broth, orange juice, soy sauce, and mirin. Bring to a boil and then lower the heat to low. Cover the pan and cook until the eggplant and onion are quite tender and the sauce becomes slightly thickened, about 10 minutes. Add the mint and sesame oil, stir to combine, and serve.

CURRIED CAULIFLOWER
with YOGURT *and* MINT SAUCE

Curry gives plebeian cauliflower a flavorful shot in the arm. As the cauliflower bastes in the butter, it becomes smooth and silky. The cool, minty yogurt sauce acts as a foil to the spiciness of the cauliflower.

½ cup plain yogurt

¼ cup olive oil

2 shallots, 1½ thinly sliced, the rest finely chopped

1 teaspoon whole cumin seeds

1½ tablespoons curry powder

Pinch of red pepper flakes

2 bay leaves

3 tablespoons unsalted butter

1 head of cauliflower, leaves trimmed, tough core removed, florets cut into small pieces

1 teaspoon kosher salt

½ teaspoon freshly ground black pepper

2 to 3 tablespoons chopped fresh mint

1 scallion, roots trimmed and cut into very thin rounds

PUT the yogurt into a fine-mesh strainer and let it drain for at least 20 minutes. Heat the oven to 400°F. Heat the olive oil in a large sauté pan over medium-high heat. Add the sliced shallots and let them cook until browned in spots. Lower the heat to medium, add the cumin seeds, and fry until fragrant, about 15 seconds. Add the curry powder, red pepper flakes, and bay leaves, and let everything sizzle for a few seconds. Add the butter, and when it has melted, add the cauliflower, salt, and pepper. Toss the cauliflower well to coat it evenly with the butter and spices and cook, stirring occasionally, for about 5 minutes. Put the pan in the oven and cook the cauliflower, stirring occasionally, until the cauliflower is tender, about 10 minutes.

MEANWHILE, combine the yogurt with the remaining chopped shallots and the chopped mint. Stir to combine and season with salt and pepper to taste.

SPRINKLE the cauliflower with the scallion and serve with the yogurt sauce on the side.

GARLICKY CHERRY TOMATO CONFIT *with* TOASTED PINE NUTS

Few can resist buying pints and pints of cherry tomatoes from the farm stand. But what to do with them all? In this recipe, they get baked in olive oil until their juices become concentrated and even more flavorful. The addition of pine nuts makes this dish very rich, so a little goes a long way; serve the tomatoes as a relish with grilled lamb or fish.

2 tablespoons olive oil

½ small onion, thinly sliced

4 garlic cloves, finely chopped

1 pint cherry tomatoes

2 tablespoons red wine vinegar

½ teaspoon kosher salt

Pinch of red pepper flakes

Pinch of sugar

2 tablespoons toasted pine nuts (see page 4), chopped and sprinkled with a little salt

2 fresh basil leaves, washed, dried, and cut into a fine chiffonade (see page 4)

HEAT the oven to 350°F. Heat the olive oil in a saucepan over medium heat. Add the onion and cook, stirring occasionally, until tender, about 7 minutes. Add the garlic and tomatoes and cook another 3 to 4 minutes. Add the vinegar, salt, red pepper flakes, and sugar. Transfer the mixture to a small baking dish. Cook the tomatoes in the oven until very tender but mostly intact, about 12 minutes.

RAISE the oven temperature to 425°F. Add the pine nuts and continue to bake until the juices from the tomatoes have been released into the dish and have reduced, 8 to 10 more minutes. (How long to cook the tomatoes depends on your preference; you can serve them while they are still quite red and intact, using a slotted spoon, or continue to bake them until they are quite browned with very little juice left in the dish, but do not let them burn.) Sprinkle with additional salt and the basil and serve hot or at room temperature.

BROILED TOMATOES *with* CRISPY BREAD CRUMBS

SERVES 4

Nothing could be easier to make than these tomatoes, yet they are always a favorite. The tomatoes should be ripe, but not too ripe or they might burst during baking. Try them with the rib-eye steak on page 212, or do as the English do and offer them with roast beef.

5 tablespoons olive oil

4 large ripe tomatoes, stemmed and sliced in half horizontally

Kosher salt and freshly ground black pepper

4 to 6 tablespoons seasoned bread crumbs (see Bistro Pantry, page 7)

HEAT the oven to 425°F. Heat 2 tablespoons of the olive oil in an ovenproof pan large enough to hold the tomatoes easily without touching over medium-high heat. Season the tomatoes with salt and pepper and sear them on the cut side until well browned. Turn the tomatoes over and sprinkle the bread crumbs onto the seared side of the tomato halves. Drizzle with the remaining olive oil and cook the tomatoes in the oven until they are tender and the bread crumbs are crispy, 8 to 10 minutes. (If necessary, broil the tomatoes for an additional 1 to 2 minutes to brown the bread crumbs.)

BRUSSELS SPROUTS *with* HAZELNUTS *and* MINT

SERVES 4

Here are Brussels sprouts for people who think they don't like Brussels sprouts. The richness of the hazelnuts, the fresh flavor of the mint, and the sweet-and-sour note from the balsamic vinegar make this an easy dish to love.

2 pints Brussels sprouts, trimmed

3 tablespoons unsalted butter

6 tablespoons chopped, toasted hazelnuts (see page 4)

2 tablespoons roughly chopped fresh mint

1 teaspoon balsamic vinegar

Kosher salt and freshly ground black pepper

BRING a large pot of salted water to a boil. With a paring knife, cut an X in the bottom of each Brussels sprout for quicker, more even cooking. Boil the sprouts until tender when pierced with a paring knife, 6 to 10 minutes, then drain.

HEAT 2 tablespoons of the butter in a large sauté pan over medium heat. Add the sprouts and cook until they begin to brown, about 8 minutes. Add the nuts and the remaining tablespoon of butter. Cook for an additional 3 to 4 minutes. Remove from the heat and add the mint and vinegar and toss to combine. Season with salt and pepper to taste and serve.

BRAISED FENNEL

Fennel is a vegetable that I serve when I throw a dinner party. The flavor—with its hint of licorice—is somewhat unexpected, but it always complements when served with fish and chicken.

2 fennel bulbs

1 tablespoon olive oil

2 tablespoons unsalted butter

½ small onion, thinly sliced

Kosher salt and freshly ground black pepper

¼ teaspoon fennel seeds

Pinch of red pepper flakes

Pinch of herbes de Provence (see Bistro Pantry, page 9)

½ cup dry white wine

1 tablespoon anisette or Pernod (optional)

¾ cup chicken broth (see Bistro Pantry, page 10)

HEAT the oven to 325°F. Remove a few of the feathery fronds from the fennel and reserve. Trim the stalks off the fennel bulbs and remove any tough outer layers. Cut the fennel into quarters lengthwise.

HEAT the olive oil and 1 tablespoon of the butter in a large ovenproof sauté pan over medium-high heat. Add the fennel and onion. Season with salt and pepper and brown the fennel on all sides, about 8 minutes. Add the fennel seeds, red pepper flakes, and herbes de Provence, and cook for about 1 more minute. Add the white wine, the anisette or Pernod, if using, and the chicken broth. Bring to a boil. Cook the fennel in the oven until tender when pierced with the tip of a small knife, about 45 minutes. Lift the fennel out of the pan with tongs and arrange it on a platter. Chop the fennel fronds and add them to the pan. Cook the liquid over medium-high heat until reduced by half. Add the remaining tablespoon of butter and whisk until combined. Taste and season with additional salt and pepper if needed. Spoon the onion and juices over the fennel and serve.

LEMONY BRAISED ENDIVE

This is just delicious with the Bacon-Wrapped Scallops on page 154, especially if you pour some of the juices from the scallop pan over the endive.

1 tablespoon salt, plus more to taste

1 tablespoon sugar

Juice of 1 lemon

4 heads of Belgian endive

1 to 2 tablespoons unsalted butter

Freshly ground black pepper

1 tablespoon chopped fresh parsley

IN a medium pot, combine 7 cups water with the salt, sugar, and lemon and bring to a boil.

MEANWHILE, trim the endive of any bruised leaves. Using a paring knife, score the base of each head with an X. Place the endive in the water. Place a small plate or pot cover on top of the endive to keep it submerged as it cooks. Reduce the heat to a robust simmer and cook until the endive is tender when pierced with the tip of a paring knife, about 10 minutes. Use tongs to remove the hot plate or pot cover and then remove the endive from the water and let it drain.

HEAT the butter in a large sauté pan over medium-high heat until hot. Add the endive, sprinkle with a little salt and pepper, and brown the endive on both sides, about 7 minutes. Sprinkle with parsley and serve.

ORZO-STUFFED RED PEPPERS *with* FETA, OLIVES, *and* OREGANO

SERVES 4

I became a fan of stuffed peppers only recently. The ones I remember from my prep-school cafeteria were limp and filled with overcooked rice and unflavored ground beef. This meat-free version helps erase that awful food memory: The tiny rice-shaped pasta called orzo, cooked al dente, takes the place of rice; peppers, cooked uncovered, get a delicious roasted flavor, and feta and lemon give the filling brightness and zing.

These stuffed peppers are substantial enough to eat on their own as a light lunch or dinner, but I love how their Greek-inspired flavors pair with lamb, such as the grilled leg of lamb on page 225. If the whole peppers are too large to serve as a side dish, you can cut them in half lengthwise (after cooking) to make 8 smaller portions.

¾ cup raw orzo

4 tablespoons olive oil

1 medium red onion, chopped

2½ ounces kale, washed and dried well, and torn into 1- to 2-inch pieces (about 2 cups)

Kosher salt and freshly ground black pepper

4 ounces feta cheese

1 teaspoon chopped fresh oregano or ½ teaspoon dried oregano

1½ teaspoons chopped fresh thyme

1 tablespoon chopped fresh parsley

8 Kalamata olives, pitted and chopped

Grated zest of ½ lemon

1 to 2 tablespoons fresh lemon juice (from ½ lemon)

4 medium red bell peppers, preferably the good-looking Holland peppers, which stand up best

1½ cups dry white wine or water

HEAT the oven to 350°F.

BRING a medium pot of salted water to a boil. Cook the orzo until al dente. Drain and cool. You should have about 1⅔ cups cooked orzo.

HEAT 2 tablespoons of the olive oil in a large sauté pan over medium-high heat. Add the onion and cook, stirring occasionally, until tender, about 5 minutes. Add the kale and cook, stirring, until wilted and tender, another 5 to 7 minutes. Season with a little salt and pepper and reserve.

IN a bowl, combine the onion and kale with the cooked orzo, feta cheese, oregano, thyme, parsley, olives, lemon zest, and 1 tablespoon of the lemon juice. Toss gently until combined and season with salt and pepper.

SLICE off the top ½ inch of each pepper and reserve. With a paring knife, cut away the white ribs inside the pepper. Turn the pepper over and tap out the seeds. Taste the orzo filling and add any additional lemon juice, salt, and pepper to taste. Divide the filling among the peppers and then replace the top of each pepper.

STAND the peppers in a medium baking dish and sprinkle them with the remaining 2 tablespoons olive oil and additional salt and pepper. Pour the white wine into the pan and cook the peppers in the oven until the peppers are very tender and slightly blackened on top, about 1½ hours.

Desserts

BISTRO DESSERTS
are generally comforting and understated,
but they also have a certain air of
sophistication about them. Because they
can follow a very hearty meal, they tend
to be small in size but are always intensely
flavored. Quite often they feature the fruit
of the season simply presented or the
straightforward flavor of chocolate.

ONE OF MY FAVORITE desserts is a simple fruit tart with a spoon of crème fraîche. Custards are also a wonderful way to end a meal, and the ways to flavor them are as varied as your imagination. For example, I love maple crème brûlée because it tastes like New England to me. Peg Carmen is the best bistro dessert cook I know. She worked at the restaurant for years and she crafted desserts with an understated, home-style elegance. Her ideas and mine seemed to come together in an easy and perfectly natural way, and her offerings complemented the season without making the menu sound like a fruit stand advertisement. Many of the desserts in this chapter were adapted and tested by Peg.

As you read through the recipes, you will notice that many of them suggest that you add a sauce, or a topping, or a cookie to serve with them. At the restaurant, our desserts comprise at least two components and often more. If you have some time (or have planned ahead and frozen some cookies), a multitiered approach to dessert is a great treat. But it's not essential. Know that such offerings as the Peach Galette (page 283) or the Caramel-Chocolate Pots de Crème (page 304) can really hold their own without their respective adornments—a Blueberry-Caramel Sauce (page 284) and Brown Sugar–Pecan Shortbread (page 306)—and that those adornments in turn can be used in other recipes or, in the case of the shortbread, enjoyed on its own.

Unlike savory cooking, baking requires a slightly more exacting approach. Use large eggs (not extra large or jumbo), especially for the custards; heavy cream (not light cream or half-and-half if you want it to whip or set up right); and spoon the flour into the measuring cup, and then level with a knife (don't pack the flour in). Both Peg and I like to use kosher salt in our desserts. If you substitute table salt, keep in mind that you will actually be adding more salt per measure, since table salt has finer crystals.

Many of these recipes call for separating egg whites from yolks. The best way to do this is with three bowls. Separate an egg white into one bowl, either by passing the yolk back and forth between the two shell halves or by letting the white run through your fingers. Put the yolk into another bowl (this can be the one in which they are to be mixed). Before cracking the next egg, put the separated white into the third bowl (this can be the bowl in which the whites are eventually to be whisked). Now when you separate the next egg, if some yolk falls into the second egg white you won't have ruined the first separated white as well.

CONSIDER A CHEESE COURSE. In France, a cheese course is often served before dessert or even in lieu of dessert, a practice becoming more common at restaurants here and with people entertaining at home. At our restaurant, we have always offered a cheese course comprising three or four cheeses, with a wide variance of tastes and textures on the plate. (More than that number and I find that I have trouble distinguishing one from another.)

At home, we pass around a large piece of black slate on which sit three or four cheeses of different flavors and textures that have been allowed to come to room temperature to bring out their full flavor. We almost always feature a nice fresh, soft goat cheese as well as a hard cheese, such as an English Cheddar, and always a big, bold, blue cheese, either from France or made in the States. We also pass around slices of good bread (never crackers, which I find interfere with the texture of the cheese). Served with some good crusty bread, a few salted walnuts, and maybe—but not always—sliced apple or pear, a cheese course is a perfect way to accompany the last of the wine in your glass. For a more formal approach, you can put small servings of three or four cheeses on individual plates and present them that way. Cheese is becoming a fun part of the meal in America, as it has been for years in Europe, and that is a good thing. Not only is it easier than ever to get good European cheese, but there are also more artisanal-style cheeses being made here. I buy mine from a wonderful store in Cambridge, Massachusetts, called Formaggio Kitchen, which also offers mail-order (see Sources).

SOUFFLÉED LEMON CUSTARD

SERVES 6 TO 8

When we were opening the restaurant in 1987, we wanted to feature a dessert that would be a refreshing way to end a meal. Jody Adams, my sous-chef at the time, suggested resurrecting an old Craig Claiborne recipe.

Not quite a soufflé and not quite a custard, the recipe is foolproof as long as the ingredients are not overmixed at the end. After baking in a water bath, the top puffs up and becomes gorgeously browned while the interior sets into soft, creamy custard. If you like your lemon desserts really lemony, you can add a couple more tablespoons of lemon juice. We serve the souffléed custard with a crisp cookie, such as the Lemon Lavender Sugar Cookie (recipe follows), and some fresh berries.

8 tablespoons unsalted butter, softened at room temperature

1½ cups sugar

6 large eggs, separated

1 cup fresh lemon juice (from about 8 lemons)

Pinch of kosher salt

⅔ cup sifted all-purpose flour

1 teaspoon grated lemon zest

2 cups whole milk

1 cup heavy cream

HEAT the oven to 350°F. In a stand mixer using the paddle attachment, cream the butter and 1 cup of the sugar at high speed until fluffy, about 5 minutes. Turn the mixer down to medium speed and add the egg yolks one at a time, beating after each addition. Add the lemon juice, salt, flour, and lemon zest all at once, and mix by hand until just barely combined. Stir in the milk and cream and mix by hand again. The mixture will look lumpy at this stage but don't worry.

IN a stand mixer using the whisk attachment, begin beating the egg whites on low speed. Gradually add the remaining ½ cup sugar and increase the speed to high. Continue beating the whites until they hold medium peaks. (Overbeating the whites will dry them out.) Using a large rubber spatula, gently fold a third of the egg whites into the custard mixture. Gently fold in the remaining whites until just barely combined. Some of the whites may still be floating on the top, which is just fine; overmixing will prevent the whites from puffing up nicely.

POUR the mixture into a 10-inch cake pan (or equivalent dish) that's at least 2 inches high.

BAKE THE CUSTARD IN A WATER BATH

Put the cake pan in a high-sided baking dish or in a roasting pan and fill the pan with warm water about one-third of the way up the sides of the cake pan. Bake until the custard is just barely set and the top is well browned, 40 to 50 minutes. Allow to cool to room temperature. Using a large spoon or spatula, scoop out the souffléed custard, making sure each serving gets some of the puffed-up top and some of the creamy custard.

LEMON-LAVENDER SUGAR COOKIE

Lavender buds are available from health food stores and some supermarkets. (Lavender for potpourri will not work!) If you can't buy (or grow) any, you can certainly order some by mail (see Sources). If you have to omit the lavender, you'll still get a good, lemony cookie.

12 tablespoons unsalted butter, softened at room temperature

¾ cup sugar

1 tablespoon grated lemon zest

1 tablespoon dried lavender buds (see Sources)

1 large egg

2 teaspoons vanilla extract

¼ teaspoon kosher salt

2¼ cups all-purpose flour

IN a stand mixer with the paddle attachment, cream the butter and sugar until the mixture looks light and fluffy. Add the lemon zest and lavender and mix briefly to combine. Add the egg, vanilla, and salt, and mix briefly to combine. Gradually add the flour, mixing on low speed until thoroughly combined. Gather the dough into a disk, wrap it in plastic wrap, and refrigerate it for at least an hour before rolling.

HEAT the oven to 325°F. On a floured surface, roll the dough out to a thickness of about ¼ inch. Cut out shapes with a biscuit or cookie cutter. (The scraps can be rerolled and cut once before the cookie becomes tough.) Bake the cookies until they begin to brown around the edges, 10 to 15 minutes. Cool on a wire rack before serving or storing.

PEACH GALETTE *with* BLUEBERRY-CARAMEL SAUCE

SERVES 6 TO 8

I love how the cornmeal gives this tart dough a rustic "bite." It can make the tart a little trickier to roll out; but just patch any tears with a piece of dough—no one will be able to tell! This is delicious served plain, with a scoop of vanilla ice cream, or with Blueberry-Caramel Sauce (recipe follows).

FOR THE GALETTE DOUGH

1¼ cups all-purpose flour

¼ cup yellow cornmeal

½ teaspoon kosher salt

3 tablespoons sugar

10 tablespoons unsalted butter, cut into small pieces and well chilled

4 to 5 tablespoons ice water

1 large egg yolk beaten with 1 teaspoon water (for brushing the tart)

FOR THE FILLING

5 or 6 peaches, peeled and sliced (about 5 cups)

1 tablespoon fresh lemon juice

¼ cup sugar

1 tablespoon all-purpose flour

¼ teaspoon ground ginger

½ teaspoon vanilla extract

Pinch of kosher salt

TO MAKE THE GALETTE DOUGH

In a stand mixer using the paddle attachment, combine the flour, cornmeal, salt, and 1 tablespoon sugar. Add the cold butter all at once. Mix on low speed until the mixture begins to resemble coarse cornmeal with some larger chunks. Using a fork or your fingertips, add the ice water 1 tablespoon at a time, tossing it with the dough. After the fourth tablespoon has been added, squeeze a small amount of dough in your hand. If the mixture does not stay together and looks dry, add another tablespoon of water. If necessary, add even more water, drop by drop, until the dough just holds together. Dump the dough onto a piece of plastic wrap and gather it up to form a flat, round disk. Wrap it well in the plastic wrap and refrigerate it for at least an hour.

TO MAKE THE FILLING

Combine all of the filling ingredients in a large bowl and toss gently to combine.

TO ASSEMBLE AND BAKE THE GALETTE

Heat the oven to 400°F. Line a baking sheet with parchment paper. On a floured surface, roll out the dough into a 14- to 15-inch circle; trim any rough edges, if necessary, to maintain a round shape. Transfer the dough to the baking sheet, allowing any excess to hang over the sides. Pour the filling onto the dough, leaving a 2-inch edge of dough with

(continued)

no filling on it. Fold the dough over the fruit toward the center, pleating and overlapping as necessary. Brush the edges of the dough with the egg wash and sprinkle the galette with the 2 tablespoons sugar.

BAKE until the crust is golden brown and the filling is bubbling, 45 to 50 minutes. Remove from the oven and let cool a little before cutting.

BLUEBERRY-CARAMEL SAUCE

MAKES ABOUT 2½ CUPS

This sauce is also fabulous spooned over vanilla (or peach) ice cream.

3 cups sugar

2 cups blueberries, washed and picked over

¼ cup fresh lime juice

IN a medium saucepan over medium-high heat, cook the sugar to a light amber color. (Check the color by drizzling some onto a white plate.) Don't worry if the sugar hardens while cooking; simply stir it and continue cooking until it smooths out.

ADD the blueberries and ½ cup water to the caramel; be careful, as the caramel will bubble and steam a great deal. Stir the blueberries into the caramel as well as possible (the sauce will harden when the cold blueberries are added, but will loosen up again as the blueberries heat up). Cover the pan and reduce the heat to low. Allow the sauce to simmer with the lid on until most of the blueberries have popped and are exuding their juices, about 5 minutes. Remove the lid and stir the sauce to further dissolve any hardened bits of caramel. (Don't worry if there are some lumps; they will be strained out.)

STRAIN the sauce to remove any blueberry skins, seeds, and hard pieces of caramel. Add the lime juice and return to a saucepan. Cook further over medium heat until the sauce can be spooned onto a room-temperature plate and keep its shape without being too runny. Serve at room temperature.

> **Note:** To make a rhubarb-raspberry galette, combine the following filling ingredients and use them in place of the peaches: 4 cups chopped rhubarb (about a ½-inch dice), 1 cup raspberries, 1 cup sugar, 2 tablespoons all-purpose flour, and a pinch of kosher salt. Try the galette with the caramel sauce on page 314, made with a couple of tablespoons of rum or brandy added to it at the end of cooking.

APPLE TARTE TATIN

SERVES 6 TO 8

When I make this classic upside-down French tart, I want to be sure that it's rich with deep brown caramel. That's why I brown the sugar first, before the apples even go into the pan. (I also don't turn the apples as you often see directed for this dessert.) I generally use a cast-iron pan to make this dish, but you can find specialized tarte Tatin pans. Serve with whipped cream, Sweetened Crème Fraîche (recipe follows), or vanilla ice cream.

1 recipe Hamersley's Bistro Tart Dough (page 115)

5 to 6 Granny Smith apples, peeled, cored, and quartered

1 teaspoon cinnamon

1 cup sugar

4 tablespoons unsalted butter, cut into small pieces

1 large egg, beaten

ON a lightly floured surface, roll the rested dough into a 12- to 13-inch circle. Trim rough edges, if necessary, to maintain a round shape. Transfer the dough to a sheet pan, cover with plastic wrap, and refrigerate.

HEAT the oven to 400°F.

TOSS the apples with the cinnamon and ¼ cup of the sugar.

IN a 10-inch cast-iron pan or other heavy-based, ovenproof skillet, heat the remaining ¾ cup sugar over medium-high heat, stirring to remove lumps, until the sugar has turned a dark amber. (Check for color by drizzling some onto a white plate.) Add the butter and stir it into the caramel until melted and homogenous; be careful, as the butter will make the caramel sputter.

REMOVE the pan from the heat. Beginning on the outside of the pan, carefully set the apple quarters in the caramel, arranging them in a circle so that they all face the same way. Set them very close to one another, trying to get as many as possible into the pan. Fill in the center of the pan with as many of the remaining apples as will fit. Put the pan back on the heat and allow the apples to cook on top of the stove for about 5 minutes. Remove the pan from the heat. Place the cold pie dough over the apples, tucking the edges into the sides of the pan. Work carefully so as not to burn your fingers, but also quickly so as not to melt the dough. Brush the dough with the beaten egg and immediately put the pan in the oven.

BAKE for 15 minutes. Lower the temperature to 375°F and bake until the crust is nicely browned and the caramel is bubbling around the edges of the pan, another 15 minutes. Carefully remove the tart from the oven and cool it on a rack for about 20 minutes. Invert the tart onto a serving platter. If any apples stick to the underside of the pan, simply return them to their rightful spot on the tart. Tarte Tatin is best served right away, but it can stand at room temperature and be reheated briefly in the oven, if that suits your schedule better.

SWEETENED CRÈME FRAÎCHE

MAKES ABOUT 1¼ CUPS

1 cup crème fraîche, purchased or homemade (see Bistro Pantry, page 7)

2 to 4 tablespoons heavy cream

2 to 4 tablespoons sugar

1 teaspoon vanilla extract

WHIP the ingredients together in a stand mixer, using the whisk attachment, until the mixture lightens and holds soft peaks. Taste and add additional sugar or cream.

CHOCOLATE MOUSSE CAKE

This recipe makes enough of the chocolate cake base for two cakes. Freeze the second cake base, well wrapped in plastic wrap, for the next time you want to make this dessert. For extra punch, serve the cake with some Coffee Crème Anglaise (page 290).

FOR THE CHOCOLATE CAKE BASE

3 ounces unsweetened chocolate, chopped

8 tablespoons unsalted butter, cut into small pieces

¾ cup hot black coffee

1 cup sugar

1 cup all-purpose flour

½ teaspoon baking soda

Pinch of kosher salt

1 large egg

1 teaspoon vanilla extract

FOR THE CHOCOLATE MOUSSE

9 ounces bittersweet chocolate, chopped

6 tablespoons unsalted butter, cut into small pieces

1 cup heavy cream

4 large eggs, separated (see Note)

½ teaspoon vanilla extract

2 tablespoons sugar

TO MAKE THE CHOCOLATE CAKE BASE

Heat the oven to 350°F.

LINE a 13 × 18-inch rimmed baking sheet with parchment paper. Put the chocolate and butter in a medium bowl, pour the hot coffee over both, wait about 5 minutes until they melt, and then whisk to combine. When thoroughly melted and combined, add the sugar and whisk until dissolved, just a minute or two. Sift the dry ingredients over the bowl of chocolate and whisk to combine. Add the egg and vanilla and continue to whisk until the batter is smooth. Pour the batter onto the prepared sheet pan and spread it as evenly as possible; it will be a very thin layer. Be sure to get it into the corners. Bake until the cake springs back in its center when touched, 10 to 12 minutes. Remove the cake from the oven and let it cool to room temperature.

WHEN cool, cut out two cake circles the size of the springform pan you are using—an 8½-inch or a 9-inch pan works best—using the bottom of the pan as a template. Line the springform pan with one of the cake circles. (Wrap the other circle well in plastic wrap and save for another use.)

TO MAKE THE CHOCOLATE MOUSSE

Set a medium heatproof glass or stainless steel bowl over a pot of simmering water. Add the chocolate and butter and mix, stirring frequently, until melted. Remove the pot from the heat.

WITH a wire whisk or in a stand mixer with the whisk attachment, beat the cream to medium peaks (the cream holds its shape when the whisk is lifted). Refrigerate the whipped cream while preparing the rest of the mousse.

WHISK the egg yolks and the vanilla into the chocolate-butter mixture and set aside.

WITH a wire whisk or the whisk attachment of a stand mixer, beat the egg whites until foamy. Gradually add the sugar and continue to beat the whites to medium peaks (the whites hold their shape when the whisk is lifted). Using a large rubber spatula, gently fold the whites into the chocolate in thirds, being careful not to deflate the volume of the egg whites. Add the next third just before the mixture is homogenous (when there are still some streaks of whites remaining, go ahead and add another third of whites).

WHEN the whites are almost thoroughly mixed in, begin folding in the cream in two stages: Add half of the cream, fold, and then add the rest, carefully folding it until thoroughly mixed.

POUR the mousse into the cake-lined springform pan and smooth the top. Refrigerate at least 6 hours. Before unmolding, carefully run a spatula or thin knife around the cake on the inside of the pan. Remove the sides of the pan, slice, and serve.

Note: Although it's estimated that only 1 in 20,000 eggs from chickens bred in the United States contains salmonella, certain people—the elderly, small children, and anyone with a compromised immune system—should probably avoid eating any raw eggs. In such cases, a pasteurized egg product would be more suitable.

CRÈME ANGLAISE

Crème anglaise is my favorite dessert sauce. I think it adds to the clout of any dessert. Try a little with the Chocolate Mousse Cake on page 288, the Apple Tarte Tatin on page 286, the Summer Berry Pudding (page 294), or poured over a bowl of perfectly ripe berries. I make this classic custard sauce in all different flavors to suit the dessert it's accompanying. Some examples follow, but you might want to experiment with your own variations.

1 cup heavy cream

1 cup whole milk

1 vanilla bean or 1 teaspoon vanilla extract

½ cup sugar

6 large egg yolks

COMBINE the cream and milk in a medium saucepan. Split the vanilla bean lengthwise, if using. With a paring knife, scrape the inside of the vanilla bean into the saucepan and add the pod halves. (If using vanilla extract, add it later.) Scald the milk and cream by bringing it to a brief boil.

IN a medium bowl, whisk the sugar and egg yolks together. Slowly whisk about ¼ cup of the hot cream mixture into the eggs, wait a minute for the eggs to temper, and then whisk in the remaining cream mixture. Pour this mixture into a clean saucepan and reduce the heat to low. Cook gently, stirring constantly with a wooden spoon, until the sauce thickens. It should coat the back of the spoon, and when you draw a line through

the sauce on the spoon, it should hold that line. If using vanilla extract instead of a vanilla bean, add it now. Strain the sauce into a bowl and put the bowl into another larger bowl filled with ice. Stir the sauce every few minutes until cool.

FOR COFFEE CRÈME ANGLAISE
Follow the recipe for Crème Anglaise, adding 2 tablespoons espresso to the sugar–egg yolk mixture before adding the cream mixture.

FOR GINGER CRÈME ANGLAISE
Follow the recipe for Crème Anglaise, adding 1 to 2 teaspoons grated fresh ginger to the cream-milk mixture when scalding.

RICE PUDDING CAKE *with* APRICOT SAUCE *and* CANDIED PISTACHIOS

SERVES 8 TO 10

This not-too-sweet dessert will please both rice pudding fans and those who find it too porridgelike for their taste.

4½ cups whole milk

Grated zest of 1 lemon

1 vanilla bean or 2 teaspoons vanilla extract

1 cup Arborio rice

Pinch of kosher salt

¾ cup sugar

¼ cup graham cracker crumbs

4 large whole eggs

2 large egg yolks

Confectioners' sugar for dusting

Apricot-Sauternes Sauce (recipe follows)

Candied Pistachios (recipe follows)

COMBINE the milk and lemon zest in a large saucepan. If using a vanilla bean, cut it in half lengthwise, scrape out the seeds, and add it, as well as the pod halves, to the milk. (If using vanilla extract, you'll add it later.) Bring the milk to a boil, strain the milk, and return it to medium heat.

SLOWLY whisk the rice into the milk and add the salt. Stir until the rice mixture comes back to a simmer. Reduce the heat to low and cook, whisking every few minutes to ensure that the rice grains remain separate, until most of the milk is absorbed into the rice and the rice is tender, 30 to 40 minutes.

STIR in the sugar and the vanilla extract, if you didn't use a vanilla bean, and cook for about 2 minutes until the sugar has dissolved. Remove the rice from the heat, and let it cool to a warm room temperature.

HEAT the oven to 300°F.

WHILE the rice cools, butter the bottom and sides

of a 9-inch round cake pan. Cut a circle out of parchment paper to fit the bottom of the pan and fit it into place. Dust the sides of the pan with the graham cracker crumbs and then shake out the excess crumbs.

IN a separate bowl, whisk together the whole eggs and egg yolks. Stir the eggs into the rice until well combined.

POUR the rice mixture into the cake pan. Bake until the center of the cake is set and feels somewhat firm to the touch, 45 to 50 minutes. Don't let the cake overcook or it will puff up and its texture will be ruined. Don't worry about the "skin" that forms; this will be the bottom of the cake.

COOL the cake to room temperature and then run a small knife around the cake to loosen it from the pan. Invert the cake onto a serving plate. Remove the parchment, if necessary, and dust with some confectioners' sugar. Serve with the apricot sauce and the pistachios.

APRICOT-SAUTERNES SAUCE

This sweet yet sophisticated sauce could also jazz up pound cake or bread pudding. If you don't have Sauternes, a sweet Riesling or a Muscat Beaumes-de-Venise would also work well.

¾ cup chopped, dried apricots, cut into a medium or small dice (each apricot should be in 6 to 8 pieces)

⅓ cup sugar

1 tablespoon fresh lemon juice

¼ cup Sauternes

BRING about 2½ cups water to a boil. Put the chopped apricots in a bowl and cover with the boiling water. Let cool to room temperature. As they reconstitute, the apricots will become plump.

IN a small saucepan, combine the sugar with ⅓ cup water and bring to a boil to dissolve the sugar. Drain the plumped apricots and add them and the lemon juice to the pan. Reduce the heat to low. Simmer for about 5 minutes, stirring every few minutes, until the sauce becomes somewhat flavorful and somewhat syrupy.

REMOVE from the heat and stir in the Sauternes. Cool to room temperature.

CANDIED PISTACHIOS

Turbinado sugar, which is slightly less refined than granulated, makes the pistachios feel less overtly sugary; regular granulated sugar will work, but with slightly different results.

1 cup shelled pistachios

2 tablespoons simple syrup (see Note)

2 tablespoons sugar, preferably turbinado

½ teaspoon kosher salt

HEAT the oven to 350°F. Line a baking sheet with parchment paper or a Silpat baking mat.

IN a medium bowl, toss the pistachios with the simple syrup, making sure to coat the nuts evenly. Combine the sugar and salt. Working quickly, add the sugar and salt to the coated pistachios and toss to coat (just a few seconds). Immediately transfer the nuts to the lined baking sheet and bake for 10 minutes. Remove and cool completely before using. When the nuts are completely cool they should be crisp and not at all sticky. If necessary, put them back into a hot oven for another 2 minutes to crisp them. Store the cooled nuts in a tightly sealed container to retain crispness.

> **Note:** To make simple syrup, combine equal amounts of sugar and water in a small saucepan. (For this recipe, ½ cup sugar and ½ cup water will be ample, but you might as well make more, say 1 cup of each, since simple syrup keeps well and is great for sweetening iced tea and lemonade as well as cocktails like margaritas; since the sugar is already dissolved, it won't leave grains behind in the glass.)
>
> Bring the sugar and water to a boil, stirring to dissolve the sugar, then lower to a simmer for a few minutes. Remove from the heat, cool, and strain. Cover and refrigerate. For an easy berry sauce, add a few drops of syrup to fresh or frozen berries with a little lemon juice; purée and strain. Or simply toss a few drops of syrup with fresh berries to give them a shine.

SUMMER BERRY PUDDING

SERVES 6

Many summers ago Fiona suggested we make this English dessert for a dinner party. It was a huge hit, and ever since then we've been offering it at the restaurant, but only in the months when our local berries are at their peak. Summer pudding is classically made with firm, white bread, but I like the extra richness brioche brings to it. Challah would also work nicely, while pound cake, which may be more available than either challah or brioche, would make this dessert richer and sweeter still.

1 loaf of brioche

8 cups assorted berries (I use equal parts raspberries, blueberries, and quartered strawberries; substitute berries that are ripe and in season)

¾ cup sugar

2 teaspoons grated lemon zest

2 tablespoons fresh lemon juice

Sweetened whipped cream or crème fraîche (see Bistro Pantry, page 7) for serving

LINE a 1½-quart soufflé dish with plastic wrap, making sure that there is excess wrap hanging over the sides.

TRIM the crust off the brioche and slice the bread into ¼-inch slices. (You can slice it the long way, end to end, to get larger slices.)

COMBINE the berries, sugar, lemon zest, and lemon juice in a medium saucepan. Cook over medium heat until the berries exude juices, about 5 minutes. Reserve 1 cup of the berries and about ½ cup of their juice for the sauce.

LINE the bottom of the soufflé dish with the sliced brioche, cutting and piecing the bread together to

form a single layer. Ladle or spoon half of the berries and juice evenly on top of the brioche. Place another layer of brioche, once again piecing the bread together where necessary, on top of the berries. Ladle all of the remaining berries and juice—except for what you reserved for the sauce—evenly on top of the brioche. Fit the final layer of brioche on top of the berries. (You should have three layers of brioche and two layers of berries.)

COVER the pudding with the excess plastic wrap. Put a plate large enough to just cover the surface of the pudding on top and set a 1- to 2-pound weight (I use a pound of butter, but a can of tomatoes would work, too) on top of the plate. Put the weighted mold in a shallow bowl or on a rimmed sheet pan to catch any overflowing juice. Refrigerate for at least 8 hours.

TO make the sauce, purée the reserved berries and juice in a blender or a food processor. Strain through a fine-mesh strainer to remove any seeds.

TO SERVE

Remove the weight and plate from the top of the pudding and peel back the plastic wrap. Invert the mold onto a serving plate with sides to catch any juice. Remove the plastic wrap completely. Let the pudding stand for about an hour before slicing. Using a serrated knife, cut the pudding into slices. Serve with the puréed sauce and sweetened whipped cream or crème fraîche.

PROFITEROLES

Yes, they are incredibly old-fashioned in a 1960s sort of way, but profiteroles are the perfect ending to a bistro-style meal. Make them way in advance (they freeze very well) and fill them with your favorite ice cream. Top with Easy Chocolate Sauce (page 298) or a fruit sauce made from puréeing ripe berries with a little sugar and lemon juice.

8 tablespoons unsalted butter, cut into pieces

½ cup milk

½ teaspoon kosher salt

1 tablespoon sugar

1 cup all-purpose flour

2 large whole eggs

3 large egg whites

Ice cream or filling of your choice

Easy Chocolate Sauce (page 298)

Confectioners' sugar

Mint leaves (optional)

HEAT the oven to 350°F.

IN a saucepan, combine the butter, milk, and ¼ cup water, and bring to a boil. Add the salt, sugar, and flour all at once. Remove the pan from the heat and beat the mixture vigorously with a wooden spoon or a firm, heatproof spatula. The dough will become smooth and will pull away from the sides of the pan. Put the pan back on medium heat, beating it vigorously again, until the mixture looks a little drier and more matte, about 30 seconds.

TURN off the heat and beat the dough for another minute or two to release the steam. Transfer the mixture to a bowl to halt its cooking. Add one of the whole eggs and beat to combine. As you add the egg, the mixture will look loose with pieces floating in it. But as you continue to beat the mixture, it will come together again and look smooth. Add the egg whites and beat the dough once again until it is smooth and shiny. (This can be done in a mixer using the paddle attachment.)

LIGHTLY grease two baking sheets. Using a pastry bag with a tip measuring about ⅜ inch across, pipe the dough into rounds onto the sheets, leaving about an inch between each one. Beat the remaining egg and brush each profiterole lightly with it, being careful not to let it drip onto the baking sheet, which will inhibit the profiteroles' ability to rise.

BAKE until the profiteroles are very well browned, about 25 minutes. Lower the heat to 225°F and continue to bake for an additional 15 minutes. Remove the sheet from the oven and turn each

(continued)

profiterole over. Poke a small hole in the center of each bottom. (You can use a small tip from your pastry bag set to do this.) Put the profiteroles back on the baking sheet, hole side up. Turn the oven off and place the profiteroles back in the oven for another 10 to 12 minutes to finish drying out. Test one by cutting it open to see if the inside is sufficiently dried. Let the profiteroles cool to room temperature. (If not filling the profiteroles right away, store them in an airtight container for a day or freeze them, well wrapped in plastic wrap, and thaw when ready to use. Recrisp the puffs in a 350°F oven for about 5 minutes before serving.)

WHEN ready to serve, slice the top quarter off each profiterole. Fill the bottom with ice cream or the filling of your choice. Offer two or three profiteroles per serving. Drizzle the ice cream with the chocolate sauce or top with your own favorite sauce or with fresh berries. Replace the top, sprinkle with confectioners' sugar, and decorate with mint, if you like.

EASY CHOCOLATE SAUCE

MAKES ABOUT 2 CUPS

At Hamersley's we add a little coffee to all of our chocolate desserts. Here it gives the sweet sauce a toasty undertone, making it seem a little more adult than your usual chocolate sauce. (The brandy helps there, too.)

¾ cup heavy cream

¼ cup strong coffee

2 tablespoons sugar

3 tablespoons unsalted butter

8 ounces bittersweet chocolate, broken into small pieces

2 to 3 tablespoons brandy

BRING the cream, coffee, sugar, and butter to a boil in a small saucepan. Add the chocolate pieces and stir over low heat until completely melted.

Add the brandy and stir to combine. Thin to the desired consistency with additional water. Serve with profiteroles or over your favorite ice cream.

SEASONAL FRUIT SHORTCAKES

SERVES 8 TO 10

At Hamersley's Bistro, the menu changes to reflect the seasons. We feature a lot of seasonal fruit, especially in tarts. But I think it's these shortcake biscuits that really show off the best that the season has to offer. Make these only when you have fruit that's so ripe and delicious that it would be a shame to cook it. Simply toss the fruit with some sugar—also, a touch of Grand Marnier or Triple Sec is nice with strawberries—and let it macerate for a bit. Serve the biscuits with some sweetened whipped cream or Sweetened Crème Fraîche (page 287).

2 cups all-purpose flour

¼ cup sugar, plus extra for tops of biscuits

1 tablespoon plus 1 teaspoon baking powder

8 tablespoons unsalted butter, cut into small pieces and well chilled

2 large egg yolks

1 teaspoon vanilla extract

½ cup heavy cream, plus extra for tops of biscuits

HEAT the oven to 425°F. Using the paddle attachment of a stand mixer, combine the flour, sugar, and baking powder. Add the butter all at once and mix on low speed until it resembles coarse cornmeal with some larger chunks of butter. In another bowl, whisk together the egg yolks, vanilla, and cream. Add this to the flour and butter and mix on low speed until the dough just begins to come together. It should look ragged at this point. Stop the mixer and feel the dough; it should feel quite moist and should press together quite easily. If it's too dry, add a little more cream. Gather the dough together by pressing with your hands, but do not knead! Gently form the dough into a flattened circle about 1 inch thick, making sure the thickness is the same on the edges as it is in the center.

LINE a baking sheet with parchment paper. Flour a round cookie cutter or biscuit cutter (I use one that's 2½ inches). Cut as many biscuits as you can from the dough, making sure to flour the cutter between cuts. Gently press together the scraps and cut more biscuits from the remaining dough. Put the biscuits on the baking sheet, leaving room between them. Brush the tops with heavy cream and sprinkle them with sugar.

BAKE until the tops are golden brown, 12 to 15 minutes. Serve warm or reheat before serving. Slice with a serrated knife and fill with ripe berries or sliced stone fruits. Top with some whipped cream or sweetened crème fraîche, if you like.

PEAR-CRANBERRY CRUMBLE

This is a great fall dessert. You could also make the crumble in individual ramekins; just check on it sooner, as it will likely cook more quickly in the ramekins.

FOR THE CRUMBLE TOPPING

1 cup all-purpose flour

¾ cup old-fashioned (not quick cooking) oatmeal

½ cup plus 2 tablespoons packed brown sugar

Pinch of kosher salt

13 tablespoons unsalted butter, cut into small pieces and well chilled

FOR THE FILLING

5 cups peeled, sliced ripe pears

¾ cup dried cranberries, plumped in hot water

2 tablespoons fresh lemon juice

½ teaspoon vanilla extract

½ teaspoon ground cinnamon

¼ teaspoon nutmeg, preferably freshly grated

½ cup sugar

Pinch of kosher salt

2 tablespoons all-purpose flour

TO MAKE THE CRUMBLE TOPPING

In a stand mixer using the paddle attachment, combine the flour, oatmeal, brown sugar, and salt. Add the cold butter and mix on low speed until the topping just begins to come together and resembles large bits of chunky dough. (Do not mix so long that it comes together completely.) Transfer the topping to a shallow container, breaking it up a bit. Cover and refrigerate for at least 2 hours.

TO MAKE THE FILLING

Heat the oven to 350°F. Combine the pears, cran-berries, lemon juice, vanilla, cinnamon, nutmeg, sugar, salt, and flour. Toss the ingredients lightly to coat evenly and pour into a 1½-quart baking dish. Top with the crumble topping, breaking up any large clumps with your fingers and spreading it evenly. At this point, there may be areas that aren't completely covered with topping, but don't worry because it will spread a bit as it bakes. Bake until the topping begins to brown and the filling is bubbling, about 40 minutes. Remove the crumble from the oven and let it cool somewhat before serving.

MAPLE CRÈME BRÛLÉE

I'm not a big gadget guy, but if you really like making crème brûlée, and you don't already have a blowtorch, you might want to get one. Nothing beats its direct flame for even caramelization on the top of the custards. You can find small ones at the hardware store, or you can buy a mini-blowtorch made for the home kitchen at a good kitchen store. It's best to make these custards a day ahead, although they can be made early that day and chilled in the refrigerator for at least 4 hours.

1 vanilla bean or 1 teaspoon vanilla extract

2 cups heavy cream

1 large whole egg

4 large egg yolks

½ cup maple syrup (grade B works well)

Pinch of kosher salt

1 to 1½ tablespoons sugar

IF using a vanilla bean, cut it in half lengthwise, scrape out the seeds, and add it, as well as the pod halves, to the cream in a medium saucepan. Bring the cream to a boil and then remove it from the heat.

COMBINE the whole egg, the yolks, and the maple syrup in a medium mixing bowl. Slowly whisk about ½ cup of the hot cream into the eggs and wait a minute for the eggs to temper. Then whisk in the remaining cream and salt. Strain the custard through a fine-mesh strainer to remove the vanilla bean and any bits of stray egg that may remain. If using vanilla extract, add it to the strained custard.

HEAT the oven to 300°F. Divide the custard evenly among 4 ramekins. Put the filled ramekins into a baking pan or roasting pan and pour enough hot water into the pan to come about halfway up the sides of the ramekins. Bake the custards in the center of the oven until the custards are just set with a slight jiggle in the center, 50 to 55 minutes.

REMOVE the pan from the oven and remove the ramekins from the water bath. Cool at room temperature for about 30 minutes before refrigerating for at least 4 hours.

JUST before serving, sprinkle the custards with enough sugar for a complete, even coating, about 1 teaspoon each. Then caramelize the sugar in one of the following ways.

WITH A BLOWTORCH
With the flame about 2 inches away, slowly guide

the flame back and forth over the surface of each custard, moving on when the sugar has melted and browned.

IN THE OVEN

Place the oven rack about 2 inches from the broiler and heat the broiler. Arrange the custards on the baking sheet and broil until the sugar melts and browns, 1 to 2 minutes. Move the baking pan around if some custards are browning faster than others. The tops will harden as they cool.

CARAMEL-CHOCOLATE POTS DE CRÈME

SERVES 6

Here is a dessert for people who can't decide which they like more: butterscotch pudding or chocolate pudding. The flavor of the caramel actually seems to deepen and improve after a day or so.

FOR THE CARAMEL CUSTARD

1½ cups heavy cream

1¼ cups sugar

½ cup milk

6 large egg yolks

1 teaspoon vanilla extract

¼ teaspoon kosher salt

FOR THE CHOCOLATE CUSTARD

3 ounces bittersweet chocolate, chopped

4 large egg yolks

5 tablespoons sugar

Pinch of kosher salt

1¼ cups heavy cream

¼ cup milk

TO MAKE THE CARAMEL CUSTARD

Heat the oven to 300°F. In a medium saucepan, bring the cream to a boil and remove from the heat. Meanwhile, in another medium saucepan, over medium-high heat, cook the sugar until it's very dark amber, almost brown. (Check the color by drizzling some onto a white plate.) Don't worry if the sugar hardens while you're caramelizing it; simply stir it and continue cooking it until it smooths out.

WHEN the caramel has reached a dark amber color, slowly stir in the hot cream, a little bit at a time to ensure that the caramel dissolves into the cream. Be careful; the mixture will bubble and steam a great deal. Add the milk and remove it from the heat.

IN a medium bowl, whisk together the egg yolks, vanilla, and salt. Slowly whisk a little of the hot caramel-cream mixture into the eggs and wait a minute to temper them. Whisk in the rest of the cream mixture, a little bit at a time. Strain to remove any lumps. Divide the custard evenly among 6 ramekins (the custard will not completely fill the ramekins). Put the filled ramekins into a baking pan or roasting pan and pour enough hot water into the pan to come about halfway up the sides of the ramekins. Bake the custards in the center of the oven until the custards are just set with a slight jiggle in the center, 30 to 40 minutes. (The custards may not all be done at the same time; you may have to remove some from the water bath before the others are finished.) Remove the ramekins from the water bath and refrigerate for at least an hour and up to a day before making the chocolate custard. (Refrigerate the custards uncovered first in order to prevent condensation. After they have cooled, cover them with plastic wrap, if you like.)

TO MAKE THE CHOCOLATE CUSTARD

Put the chopped chocolate in a medium heatproof glass or stainless-steel bowl that will fit snugly over a pot of simmering water. In another bowl, whisk together the yolks, sugar, and salt.

IN a medium saucepan, bring the cream just to a boil. Pour the cream over the chocolate and let sit for a minute to start the chocolate melting. Gently whisk the cream and chocolate together until completely smooth. Add the milk to the chocolate mixture, put the bowl over a pot of simmering water, and whisk gently to create a smooth, homogenous consistency. Add a little of the warm chocolate mixture to the yolk-sugar mixture to temper the eggs. Then add the egg mixture to the chocolate mixture. Cook slowly over the simmering water, stirring constantly with a heatproof rubber spatula, until the mixture thickens considerably, 12 to 15 minutes. The custard is properly cooked when it coats the spatula thickly and when you draw a line through the custard on the spatula, it holds that line.

REMOVE the chocolate custard from the heat and slowly pour (or ladle) it over the chilled caramel custards, dividing equally. Return the custards to the refrigerator and continue to cool until the chocolate layer is set (another hour or so). The custards can be assembled a day ahead and kept refrigerated. They taste best when allowed to sit at room temperature for about an hour before serving.

BROWN SUGAR—PECAN SHORTBREAD

MAKES 36 COOKIES

When we serve custards and soufflés at the restaurant, we often send out a crisp cookie as an accompaniment. These are great with the Caramel-Chocolate Pots de Crème (page 304), but they're also very nice on their own with a cup of tea.

2 cups all-purpose flour

⅔ cup packed light brown sugar

5 tablespoons cornstarch

½ teaspoon kosher salt

16 tablespoons cold, unsalted butter, cut into small pieces

2 teaspoons vanilla extract

1 cup finely chopped toasted pecans (see page 4)

HEAT the oven to 350°F. Line a 9-inch square pan with parchment paper, letting some excess paper extend beyond the edges of the pan. Line a couple of baking sheets with parchment paper as well.

WITH the paddle attachment of a stand mixer, combine the flour, sugar, cornstarch, and salt. Add the butter and vanilla and mix on low speed until the dough is thoroughly mixed and begins to clump together. Add the pecans and mix just enough to incorporate them. The dough will look rather dry and crumbly at this point and won't come together.

PRESS the dough into the lined 9-inch pan and chill the dough for 30 minutes. Using the excess parchment paper, lift the dough out of the pan in one square. Cut the dough into 1½-inch squares (6 across, 6 down). Transfer the cut shortbread to the lined baking sheets and bake until they feel firm to the touch and just begin to turn golden brown, 15 to 20 minutes. The cookies should not develop too much color, and their sharp square edges will become a bit rounded as they bake. Cool completely on a wire rack before serving or storing in an airtight container.

CHOCOLATE TRUFFLE CAKE

This rich, dense cake benefits from a little sauce on the side. You could go with a crème anglaise or try one of these more unexpected sauces (recipes follow). I like them both so much, I couldn't pick just one of them to feature in this book.

8 ounces bittersweet chocolate, chopped

4 ounces unsweetened chocolate, chopped

16 tablespoons unsalted butter, plus more for greasing the pan

½ cup hot brewed coffee

1 teaspoon kosher salt

1 teaspoon vanilla extract

5 large eggs, at room temperature

½ cup sugar

1½ tablespoons all-purpose flour

HEAT the oven to 350°F. Cut a piece of parchment paper to fit the bottom of a 9-inch round cake pan. Line the bottom of the pan with the parchment paper and then butter the paper.

SET a medium heatproof glass or stainless steel bowl over a pot of simmering water so that the bottom of the bowl fits snugly without touching the water. Melt the chocolate and the butter over the simmering water. Remove the bowl from the heat. Add the coffee, salt, and vanilla.

IN a stand mixer using the whisk attachment, beat the eggs and sugar together until the mixture lightens and begins to hold ribbons, 3 to 4 minutes. Fold the eggs into the chocolate mixture. Stir in the flour.

POUR the batter into the prepared pan. Set the cake pan into a larger baking pan or roasting pan and add hot water to the larger pan to about 1 inch deep. Bake until the cake is mostly set with a slight jiggle in the center, 40 to 45 minutes. Remove the cake from the water bath and let it cool to room temperature. To turn the cake out onto a serving plate, the cake must be at room temperature or cold (cold works best). Run a thin knife around the inside of the cake pan. Invert it onto a regular plate, remove the parchment, and invert it again onto the serving plate. Serve at room temperature.

PORT-CHERRY SAUCE

Try serving a little of the port you used in the sauce along with the dessert.

1 cup dried, tart cherries

½ cup port

½ cup sugar

2 tablespoons fresh lemon juice

BRING 1 cup water to a boil in a medium saucepan. Add the cherries, turn the heat to low, and cook for about 5 minutes to plump the cherries. Add the port, sugar, and lemon juice to the pan, and continue to simmer until the sauce thickens slightly, about 10 minutes. Cool to room temperature before serving.

ORANGE SAUCE

If you use blood oranges for the sauce, it will be a beautiful rosy color. Standard oranges will taste just as good, but will make the sauce a light yellow.

¾ cup sugar

1 tablespoon grated orange zest

¼ cup fresh orange juice (use blood oranges when available)

¼ cup fresh lemon juice

1 large egg yolk

3 large whole eggs

Pinch of kosher salt

6 tablespoons unsalted butter, cut into pieces

2 tablespoons Grand Marnier or other orange liqueur

IN a medium saucepan over medium heat, whisk together the sugar, zest, orange juice, lemon juice, egg yolk, whole eggs, and salt. Add the butter and cook, stirring constantly, until the first sign of a boil, about 5 minutes. Remove the sauce from the heat and strain into a bowl. Cool the sauce to room temperature and add the Grand Marnier. The sauce will keep for a week, covered, in the refrigerator, but is best served at room temperature.

MERINGUES

What to Do with all of those leftover egg whites? Make meringues! They're great on their own as a light, sweet treat at the end of a heavy meal, and kids just love them. Don't make them on a very humid day; the meringues will lose their crispness with heartbreaking speed.

2 large egg whites at room temperature

¼ teaspoon kosher salt

¼ teaspoon cream of tartar

½ cup sugar

½ teaspoon vanilla extract

HEAT the oven to 225°F. Line two baking sheets with parchment paper.

USING the whisk attachment on a stand mixer, beat the egg whites on medium speed. When the whites begin to look foamy, add the salt and cream of tartar. Turn the speed up to medium-high and continue to whip, gradually adding the sugar 1 tablespoon at a time. When medium-stiff peaks are achieved, add the vanilla, turn the speed up to high, and beat the whites to stiff peaks. They should look shiny and opaque but not dry.

IMMEDIATELY spoon the meringue onto the baking sheets. I drop them onto the pan with a tablespoon, leaving room between each, to make cookies about 1½ inches in diameter.

BAKE for 1½ hours, turn off the oven, and leave the cookies in the oven for an additional hour or more (even overnight) to continue to dry out. Store in an airtight container. You can freeze meringues, well wrapped in plastic. Allow them to defrost in the refrigerator before using.

Note: To make chocolate chip meringue cookies, add ¾ cup chopped bittersweet chocolate or mini–chocolate chips just before baking. (Be careful not to deflate the egg whites when folding in the chocolate.) For hazelnut meringues, add ¾ cup ground hazelnuts tossed with 1 tablespoon confectioners' sugar.

RAISIN-HAZELNUT BISCOTTI

A couple of biscotti, served with coffee or a glass of sherry for dipping, is a wonderful way to end a meal. This and the two recipes that follow are some of my favorites.

2¾ cups all-purpose flour

1⅔ cups sugar

1 teaspoon baking powder

½ teaspoon kosher salt

2 teaspoons anise seed

3 large whole eggs

3 large egg yolks

2 teaspoons vanilla extract

1 cup toasted hazelnuts (see page 4)

¾ cup golden raisins

HEAT the oven to 350°F. Line a 13 × 18-inch sheet pan with parchment paper.

COMBINE the flour, sugar, baking powder, salt, and anise seed in the bowl of a stand mixer.

IN a separate bowl, whisk together the whole eggs, egg yolks, and vanilla. Add to the dry ingredients and mix on low speed to combine, stopping to scrape the bowl occasionally; the dough will be rather crumbly at this point. Add the nuts and raisins and mix on low speed to combine.

TO SHAPE AND BAKE THE BISCOTTI

Dump the dough out onto a floured surface. With well-floured hands, shape the dough into a log. The dough will be rather sticky and may not retain its shape. Using a liberal amount of flour on your hands, quickly transfer the log to the prepared sheet pan and shape into a long, flattish log

that touches the ends of the sheet pan the long way and is a consistent thickness for its entire length.

BAKE the biscotti log until it develops a light golden color and feels rather firm to the touch, 35 to 40 minutes. Cool to room temperature.

LOWER the oven temperature to 300°F.

LINE two baking sheet pans with parchment paper. With a serrated knife, slice the biscotti about ¼ inch thick. Lay the biscotti slices flat on the lined baking sheets and bake for about 15 minutes until they begin to dry out. The cookies will not feel entirely crisp until they are completely cool, so remove them while they still have a bit of spring. When they are cool, test them again. If they need to be more crisp, return them to the oven for a few more minutes. Store in an airtight container when completely cool.

BLACK PEPPER *and* CINNAMON SPICED BISCOTTI

Here black pepper and cinnamon team up in an intriguing hot and spicy combination.

2¾ cups all-purpose flour

1½ cups packed dark brown sugar

1 teaspoon baking powder

½ teaspoon kosher salt

1 teaspoon freshly ground black pepper

1½ teaspoons ground cinnamon

¼ teaspoon ground cloves

¼ teaspoon ground nutmeg

1 teaspoon ground ginger

3 large whole eggs

3 large egg yolks

2 teaspoons vanilla extract

HEAT the oven to 350°F. Line a baking sheet with parchment paper.

COMBINE the flour, brown sugar, baking powder, salt, and spices in the bowl of a stand mixer.

IN a separate bowl, whisk together the whole eggs, egg yolks, and vanilla. Add to the dry ingredients and mix on low speed to combine, stopping to scrape the bowl occasionally; the dough will be rather crumbly at this point.

FOLLOW the procedure for shaping and baking as described on page 311.

CITRUS BISCOTTI

These biscotti get much of their bright flavor from the citrus zest. When zesting the fruit, try to get only the colored part of the skin and not the bitter white pith beneath.

2¾ cups all-purpose flour

1⅔ cups sugar

1 teaspoon baking powder

½ teaspoon kosher salt

3 large whole eggs

3 large egg yolks

2 teaspoons vanilla extract

2 tablespoons grated citrus zest (lemon, lime, or orange, or a combination)

HEAT the oven to 350°F. Line a baking sheet with parchment paper.

COMBINE the flour, sugar, baking powder, and salt in the bowl of a stand mixer.

IN a separate bowl, whisk together the whole eggs, egg yolks, and vanilla. Add to the dry ingredients and mix on low speed to combine, stopping to scrape the bowl occasionally; the dough will be rather crumbly at this point. Add the zest and mix on low speed to combine.

FOLLOW the procedure for shaping and baking as described on page 311.

INDIVIDUAL WARM APPLE TARTS *with* CHINESE FIVE-SPICE POWDER, CARAMEL, *and* CRÈME FRAÎCHE

SERVES 6

I first tasted a tart like this in the famous Poilâne Bakery in Paris. Cooking the apples first lets you alter their flavor depending on your mood. Here I've added a little Chinese five-spice powder. That might seem strange, but the spice mix features the usual apple dessert suspects—cinnamon and cloves. (In fact, I first used it when I was out of cinnamon.) Chinese five-spice powder also includes star anise, fennel seeds, and Szechwan peppercorns. Used sparingly, it adds a subtle, tingly heat and a little intrigue to otherwise familiar flavors. You can find five-spice powder at most supermarkets.

FOR THE TARTLET SHELLS

1 recipe Hamersley's Bistro Tart Dough
(page 115)

FOR THE FILLING

4 tart baking apples, such as Granny Smith

2 tablespoons unsalted butter

1 tablespoon sugar

1 teaspoon Chinese five-spice powder

FOR THE CARAMEL SAUCE

½ cup sugar

1 tablespoon light corn syrup

¼ cup heavy cream

2 tablespoons unsalted butter

¼ teaspoon vanilla extract

TO ASSEMBLE AND SERVE

2 large eggs, lightly beaten

1 tablespoon heavy cream

1 tablespoon sugar

6 tablespoons Sweetened Crème Fraîche
(page 287)

TO MAKE THE TARTLET SHELLS

Line two baking sheets with parchment paper. Shape the dough into six 2-ounce balls. On a lightly floured surface, roll the balls out into disks about 6 inches across. Don't worry about making them perfectly round; imperfection is part of the charm of these tarts. Place the circles on the baking sheets. Fold about ½ inch of the edge of each

disk back over onto itself, pleating as you go. Refrigerate the dough for at least 20 minutes and up to 2 days, covered in plastic wrap.

TO MAKE THE FILLING

Peel the apples, cut them in half, and core them. Cut each half into 4 wedges. Heat the butter in a large nonstick sauté pan over medium heat until it bubbles. Add the apples and toss them in the butter. Sprinkle the sugar and five-spice powder over the apples and cook over medium heat, stirring occasionally, until the apples are just tender, 6 to 8 minutes. Remove from the heat and let cool.

TO MAKE THE CARAMEL SAUCE

Combine the sugar and corn syrup in a medium saucepan. Cook over medium-high heat, stirring occasionally with a wooden spoon. Periodically check the color by dabbing a bit onto a white plate. (Be very careful, as the sugar is extremely hot.) When the sugar has turned a dark amber, remove it from the heat. In another saucepan, bring the cream to a boil. Stir in the butter and vanilla. Slowly and carefully add the cream to the caramel,

stirring with a wooden spoon. Keep the caramel sauce warm or gently reheat it before serving.

TO ASSEMBLE AND SERVE

Heat the oven to 350°F. Whisk the eggs and cream together. Divide the apple filling among the disks, placing it in the center of each round just up to the pleated edge. Using a pastry brush, brush the edges of each tart with the egg-cream mixture. Sprinkle about ½ teaspoon sugar over each tart. Bake the tarts until golden brown on the bottom, 20 to 25 minutes. Serve hot out of the oven with the caramel sauce and a tablespoon of crème fraîche on the side. The tarts taste best served immediately, but they can also be cooled completely and reheated in the oven for 5 minutes before serving.

SOURCES

ANCHO CHILE PEPPERS: You can order ancho chiles, as well as all kinds of other chiles, from Adriana's Caravan (*adrianascaravan.com;* 800/316-0820) and Melissa's (*melissas.com;* 800/588-0151).

CHEESE: I love the artisan cheeses offered at Formaggio Kitchen in Cambridge, Massachusetts. You can visit their website at *formaggiokitchen.com* or call 888/212–3224 to place an order. Formaggio Kitchen is also a great source for interesting oils, vinegars, and other high-quality pantry items.

COUNTRY HAM: Country ham, such as Smithfield ham, has been brined and smoked. It's easy to find in the South where it's produced and not so easy to find in other areas of the country. You can order it by mail from *thevirginiacompany.com* (800/568–2746). I'm also partial to the corncob-smoked ham from Harrington's of Vermont (*harringtonham.com;* 802/434–4444).

DUCK PRODUCTS: To order foie gras, whole duck, duck breasts, duck legs, duck fat, and confit by mail try Hudson Valley Foie Gras (*hudsonvalleyfoiegras.com;* 845/292–2500) or D'Artagnan (*dartagnan.com;* 800/327–8246).

GAME BIRDS AND OTHER POULTRY: To order squab, quail, or other poultry, try D'Artganan (*dartagnan.com;* 800/327-8246).

KITCHEN TOOLS: For great tools at great prices, I like JB Prince in New York City (*jbprince.com;* 800/473–0577).

LAVENDER BUDS: You can find lavender buds and a wide variety of other offerings, including spices, cheeses, meats, and fish at Dean & DeLuca (*deananddeluca.com;* 800/221–7714).

LENTILS: You can find French green lentils (often called lentils du Puy) at many specialty food stores. A good online source is *thefoodstores.com* (888/328–3663).

MEATS AND PRODUCE: If you live in the greater Boston area, you might want to check out John Dewar Co., in Newton, for its fabulous meats (617/964–3577) and Verrill Farms in Concord for its wonderful produce (508/369–4494).

PRESERVED LEMONS: Adriana's Caravan (*adrianascaravan.com;* 800/316-0820) carries preserved lemons as well as all kinds of spices, chiles, and other international ingredients.

SMOKED SHRIMP: Ducktrap River Fish Farm sells its smoked fish to many supermarkets, but you can also order such items as smoked shrimp and fresh Maine lobster directly from the Belfast, Maine–based company by visiting *ducktrap.com* or calling them at 800/828–3825. Another favorite local purveyor is Captain Marden's Seafoods in Wellesley, Massachusetts. They'll ship outstanding seafood to you if you call 800/666–0860 or visit their website at *captainmardens.com.*

TASSO: You can order this Cajun specialty from *magicseasonings.com* (800/457–2857).

TRUFFLES AND WILD MUSHROOMS: Urbani Truffles is a great source for truffles and truffle products as well as high-quality wild mushrooms (*urbani.com;* 800/281–2330).

BIBLIOGRAPHY

Like many people, I live and travel vicariously through cookbooks. In that way, Paula Wolfert took me with her to the southwest of France and Morocco. I traveled to Provence with Richard Olney. And Elizabeth David taught me about French provincial cooking in a way that inspired me to seek out those regions and to taste for myself the dishes she described. The following works have influenced my cooking throughout the years or have been used as a reference for this project—and, in many cases, both.

Bertolli, Paul, et al. *Chez Panisse Cooking.* Random House, 1994.

Child, Julia, et al. *Mastering the Art of French Cooking, Volumes I and II.* Alfred A. Knopf, 1961 and 1970.

David, Elizabeth. *French Provincial Cooking.* Penguin, 1999.

De Ravel, Anne, and Andres Daguin. *Foie Gras, Magret and Other Good Foods from Gascony.* Random House, 1988.

Hazan, Marcella. *Marcella Cucina.* HarperCollins, 1997.

Kimball, Christopher. *The Cook's Bible.* Little, Brown & Company, 1996.

Olney, Richard. *Simple French Food.* Atheneum, 1974.

Prosper, Montagné. *Larousse Gastronomique,* edited by Charlotte Turgeon and Nina Froud. Crown, 1961.

Rombauer, Irma S., et al. *The Joy of Cooking.* Scribner, 1997.

Saveur Editors. *Saveur Cooks Authentic French.* Chronicle Books, 1999.

Soltner, André. *The Lutèce Cookbook.* Alfred A. Knopf, 1995.

Wells, Patricia. *Bistro Cooking.* Workman Publishing, 1989.

INDEX

Acorn squash
    autumn vegetable stew with Cheddar-garlic
        crumble crust, 113–14
    harvest salad of roasted vegetables with romesco
        sauce, 43–45
Aïoli, 10, 16
Almond(s)
    curry, date, chile, and almond crust, sear-roasted
        rack of lamb with, 232–33
    in romesco sauce, 45
Anchovy(ies), 8
    butter, salmon wrapped in leeks with, 156–57
    pissaladière, 93–94
Angel hair pasta, with seared chicken livers, peanuts,
        and cucumber, 130–31
Apple(s)
    apple tarte Tatin, 286–87
    cider and crisp apple mignonette sauce, 71
    and endive salad, foie gras terrine with, 84–85
    individual warm apple tarts with Chinese five-
        spice powder, caramel, and crème fraîche,
        314–15
    roast pork with onions, sage, and, 241–42
Apricot sauce, rice pudding cake with candied
        pistachios and, 291–92
Armagnac, pot-roasted pork with prunes, walnuts,
        and, 244–45

Artichoke(s)
    roasted, with garlic and pancetta bread crumbs,
        256
    and Swiss chard gratin, 107
Arugula
    salad, with fresh figs, Gorgonzola, and bacon, 38
    sliced peach, arugula, and walnut salad, salt-
        cured foie gras with, 82–83
Asiago cheese
    crispy polenta triangles with chanterelles and,
        144–45
    Fiona's hearty lentil soup with bacon and, 55
    shaved, roasted asparagus with pancetta and, 261
Asparagus, roasted, with pancetta and shaved
        Asiago, 261
Avocado and orange salad with honey and ginger
        dressing, 36–37

Bacon
    arugula salad with fresh figs, Gorgonzola, and,
        38
    bacon-wrapped scallops with beurre blanc, 154
    beef short ribs braised in dark beer with red
        onions and, 214–15
    caramelized onion, bacon, and potato tart, 119

frisée salad with lardons and poached egg, 41–42

hearty lentil soup with Asiago cheese and, 55

Lu Lu's favorite linguine, 129

rabbit braised in red wine with pearl onions, chanterelles, and, 236–37

smoky, beef braised in red wine with mushrooms and, à la Bourguignonne, 218–19

and spinach salad, calf's liver with warm mustard dressing and, 248–49

Balsamic vinegar, duck confit with roasted shallots and, 198

Basil, tomato, and fennel salad with lemon vinaigrette, 39

Beans

green: lobster with corn, tomatoes, citrus vinaigrette, and, 170–71; summer vegetable ragout with creamy polenta, 140–41

Hamersley's cassoulet, with pork, duck confit, and sausage, 78–79

slow-roasted leg of lamb with white beans and escarole, 234–35

Beef

blue cheese-stuffed burger, Wolfgang's, with port and green peppercorn sauce, 216

braised in red wine, with mushrooms and smoky bacon à la Bourguignonne, 218–19

grilled flank steak with coffee and black pepper marinade, 213

sear-roasted rib steak with garlic butter, 212

short ribs, braised in dark beer with bacon and red onions, 214–15

skillet-cooked skirt steak with blue cheese butter, 217

stock, 22

Beer, dark, beef short ribs braised in, with bacon and red onions, 214–15

Beet(s)

fresh goat cheese, roasted beet, and walnut tart, 120–21

and ginger soup, puréed, 52

grilled mackerel with fennel, lime vinaigrette, and, 166–67

roasted, in salad with toasted walnuts, watercress, and creamy horseradish dressing, 47

Bell peppers, 10

chicken pipérade, 188

orzo-stuffed red peppers with feta, olives, and oregano, 274–75

peperonata, baked polenta squares with white truffle oil and, 142–43

red, roasted: brandade with toasts and, 89; in open-faced sandwich with goat cheese and black olive spread, 98; in romesco sauce, 45

summer vegetable ragout with creamy polenta, 140–41

Berries, summer berry pudding, 294–95

Beurre blanc, bacon-wrapped scallops with, 154

Biscotti

black pepper and cinnamon spiced, 312

citrus, 313

raisin-hazelnut, 311

Black pepper. *See* Pepper

Black truffles, creamy gratin of celery root, onions, and, 111

Blueberry-caramel sauce, peach galette with, 283–84

Blue cheese. *See also* Gorgonzola; Roquefort

butter, skillet-cooked skirt steak with, 217

-stuffed burger, Wolfgang's, with port and green peppercorn sauce, 216

Bluefish, barbecued, with smoked shrimp butter, 175

Bouillabaisse, New England, with rouille and croutons, 173–74

Brandade with roasted red peppers and toasts, 89

Bread crumbs, 7–8

crispy, broiled tomatoes with, 270

pancetta and garlic, roasted artichokes with, 256

seasoned, 13

Broth. *See* Stock

Brown butter, trout with lemon, parsley, and, 161

Brown sugar-pecan shortbread, 306

Brussels sprouts

harvest salad of roasted vegetables with romesco sauce, 43–45

with hazelnuts and mint, 271

Butter, 7
Butternut squash, risotto with maple syrup and,
    135

Cabbage, red, sweet-and-sour, 263
Cakes
    chocolate mousse cake, 288–89
    chocolate truffle cake, 307
    rice pudding cake with apricot sauce and
        candied pistachios, 291–92
Calf's liver with spinach and bacon salad and warm
    mustard dressing, 248–49
Capers
    chicken paillards with lemon and, 192
    sear-roasted veal chops with cornichons and,
        223–24
Caramel
    blueberry-caramel sauce, peach galette with,
        283–84
    caramel-chocolate pots de crème, 304–5
    individual warm apple tarts with Chinese five-
        spice powder, crème fraîche, and, 314–15
Carrot(s)
    autumn vegetable stew with Cheddar-garlic
        crumble crust, 113–14
    harvest salad of roasted vegetables with romesco
        sauce, 43–45
    pickled carrot mignonette sauce, 71
    and tarragon vinaigrette, orange and ginger-
        glazed roasted swordfish with, 162–63
Cassoulet, Hamersley's, with pork, duck confit, and
    sausage, 238–40
Cauliflower, curried, with yogurt and mint sauce,
    268
Celery root
    autumn vegetable stew with Cheddar-garlic
        crumble crust, 113–14
    creamy gratin of onions, black truffles, and, 111
    remoulade, 91
Chanterelles. *See* Mushroom(s)

Cheese courses, 278–79
Cheese puffs (gougères), 75
Cherries, port-cherry sauce, 308
Chicken, 178–79
    breasts: crispy, 190–91; paillards, with lemon and
        capers, 192
    broth, 21
    chicken pipérade, 188
    coq au vin, 186–87
    roast: Hamersley's, with garlic, lemon, and
        parsley, 182–83; split, with herbed butter,
        184–85; walk-away, with onions and
        potatoes, 181
Chicken liver(s)
    country pâté, 78–79
    mousse, 80
    pâté, 33
    seared, with angel hair pasta, peanuts, and
        cucumber, 130–31
Chiles
    curry, date, chile, and almond crust, sear-roasted
        rack of lamb with, 232–33
    hot pepper sauce, 71
    in romesco sauce, 45
    spicy tripe soup with mint and couscous, 62
Chives, lemon-scented risotto with morels and,
    133
Chocolate
    caramel-chocolate pots de crème, 304–5
    chocolate mousse cake, 288–89
    chocolate truffle cake, 307
    sauce, easy, 298
Chowder, mussel and finnan haddie, 59
Chutney, spicy pumpkin-mango, duck confit with,
    199
Cider and crisp apple mignonette sauce, 71
Cinnamon and black pepper spiced biscotti, 312
Citrus vinaigrette, lobster with corn, tomatoes, green
    beans, and, 170–71
Clams
    penne with pancetta, spinach, and, 127
    sizzling, with garlic-herb butter, 69

Coffee
    and black pepper marinade, grilled flank steak
        with, 213
    coffee crème anglaise, 290
Confit
    cherry tomato, garlicky, with toasted pine nuts,
        269
    duck. *See* Duck, confit
Cookies
    biscotti: black pepper and cinnamon spiced, 312;
        citrus, 313; raisin-hazelnut, 311
    brown sugar-pecan shortbread, 306
    lemon-lavender sugar cookies, 282
Coq au vin, 186–87
Coriander
    Japanese eggplant with mint, ginger, and, 267
    and orange vinaigrette, braised leeks with,
        258–59
Corn
    lobster with tomatoes, green beans, citrus
        vinaigrette, and, 170–71
    sugar snap, in summer vegetable ragout with
        creamy polenta, 140–41
Cornichons, sear-roasted veal chops with capers and,
    223–24
Country pâté, 78–79
Couscous
    spicy lamb shanks with preserved lemons and,
        228–31
    spicy tripe soup with mint and, 62
Crab
    crabmeat risotto with peas and mint, 138
    soft-shell crab sandwich with spicy rouille, 99
Cranberries, pear-cranberry crumble, 300
Crème anglaise, 290
Crème brûlée, maple, 302–3
Crème fraîche, 7
    homemade, 12
    individual warm apple tarts with Chinese five-
        spice powder, caramel, and, 314–15
    new potato galette with olives and, 116–17
    sweetened, 287

Croutons, shaved, 44
Crumble, pear-cranberry, 300
Cucumber(s)
    chopped salad of peas, radishes, and, with
        tarragon vinaigrette, 46
    seared chicken livers with angel hair pasta,
        peanuts, and, 130–31
    soup, cold, with chopped tomato salad, 51
Curry, date, chile, and almond crust, sear-roasted
    rack of lamb with, 232–33
Custard(s)
    caramel-chocolate pots de crème, 304–5
    crème anglaise, 290
    lemon, souffléed, 280–81
    maple crème brûlée, 302–3
    Roquefort and hazelnut, souffléed, 73

Dandelion, open-faced omelet with morels, scallions,
    and, 74
Date, curry, chile, and almond crust, sear-roasted
    rack of lamb with, 232–33
Desserts, 277–315. *See also* Cakes; Cookies;
    Custard(s); Tarts, sweet
    meringues, 310
    pear-cranberry crumble, 300
    profiteroles, 297–98
    sauces for, 284, 292, 298, 308–9
    seasonal fruit shortcakes, 299
    summer berry pudding, 294–95
Duck, 179–80. *See also* Foie gras
    breast, seared, with plums and port, 201–2
    confit, 193–95; crisped, 196; with French lentil
        salad and classic bistro vinaigrette, 197; in
        Hamersley's cassoulet with pork and sausage,
        238–40; with roasted shallots and balsamic
        vinegar, 198; with spicy pumpkin-mango
        chutney, 199
    rillettes, 90
    roast, with grapefruit, garlic, and tarragon with
        wilted greens, 203–4

Garlic
aïoli, 16
butter, sear-roasted rib steak with, 212
garlic, tomato, and olive compote, seared sea
  scallops with, 152–53
garlicky cherry tomato confit with toasted pine
  nuts, 269
garlicky mashed potato cakes, 264
grilled butterflied leg of lamb with rosemary
  and, 225
Hamersley's roast chicken with lemon, parsley,
  and, 182–83
-herb butter, sizzling clams with, 69
and pancetta bread crumbs, roasted artichokes
  with, 256
red onions braised in red wine with thyme and,
  262
roast duck with grapefruit, tarragon, wilted
  greens, and, 203–4
roasted: purée, 10, 15; whole heads, 15; and wild
  mushroom sandwich, 95
salt cod with spicy tomatoes, onions, and, 164
sautéed spinach with lemon, olive oil, and, 255
soup, creamless yet creamy, 53
veal breast stuffed with spinach, mushrooms,
  and, 220–22
Ginger
and beet soup, puréed, 52
ginger crème anglaise, 290
and honey dressing, avocado and orange salad
  with, 36–37
Japanese eggplant with coriander, mint, and, 267
and orange-glazed roasted swordfish with carrot
  and tarragon vinaigrette, 162–63
Goat cheese
fresh goat cheese, roasted beet, and walnut tart,
  120–21
fried walnut-coated, mixed greens with sherry
  vinaigrette and, 34
in open-faced sandwich with roasted red pepper
  and black olive spread, 98
oven-baked penne with onions, walnuts, and, 128

Gorgonzola. *See also* Blue cheese
arugula salad with fresh figs, bacon, and, 38
Gougères, 75
Grapefruit, roast duck with garlic, tarragon, wilted
  greens, and, 203–4
Gratin(s), 102
artichoke and Swiss chard, 107
celery root, onions, and black truffles, creamy,
  111
creamy bistro potato and leek, 106
mussels, country ham, and potatoes, 104–5
onion soup au gratin, 56–57
potatoes and caramelized onions, 103
tian of summer vegetables Provençal,
  108–10
Green beans. *See* Beans
Green peppercorns. *See* Pepper
Greens. *See also specific greens*
autumn, seared scallops with chanterelles and,
  72
wilted, caramelized sweetbreads with lemon
  and, 250–51
wilted, roast duck with grapefruit, garlic,
  tarragon, and, 203–4

Halibut, 151
Ham
gratin of mussels, country ham, and potatoes,
  104–5
polenta with tasso and sweetbreads,
  146–47
Hamburger, Wolfgang's blue cheese-stuffed, with
  port and green peppercorn sauce, 216
Hazelnut(s)
Brussels sprouts with mint and, 271
raisin-hazelnut biscotti, 311
in romesco sauce, 45
and Roquefort custard, souffléed, 73
Herbes de Provence, 9–10
Hamersley's, 14

Honey and ginger dressing, avocado and orange
    salad with, 36–37
Horseradish
    dressing, creamy, roasted beets, toasted walnuts,
        and watercress salad with, 47
    oven-roasted skate with walnut crumbs and,
        158–59
Hot peppers. *See* Chiles
Hot pepper sauce, 71

Lamb
    leg of: grilled butterflied, with garlic and
        rosemary, 225; slow-roasted, with white
        beans and escarole, 234–35
    rack of, sear-roasted, with curry, date, chile, and
        almond crust, 232–33
    shanks: Parmesan-crusted, 226–27; spicy, with
        couscous and preserved lemons, 228–31
Lavender, lemon-lavender sugar cookies, 282
Leek(s)
    braised, with coriander and orange vinaigrette,
        258–59
    creamy bistro potato and leek gratin, 106
    with fennel and cream, 260
    and potato soup, with tarragon and fennel seeds,
        54
    salmon wrapped in, with anchovy butter, 156–57
    seared quail with star anise and, 206–7
Lemon(s)
    caramelized sweetbreads with wilted greens
        and, 250–51
    chicken paillards with capers and, 192
    citrus biscotti, 313
    Hamersley's roast chicken with garlic, parsley,
        and, 182–83
    lemon-lavender sugar cookies, 282
    lemony braised endive, 273
    preserved, quick, 231; spicy lamb shanks with
        couscous and, 228–31
    sautéed spinach with garlic, olive oil, and, 255

-scented risotto, with morels and chives, 133
souffléed lemon custard, 280–81
trout with brown butter, parsley, and, 161
vinaigrette, tomato, basil, and fennel salad with,
    39
Lentil(s), 9
    French lentil salad, duck confit with classic
        bistro vinaigrette and, 197
    soup, Fiona's hearty, with bacon and Asiago
        cheese, 55
Lime
    citrus biscotti, 313
    vinaigrette, grilled mackerel with beets, fennel,
        and, 166–67
Linguine, Lu Lu's favorite, 129
Liver. *See* Calf's liver; Chicken liver(s); Foie gras
Lobster
    with corn, tomatoes, green beans, and citrus
        vinaigrette, 170–71
    lobster, fennel, and orange soup, 60–61
    lobster, mushroom, and spinach tart, 122–23

Mackerel, grilled, with beets, fennel, and lime
    vinaigrette, 166–67
Mango-pumpkin chutney, spicy, duck confit with,
    199
Maple
    maple crème brûlée, 302–3
    -parsnip purée, seared foie gras with port sauce
        and, 86–87
    syrup, risotto with butternut squash and, 135
Mayonnaise
    aïoli, 16
    rouille, 17
Meat, 209–51. *See also specific types*
    about cooking, 3, 209–11
Meringues, 310
Mignonette sauce, 70–71
Mint
    Brussels sprouts with hazelnuts and, 271

and ginger-glazed roasted swordfish with carrot
and tarragon vinaigrette, 162–63
lobster, fennel, and orange soup, 60–61
sauce, 309
Orzo-stuffed red peppers with feta, olives, and
oregano, 274–75
Oysters on the half shell, 70–71

Pancetta
and garlic bread crumbs, roasted artichokes
with, 256
penne with clams, spinach, and, 127
roasted asparagus with shaved Asiago and, 261
Pantry items, 6–11
Parmesan cheese
-crusted lamb shanks, 226–27
dressing, hearts of romaine and watercress with,
35
Parsley
Lu Lu's favorite linguine, 129
roast chicken with garlic, lemon, and, 182–83
trout with lemon, brown butter, and, 161
Parsnips
autumn vegetable stew with Cheddar-garlic
crumble crust, 113–14
harvest salad of roasted vegetables with romesco
sauce, 43–45
maple-parsnip purée, seared foie gras with port
sauce and, 86–87
Pasta, 126
Lu Lu's favorite linguine, 129
oven-baked penne with onions, walnuts, and
goat cheese, 128
penne with clams, pancetta, and spinach, 127
seared chicken livers with angel hair pasta,
peanuts, and cucumber, 130–31
Pâté
chicken liver, 33
chicken liver mousse, 80
country, 78–79

rillettes of duck, 90
terrine of foie gras with shaved apple and endive
salad, 84–85
Peach(es)
galette, with blueberry-caramel sauce, 283–84
sliced peach, arugula, and walnut salad, salt-
cured foie gras with, 82–83
Peanuts, seared chicken livers with angel hair pasta,
cucumber, and, 130–31
Pear-cranberry crumble, 300
Peas
chopped salad of cucumbers, radishes, and, with
tarragon vinaigrette, 46
crabmeat risotto with mint and, 138
grilled salmon with potatoes, mint, and, 155
sugar snap: in summer vegetable ragout with
creamy polenta, 140–41; whole red snapper
with shiitake mushrooms, water chestnuts,
and, 168–69
Pecans, brown sugar-pecan shortbread, 306
Penne
with clams, pancetta, and spinach, 127
oven-baked, with onions, walnuts, and goat
cheese, 128
Peperonata, baked polenta squares with white truffle
oil and, 142–43
Pepper, 9
black pepper and cinnamon spiced biscotti, 312
coffee and black pepper marinade, grilled flank
steak with, 213
green peppercorn(s): and port sauce, Wolfgang's
blue cheese-stuffed burger with, 216; sauce
for oysters, 70
Peppers. *See* Bell peppers; Chiles
Pine nuts
in romesco sauce, 45
toasted, garlicky cherry tomato confit with, 269
Pissaladière, 93–94
Pistachios, candied, 293
rice pudding cake with apricot sauce and,
291–92
seared foie gras with sautéed plums and, 88

Sweetbreads
  caramelized, with lemon and wilted greens,
    250–51
  polenta with tasso and, 146–47
Sweet potatoes, harvest salad of roasted vegetables
    with romesco sauce, 43–45
Swiss chard and artichoke gratin, 107
Swordfish, orange and ginger-glazed roasted, with
    carrot and tarragon vinaigrette, 162–63

Tarragon
  and carrot vinaigrette, orange and ginger-glazed
    roasted swordfish with, 162–63
  potato and leek soup with fennel seeds and, 54
  roast duck with grapefruit, garlic, wilted greens,
    and, 203–4
  vinaigrette, chopped salad of peas, cucumbers,
    and radishes with, 46
Tart dough, Hamersley's bistro, 115
Tarts, savory, 102
  caramelized onion, bacon, and potato, 119
  fresh goat cheese, roasted beet, and walnut,
    120–21
  lobster, mushroom, and spinach, 122–23
  new potato galette with crème fraîche and
    olives, 116–17
  pissaladière, 93–94
  portobello mushroom and Roquefort galette,
    118
Tarts, sweet
  apple tarte Tatin, 286–87
  individual warm apple tarts with Chinese five-
    spice powder, caramel, and crème fraîche,
    314–15
  peach galette with blueberry-caramel sauce,
    283–84
Tasso, polenta with sweetbreads and, 146–47
Techniques, 2–4
Terrine of foie gras with shaved apple and endive
    salad, 84–85

Thyme, red onions braised in red wine with garlic
    and, 262
Tian of summer vegetables Provençal, 108–10
Tomato(es)
  broiled, with crispy bread crumbs, 270
  garlic, tomato, and olive compote, seared sea
    scallops with, 152–53
  garlicky cherry tomato confit with toasted pine
    nuts, 269
  lobster with corn, green beans, citrus vinaigrette,
    and, 170–71
  salad(s), 31; with basil, fennel, and lemon
    vinaigrette, 39; chopped, cold cucumber soup
    with, 51
  spicy, salt cod with garlic, onions, and, 164
  tian of summer vegetables Provençal,
    108–10
Tools and equipment, 4–6
Tripe soup, spicy, with mint and couscous, 62
Trout with lemon, brown butter, and parsley, 161
Truffle oil, white, baked polenta squares with
    peperonata and, 142–43
Truffles, black, creamy gratin of celery root, onions,
    and, 111
Tuna au poivre, grilled, with red wine vinaigrette,
    160
Turnips, harvest salad of roasted vegetables with
    romesco sauce, 43–45

Veal
  breast, stuffed with spinach, mushrooms, and
    garlic, 220–22
  chops, sear-roasted, with capers and cornichons,
    223–24
  stock, 18–19
Vegetable(s), 253–75. *See also specific vegetables*
  autumn: roasted, in salad with romesco sauce,
    43–45; stew with Cheddar-garlic crumble
    crust, 113–14
  stock, 20